EARL SPENCER
SAINT OR SINNER?

EARL SPENCER

Saint or Sinner?

A Biography
by Richard Barber

ANDRE DEUTSCH

For Patti

Front cover photographs:
Far left © Camerapress
Second left © Dave Chancellor / Alpha
Far right © Alpha

First published in 1998 by
André Deutsch
76 Dean Street
London W1V 5HA

A CIP record for this title is available
from the British Library

ISBN 0 233 99 360 6

Typeset by Derek Doyle & Associates
Mold, Flintshire.
Printed and bound by Butler and Tanner
Frome, Somerset

Extracts from *Diana: Her True Story*, Andrew Morton,
Michael O'Mara Books Ltd and *Raine and Johnny*,
Angèla Levin, Weidenfeld & Nicholson,
included with kind permission.

CONTENTS

FOREWORD

It seemed like a relatively straightforward proposition. Less than a week after Earl Spencer had climbed down from the pulpit in Westminster Abbey, having delivered one of the most memorable funeral orations of the twentieth century, I was asked if I would write his biography. My misgivings dismissed – if the publishers had wanted an historian, I was told, they'd have approached one – I considered how best to present a clear-eyed account of a man many were hailing as a contemporary hero.

But three months, it seems, is a long time in the public spotlight. By the end of November, Charles Spencer had metamorphosed into the man in the black hat. Whatever the reason for his divorce case being heard in South Africa, Charles scarcely can have foreseen the way in which he would be portrayed by the world's media. In terms of public relations, it was a disaster. As an example of the speed with which a man can be perceived to have switched so comprehensively from good guy to bad, it is without modern parallel.

So, which is the real Earl Spencer? That is what drove my undertaking. To arrive at a conclusion, I decided to pursue three separate lines of enquiry and then to weave them together to arrive at as even-handed an appraisal as possible. Some of the material in this book has been gleaned from newspaper and magazine cuttings as well as from television and radio programmes. Then there are the new interviews – with the nanny, the schoolfriend, the headmistress and so on – that yielded original anecdotes, fresh insights. Finally, I convened, loosely speaking, a panel of expert witnesses, each chosen for the particular discipline in which he or she excels, to throw a more searching light into the dark corners of this complicated man.

To all of these people, and to anyone else quoted in the book, my thanks. But it doesn't end there. You do not dip out of a busy working life for the better part of six months without a support system, a network of friends making encouraging noises. So, my thanks too, to Melanie Cantor for introducing me to my agent, Judy Chilcote (the best telephonic hand-holder in the business), and to Hannah MacDonald, my calm, quietly confident editor at André Deutsch.

Adam Helliker, Kate Sissons and William Sitwell all proved invaluable with their journalistic advice. George Bull, Gabrielle Donnelly, Jo Foley, Alarys and Christopher Gibson, Nina Myskow, John Tagholm and Stella Wilson were always there when I needed them. Most importantly of all, I could not have completed my task on time had it not been for the cheerful professionalism of Sally Tagholm, researcher *par excellence*.

And finally, it is just conceivable that I may not always have been at my tiptop best over the last six months in my dealings with Patti, Edward, Harriet and Grace. If so, my apologies and my love, as ever.

Richard Barber
London, February 1998

1

THE FUNERAL

It was almost certainly the single most public occasion the world has yet seen. On Saturday, 6 September 1997, some 2.5 billion people across the globe – over 31 million in Britain alone – watched the funeral of the nation's golden child. Some watched in the privacy of their own homes, others on the giant screens erected in London and other cities around the world and a privileged few sat silent beneath the soaring vaulted roof of Westminster Abbey. When Diana, Princess of Wales made her final 'appearance' at the tragically foreshortened conclusion of a public life that had elevated her to the position of World's Most Famous Person, the world itself – or so it seemed – held its collective breath and then wept, silently, personally, privately, a vale of tears for the passing of the People's Princess.

If we were to lose her so prematurely, then let us at least give her a right royal send-off. And nor did the occasion disappoint. The Almighty switched on the sun in a sky of unseasonal cerulean blue. The gun carriage was draped with the Royal Standard (to which, of course, she was no longer entitled, having been unceremoniously stripped of her royal privileges, her HRH title included, at the point of her divorce from the man who would be king). It was pulled at a heartbreakingly ponderous pace and was followed in the concluding stages of its journey by the leading male players in this very public tragedy: Prince Charles and his father, the Duke of Edinburgh, on either flank; Prince Harry next to his father; Prince William next to his paternal grandfather; and, in the middle, the unmistakable frame of the ninth Earl Spencer.

At six feet three inches, Charles Spencer cuts an imposing figure. Now 34, he retains his boyish good looks: penetrating greenish brown eyes beneath that thatch of barely controlled hair in the distinctive shade of Spencer red, the sizeable frame threatening to run to fat should the good life not be kept firmly in check. That his face was set in what looked like a pretty intractable grimace might then have seemed unremarkable, but we can now picture a man contemplating his task ahead.

For the meantime, though, perhaps the single most poignant image imprinted on the mind of any parent watching the almost unbearable cortège was the sight of Prince Harry's pretty, plump little rosebud wreath adorned with a card bearing, in his best joined-up writing, the single word, 'Mummy'. It was almost too much to take, this reminder that – after all the nonsense of the fake fairy-tale marriage, beyond all the internecine strife waged within and without the Palace walls – the fabulous, flawed, infinitely frustrating Diana, would wish, above all, to be remembered as a mother.

The funeral service made you proud to be British. The Abbey had never looked lovelier and the singing of the 'Libera me, Domine', from Verdi's *Requiem*, was sublime. The readings by Diana's two older sisters, Lady Sarah and Lady Jane, and by the Prime Minister, Tony Blair, were nerve-racking, eerie (if you closed your eyes, didn't Jane sound uncannily like Diana?) and statesmanlike, by turn. Elton John, the world willing him to give his best rendition ever of the rewritten 'Candle in the Wind', rose magnificently to the occasion, securing his subsequent turn-of-the-year knighthood at a single stroke.

And then it was the turn of Charles, the ninth Earl Spencer. Matthew Engel, writing in the *Guardian*, summed up best the following five minutes – some twelve hundred words that will remain indelibly emblazoned on the memory of anyone who witnessed their electrifying delivery and which made Spencer (alongside Blair) Britain's man of that watershed year.

'Earl Spencer,' wrote Engel, 'used [the funeral Address] to come as near as anyone has done within Britain since 1745 (the year of the Jacobite rebellion) to raising the rebel standard against the monarchy. His Address was not a eulogy but a battle cry. Even before he began, one observer in Westminster Abbey thought the scene resembled the House of Commons: the Spencers in the North Lantern staring across at the Windsors in the South Lantern, a couple of sword-lengths away. But these are two families that match each other, and any political party, for internal dysfunction, for the range of their splits, feuds, sub-feuds, and even the odd lingering cross-current of affection.

'Now, they are ranged, institutionally, against each other: Montagues and Capulets for our times but with the war outlasting both love and death. The life of Diana was a tragic story. We may now be embarking on the sequel: the Tragedy of Charles III. But maybe there is never going to be a Charles III. And, if there is, then in the overblown atmosphere of this weekend, one could be forgiven for wondering whether it really will be Charles Windsor rather than Charles Spencer, the new popular hero, and a far more gifted moment-seizer than the Windsors have ever produced.'

Here is what Charles Spencer said from that Westminster Abbey pulpit:

I stand before you today, the representative of a family in grief, in a country in mourning before a world in shock. We are all united not only in our desire to pay our respects to Diana but rather in our need to do so.

For such was her extraordinary appeal that the tens of millions of people taking part in this service all over the world via television and radio who never actually met her feel that they, too, lost someone close to them in the early hours of Sunday morning. It is a more remarkable tribute to Diana than I can ever hope to offer to her today.

Diana was the very essence of compassion, of duty, of style, of beauty. All over the world, she was a symbol of selfless humanity, a standard-bearer for the rights of the truly downtrodden, a truly British girl who transcended nationality, someone with a natural nobility who was class-less, who proved in the last year that she needed no royal title to continue to generate her particular brand of magic.

Today is our chance to say thank you for the way you brightened our lives, even though God granted you but half a life. We will all feel cheated that you were taken from us so young and yet we must learn to be grateful that you came along at all. Only now you are gone do we truly appreciate what we are now without and we want you to know that life without you is very, very difficult.

We have all despaired at our loss over the past week and only the strength of the message you gave us through your years of giving has afforded us the strength to move forward.

There is a temptation to rush to canonize your memory; there is no need to do so. You stand tall enough as a human being of unique qualities not to need to be seen as a saint. Indeed, to sanctify your memory would be to miss out on the very core of your being, your wonderfully mischievous sense of humour with the laugh that bent you double.

Your joy for life transmitted wherever you took your smile and the sparkle in those unforgettable eyes; your boundless energy which you could barely contain. But your greatest gift was your intuition and it was a gift you used wisely. This is what underpinned all your other wonderful attributes and if we look to analyse what it was about you that had such a wide appeal, we find it in your instinctive feel for what was really important in all our lives.

Without your God-given sensitivity, we would be immersed in greater ignorance at the anguish of Aids and HIV sufferers, the plight of the homeless, the isolation of lepers, the random destruction of landmines. Diana explained to me once that it was her innermost feelings of suffering that made it possible for her to connect with her constituency of the rejected.

And here we come to another truth about her. For all the status, the glamour, the applause, Diana remained through-out a very insecure person at heart, almost childlike in her desire to do good for others so she could release herself from deep feelings of unworthiness, of which her eating disorders were merely a symptom. The world sensed this part of her character and cherished her for her vulnerability whilst admiring her for her honesty.

The last time I saw Diana was on July first, her birthday, in London, when, typically, she was not taking time to celebrate her special day with friends but was guest of honour at a charity fundraising evening. She sparkled, of course, but I would rather cherish the days I spent with her in March when she came to visit me and my children in our home in South Africa. I am proud of the fact that, apart from when she was on public display meeting President Mandela, we managed to contrive to stop the ever-present paparazzi from getting a single picture of her. That meant a lot to her.

These are days I will always treasure. It was as if we'd been transported back to our childhood when we spent such an enormous amount of time together, the two youngest in the family. Fundamentally, she hadn't changed at all from the big sister who mothered me as a baby, fought with me at school, and endured those long train journeys between our parents' homes with me at weekends.

It is a tribute to her level-headedness and strength that, despite the most bizarre life imaginable after her childhood, she remained intact, true to herself. There is no doubt that she was looking for a new direction in her life at this time. She talked endlessly of getting away from England, mainly because of the treatment she received at the hands of the newspapers.

I don't think she ever understood why her genuinely good intentions were sneered at by the media; why there appeared to be a permanent quest on their behalf to bring her down. It is baffling. My own, and only, explanation is that genuine goodness is threatening to those at the opposite end of the moral spectrum.

It is a point to remember that of all the ironies about

Diana, perhaps the greatest is this: that a girl given the name of the ancient goddess of hunting was, in the end, the most hunted person of the modern age.

She would want us today to pledge ourselves to protecting her beloved boys, William and Harry, from a similar fate. And I do this here, Diana, on your behalf. We will not allow them to suffer the anguish that used regularly to drive you to tearful despair.

Beyond that, on behalf of your mother and sisters, I pledge that we, your blood family, will do all we can to continue the imaginative and loving way in which you were steering these two exceptional young men so that their souls are not simply immersed by duty and tradition but can sing openly as you planned.

We fully respect the heritage into which they have both been born and will always respect and encourage them in their royal role. But we, like you, recognize the need for them to experience as many different aspects of life as possible, to arm them spiritually and emotionally for the years ahead. I know you would have expected nothing less from us.

William and Harry, we all care desperately for you today. We are all chewed up with sadness at the loss of a woman who wasn't even our mother. How great your suffering is we cannot even imagine.

I would like to end by thanking God for the small mercies he has shown us at this dreadful time; for taking Diana at her most beautiful and radiant and when she had so much joy in her private life.

Above all, we give thanks for the life of a woman I am so proud to be able to call my sister: the unique, the complex, the extraordinary and irreplaceable Diana whose beauty, both internal and external, will never be extinguished from our minds.

Although the overwhelming public response was squarely behind the Earl – applause, like a distant hailstorm, rolling in from Hyde Park and then through the Abbey itself – there were dissenters. Hugo Vickers, a royal biographer, declared himself shocked at the sentiments expressed by the Earl. 'There were elements of the speech that I found slightly brutal,' he told one reporter. 'It was a little bit bad-mannered to direct those kinds of comment at the Royal Family sitting opposite when they had made such an effort in the past few days to express their grief.' It subsequently transpired that Buckingham Palace had neither asked for nor been offered any prior sight of Earl Spencer's Address. According to a Palace spokesman, 'The whole service was very much led by the Spencer family in consultation with the Dean of Westminster. It would not have been appropriate for us to know what was in the tribute. It was a brother's heartfelt tribute to his sister.'

Anthony Holden, journalist, author and also a royal bio-grapher, notably of the Prince of Wales, was impressed by what he heard. 'I thought what Charles Spencer said was terrifically effective and I don't agree with people who think it was in any way out of place. I gave him points for what he said and for the way that he said it. It needed to be said. The reason for the applause and the reason I would guess that most people would still consider it to have been a good speech was because it was felt that the Royal Family had in some way cheated, that they had let the country down.'

Holden speaks, he says, as the self-appointed leader of what he describes as the flagpole movement. 'Because I was doing broadcasts every day after Diana's death from the platforms erected outside Buckingham Palace, I was able to see flags in a 360-degree radius, each one of them at half-mast. With one notable exception. The flagpole behind me in every broadcast until the Thursday before the funeral was devoid of any flag whatsoever. I never tired of saying that protocol was irrelevant, that there should be a flag hanging from the Buckingham Palace flagpole and that it should be at half-mast. In time, I became aware of people around me slapping me on the back and urging me to say as much when I was interviewed on the BBC.'

Which is what he duly did, with the result that all the tabloid newspapers took up the cause and the Royal Family eventually bowed to public pressure. Not that the clamour was confined to flags and poles. The Queen was urged to leave Balmoral in Scotland and come back to the capital. In what many consider to be the nick of time, she did indeed return to London and then gave an evidently honest and affecting televised broadcast to the nation. 'The royals just about saved their bacon,' says Holden. 'If the Queen hadn't done the things she did, there was the very real prospect of her being booed at the funeral and that, in my opinion, could have triggered the end of the monarchy.

'As it was, there was still a lot of resentment washing around at the time of the funeral. That's what Spencer, maybe unconsciously, milked and that's why people applauded as they did. There was also the rather uneasy feeling that the royals were trying to reclaim in death a woman who, a year before to the very week, they had expelled from the family, stripped of her HRH status, and whose name they had had deleted from prayers said in churches throughout Christendom on Sundays.

'When Prince Charles went to Paris to bring back the coffin, the mood among the crowd outside the Palace bordered on the mutinous. How dare he bring her back? they said. He was the man who ruined her life. Those were the people who will never forgive Charles for the way he – and the Queen, to an extent – treated Diana, and they were the same people who applauded Charles Spencer's speech.'

From shortly after the announcement of Diana's death until beyond her funeral, Holden worked for three American networks in London – NBC, ABC and CBS. During a break between broadcasts in the NBC studios one day, he found himself discussing the polished way in which Charles had delivered his Address from the pulpit of Westminster Abbey. 'A very senior, rather formidable producer who had flown over from New York to cover the unfolding drama overheard what I was saying. She strode over and said, "Charles Spencer used to work for me and, I can tell you, he can write and deliver a very good piece to camera." And she was right. That *was* a piece to camera – in other words, as it might have been delivered if he were reporting from the scene of some important event for a national news bulletin. His television experience had come in very handy. Watching it again, as I have done many times, you realize it was as if Charles was saying what he had to say not to the congregation but to the camera.

'He now says his words have been misinterpreted and that he never intended to be as rude in front of his godmother, the Queen, and the rest of the royals, as it might have appeared. I suggested as much in conversation with a senior Buckingham Palace courtier who merely rolled his eyes at me. Clearly, the commonly held opinion behind Palace walls was that Spencer was being wise after the event – or casuistic, to use the polite word. And yet I stand back from all of that and merely admire how polished it was. As with all the great political speeches, I thought it was very skilfully done.

'The most impressive element, in terms of writing ability, was the way in which Spencer captured the essence of Diana, her vulnerability as much as her undoubted victories.' Nor is Holden alone in this view. Sir Robert Fellowes, husband of Diana and Charles's elder sister, Jane, and soon-to-be retired private secretary to the Queen, subsequently revealed to an intimate that he thought the speech was fine – although, given the chance, he would have removed just two words. When asked which two, he is said to have replied 'blood family'. 'He thought that phrase was a bit over the top,' according to Holden. 'Otherwise, objectively speaking, Fellowes didn't have a problem with the Address.'

The other Charles, however, was said to be incandescent with rage over his brother-in-law's chosen words. 'Oh, I don't doubt it,' says Holden. 'So one can only wonder what the atmosphere must have been like at Althorp when everyone arrived there by train and car after the service. The Spencers are quite as dysfunctional a family – if not more so – as the Windsors, with an equal, if not greater, share of divorces and eating disorders in their recent history. It was plainly absurd for Charles Spencer to set himself up as any sort of paragon of how to be married.'

Mary Clarke, last nanny to the Spencer children and the person charged by the eighth Earl with preparing his son and heir to be sent away to boarding school, spent nineteen months with Charles in the early seventies. She feels she was given a privileged insight into what makes the man tick, albeit when he was still only in single figures. 'Charles was brought up to understand that the Spencers were just as much a part of English history as the Royal Family,' says Clarke. 'Some people have criticized him for daring to speak out as he did at Diana's funeral and particularly in that setting. But he wouldn't have seen it like that. He was simply saying what he really felt. Impertinence doesn't come into it. I believe he felt it was something that had to be said.

'He did feel very emotional about his sister and being Charles, with his background and place in history, he didn't feel inhibited about speaking his mind in front of the Queen. It is precisely because she's his godmother that he wouldn't have found that occasion daunting. It is a world he knows well. It would never have occurred to him that he was somehow speaking out of turn. I understand that some people might have interpreted that as arrogance but knowing him as I did, I saw it as an extension of the child who grew into the self-contained, quietly confident man. It's precocious children who make arrogant adults and Charles Spencer was never precocious, I can assure you. He was easy and loving, a child who accepted me for what I was and who gave me no trouble.

'My instinctive response when he climbed down from the pulpit to all that applause was, "Good for you!" I always believe it's good for people to speak naturally and to say exactly what they feel – as long as they're not downright rude, of course. But then he wasn't. He only said what so many of us had thought for so long: that basically his sister had been very badly treated by the Royal Family and that she had done a really rather remarkable job in carving out a role for herself. Diana, from being the girl I knew through to the woman she had become by the time she was killed, always wanted to please. Her brother knew that and was at pains to acknowledge the fact publicly.

'The only thing that saddened me about the speech was when he referred to the long train journeys shuttling between his parents. I accompanied him and Diana on those trips and that's not how I remember them. We'd read and play games; I particularly recall I Spy being a favourite way to pass the time. It was anything other than quiet. Lord Althorp always paid for us to travel first class so we often had a compartment to ourselves. On return journeys, the children would be bubbling over with stories of what they'd been up to. I always encouraged them to talk about their mother.'

Virginia Ironside is Britain's leading agony aunt, and the author of three books on bereavement. 'What emerges from studying the text of Charles Spencer's Address,' she says, 'is of someone who is sincere and who knows how to make a speech but also of someone who is full of love and anguish and vengefulness. He crystallized the public mood in that, apart from all the other emotions, we were furious that Diana had died – fury being an acknowledged symptom of bereavement – and Charles, on our behalf, vented that anger on the Royal Family. He hit the spot extremely effectively. With whom could the ordinary member of the public be furious when Diana died? With the press, of course; but with the royals, too.

'We all described the classic arc of grief that follows a death: shock; guilt (somehow, by buying all those papers, had we not contributed to her death?); anger; sadness; and, in the event, chaos. Charles read the public mood perfectly and then actually had the gall to say what he said in Westminster Abbey. That was very shocking. A funeral, and especially such a public one, should not be a platform from which to criticize other people.

As to *how* Charles managed to crystallize and then lead the public's mood at a time of such high emotion 'I suspect he's learned the art, as Diana did, too. They both came from a fractured family. Manipulation is often the only card you can play when you're children. Somehow, on that occasion, at least, he managed to emerge as a kind of saintly champion of his sister and yet without missing the trick of reminding everyone, the Windsors included, that he was a member of what he called Diana's "blood family". He talked about his sister's intuition but he's intuitive, too. He managed to steal the show at her funeral over Tony Blair, Elton John and the entire Royal Family and, what's more, he knew what he was doing. It was a terribly well-written speech.

'If we lived in medieval times, you would say that Charles Spencer was announcing to the world that he was a baron wanting to set up his own dynasty rivalling the monarch. He has an eye for the main chance, no question. That point in the Address when he went from referring to her as "Diana" to calling her "you" was a very clever way of switching people's emotions, a trick employed by all good speechmakers. All the seeds of power seemed present in him. Unfortunately, people who have suffered as children often grow into damaged adults. They're invariably ambitious. And Charles also has great wealth: it's a potent combination.'

He was good, too, says Ironside, at peppering his speech with just the right amount of intimate references: the time, for instance, brother and sister had spent in South Africa, undetected or, at least, unimpeded, by the hated hounds of the press; of her bending double when she laughed her characteristic laugh. 'But when he talked,' she says, 'of "Diana's innermost suffering", he was talking just as much about himself.' The mention of his sister's bulimia was also a smart move. 'It's no good, if you're defending your client in court to maintain that he is perfect in every respect. How much better to acknowledge someone's human failings? By the same token, it added to the strength of the speech that he mentioned her shortcomings; otherwise, it would have looked like a whitewash. Charles made Diana seem three-dimensional.'

But he was, simultaneously, working to more than one

agenda, it seems. 'The sideswipe at his parents for divorcing – the reference to those interminable train journeys shuttling between them. It must have been a pretty cathartic experience for him, an opportunity to say all the things he wanted to say in front of almost half the world.' Nor does Ironside judge him for that. 'Wouldn't we all like the chance to get up there and release our demons – and to be applauded for it into the bargain?

'One phrase that struck me perhaps more than any other was when he said how everyone was "chewed up with sadness" for William and Harry. That sounded real, something you would say in conversation but not from a public platform. He left that in deliberately, I think, to reveal a small window on himself.' The other element that struck Ironside most forcibly was Charles's reference to Diana on two occasions as a sort of substitute mother. ' "She was a big sister who mothered me as a baby," he said at one point. It made me realize that, to some extent, he did see her as a mum, unsurprising considering the ghastliness of their childhood. If you read the speech again as if it were delivered by a son talking about his mother, rather than by a brother talking about his sister, it takes on a quite different resonance. At the very least, the boundaries are blurred.

'There is much more passion in what he said than most brothers feel for their sisters. But then he felt much more deeply about her than he might otherwise have done because she had been overwhelmingly the most stable element of his childhood. Little wonder he was so angry about her death. When Diana died, in a sense Charles lost a mother for the second time in his life, his biological mother having left the family home when he was little more than a toddler. Men are popularly said to marry their mothers but Charles effectively married his sister, both Diana and Victoria being anorexic and needy young women. That's extremely unusual. He married someone with very little self-esteem who he perhaps thought would devote herself to him.'

Virginia Ironside can only wonder at Charles Spencer's state of mind now. 'I would imagine he's pretty depressed. He's had his big moment of glory because there's no question that there's something exciting about a funeral and, most particularly, this

13

one. People don't usually admit to it but there's an undeniable feeling of being special if you're close to the person who has died; and, of course, you're very busy. There is a show to put on and you're the centre of attention. When it's all over, you continue to miss the person who died but you do so no longer surrounded by any public outpourings of grief or any accompanying razzmatazz. Charles Spencer had all that in spades.'

Now, says Ironside, he has Diana for ever. 'He refused to have her HRH status reinstated. He wanted her for himself – and that's just what he's achieved. She's buried on that island at Althorp.' All of which must have left him feeling rather flat now that the extraordinary fuss has died down. 'I have a suspicion, whatever he may say to the contrary, that his much publicized court case over the divorce from Victoria gave him a welcome shot of adrenalin.

'People who protest constantly about how much they detest publicity clearly enjoy the opportunity of saying as much. His relationship with the media has always struck me as highly ambivalent but then that was also true of Diana. I believe that a part of Charles – and he may not even acknowledge this about himself – enjoys being centre-stage, seeks out controversy. If you don't want the bull to attack you, don't prick him in the neck. If you don't want the press to pursue you, don't attack them in public. It's quite easy.

'Look at his older sisters. We rarely, if ever, see mention of them in the papers. Charles is now the head of the family by virtue of his gender alone. But he brings to that role his own personality, his own set of values. If he wished to be more or less anonymous, to do what he wanted to do without drawing attention to himself, he could. Was what he said from the pulpit at Westminster Abbey genuinely helpful to William and Harry? Is that what children want to hear from an uncle at their mother's funeral? I have my doubts.'

The eighth Earl, Charles's father, Johnnie, cannot have known just how prescient were his remarks to the *Chronicle Herald* in Halifax, Nova Scotia: 'Prince William will grow up close to the Spencer side of the family,' he was reported as saying in June

1983, 'and be influenced by them as much as the royals. I know the royals can appear to swallow people up when others marry in, and the other family always looks as if it has been pushed out but that could never happen with us. We can cope with the pressures. We have been brought up with royalty and there is no question of us being pushed out. Diana would not permit it to happen; and she always gets her own way.' Moreover, these assertions reflect, as we shall see, the Spencer house's enduring vigour in dealings with the royals.

Andrew Morton, arguably the most famous – and certainly the most prosperous – of all the royal biographers (helped, not a little, by the co-operation, it was subsequently revealed, of the Princess herself), takes a typically pragmatic view of Earl Spencer's ringing words in the Abbey. 'The fact that he was able to stand up,' says Morton, 'and talk, with the Queen, his godmother, just a couple of yards away, in relatively withering terms about the Royal Family, shows a degree of focus and ferocity you wouldn't encounter, for example, in most lily-livered journalists. You wouldn't want to have a stand-up row with the Spencers. These are, and were, extremely tough people.'

He could be accused of many things but being lily-livered is not one of them. David Starkey, constitutional historian, and once described as 'the rudest man in Britain' (a badge he would appear to wear with some pride), remained resolutely undazzled by Diana during her life and continued to do so after its abrupt end. Nor is he any fan of her younger brother. 'Somebody asked for my reaction to Diana's death on the morning that we all learned the news,' recalls Dr Starkey, 'and I remember saying that, while I understood the horror of the thing, my opinion of her now that she was dead was no different from my opinion of her when she was alive: she was highly divisive. As soon as you remove the speech from the pulpit, where it acquired an utterly spurious authority, the words become meaningless.

'I felt there were two things that were deeply worrying about what he said. The first was that it seemed to me to be in grossly bad taste. It was a political funeral oration when no such thing was called for. I was commentating on the funeral for CBS alongside Dan Rather. When Charles sat down to that wave of applause, Dan turned to me and said, "David, that is the most political funeral Address I have heard since Mark Antony's for Julius Caesar. Is this guy running for office?"

'The second worrying aspect, in my opinion, was the directness of the attack on the Royal Family in the presence of the Queen, Prince Charles and William and Harry. I found that utterly tasteless and repugnant. And to be subjected to a display of moral posturing from a man known to be an adulterer was, frankly, preposterous. In the end, you are driven to the conclusion that maybe he doesn't look in the mirror enough. Certainly, he seems to lack self-awareness to a quite terrifying degree.

'The speech – and there is no point denying it – was expertly crafted and delivered, but for all that its content struck me as ludicrously overblown. He came across as a sort of medieval baron from the House of Spencer setting his cap at the House of Windsor. Diana's death, to a large extent, dissolved the public antipathy towards Prince Charles and the divorce; not immediately, of course, but that is what gradually came to pass. Charles Spencer's role at that funeral should have been confined to recalling the life and work of a woman millions of people loved very dearly.

'In the event, he delivered an oration that seemed antagonistic, exacerbating the bad feelings that had existed during and beyond that failed marriage. It was completely inappropriate for the occasion. Generosity, not bitterness, should have been the order of the day.

'Prince Charles, of course, behaved immaculately that week and especially on the day of the funeral. He's a difficult and prickly man on occasion but he is a gentleman. He obviously cares passionately about his family, he cares profoundly about public decency and he is devoted to his sons. Spencer's speech rode roughshod over all three of those sets of values just about as radically as it was possible to do. It was a remarkable testi-

16

mony to his composure that Prince Charles did not reveal what he most certainly must have been feeling.

'As for the Queen, I can only wonder at her distress. It is quite clear to me that the whole Diana episode has been about as absolutely catastrophic as her reign could have embraced. The arrival of Diana on the royal scene proved to be as damaging to the monarchy as the abdication crisis which, of course, her father's and her own succession were designed to heal. The way in which Diana rocked the boat was a disaster and a negation of everything the Queen stands for. So to have the Princess's final send-off accompanied by a speech like that must have been particularly hurtful to her.'

David Starkey, however, recognises a certain irony when he says that the speech reminded him of his sister. 'Her world was almost entirely solipsistic; everything she did, albeit for the benefit of others, was Diana-centred. When she spoke to Andrew Morton, for instance, of the disabled and the dispossessed, she said, "I hunger for them"; in other words, it was what they did to her rather than the other way around.'

Shelley-Anne Claircourt began working for Althorp in 1994. Its general manager, David Horton-Fawkes, approached her public relations company with a view to her representing the estate. She had worked with Horton-Fawkes some years earlier when they were both employed by the Savoy Hotel in London. 'The idea,' says Claircourt, 'was to raise the profile of Althorp House for corporate use – as a venue for conferences, dinners, wedding receptions and so on. My role was to work with David in promoting the house and its grounds to the general public.

'I had first met Charles some years earlier when I was still at the Savoy and he was covering the wedding of Mrs Thatcher's son, Mark, for NBC.' The first time she worked for Charles directly was when he was selling what is called a lordship title – in this instance, the lordship of the manor of Wimbledon which had been in the Spencer family since 1744 and which was bought at auction for the unexpectedly high price of £188,000 by an anonymous buyer who could henceforth style himself Lord of Wimbledon, and may even put the title in his passport but who owns nothing, cannot expect a seat in the House of Lords and is not entitled to wear the traditional ermine. The money raised paid for Althorp's antiquated plumbing to be overhauled.

'Initially,' recalls Claircourt, 'I worked very closely with David so that Lord Spencer, while being extremely approachable, was perhaps a little elusive; but he was always appreciative of whatever I'd done and let me know as much. Indeed, after helping with the media during the six days leading up to Diana's funeral, Charles had the sensitivity to write me a letter thanking me for my contribution. I'll always treasure it.

'Everything changed, of course, when Diana died. In the first two days after her death, my office had to deal with over five hundred separate press enquiries – everything from specific questions about what she would be buried wearing through to more general calls concerning the mood of her immediate family members. We acted, I suppose, as a sort of buffer zone in that we tried to shield the family in whatever small ways we could from the barrage of interest.

'I spoke to Lord Spencer after he flew back to England to organize his sister's funeral. I found it terribly difficult. Obviously, I said how sorry I was about what had happened but it sounded so inadequate somehow. He was wonderful. He seemed to know instinctively how everyone else must be feeling and immediately tried to put me at my ease. For the next week until he returned to Cape Town, he was so caught up in the details of Diana's funeral and burial that he didn't really have time left over to grieve himself. But I did hear that, when he got home, the awfulness of the whole tragedy really hit him. I didn't witness this for myself but it's not hard to imagine the traumatic effect on someone of losing a much-loved sister and in the full glare of global publicity.

'I thought his funeral Address was absolutely amazing, and courageous, too. I know there has been criticism of him saying what he said in Westminster Abbey, that it was the wrong time and the wrong place. But when could he have said what he did if not then? There is no event you could create to equal Diana's funeral. These are things he wanted to say and that he felt needed saying. It came from the heart. Yes, it was extraordinarily powerful but it's only if you isolate one or two sentences and repeat them out of context that they could be seen as being in any way insulting. In its entirety, though, the Address spoke for the whole nation. When Charles asked that we let the boys' "souls sing openly", I think he was voicing all our thoughts.

'He received about a hundred thousand letters and not one of them criticized him for what he'd said in the Abbey. He replied to over a thousand in the immediate aftermath of her death and funeral as well as sending personal letters to everyone who'd been involved in the funeral in some way; and not just hurried notes. These were handwritten, personalized letters and, considering what he must have been going through himself, I find that quite incredible.' He also issued a statement to everyone who had taken the trouble to share their grief with him over the loss of his sister. 'I would like to thank all the people from all over the world,' the statement read, 'who have communicated their grief at Diana's loss to me and my family. The flowers, the letters, the telegrams – all in their tens of thousands – have been a source of comfort and pride to us, and have genuinely helped us to mourn her death. The knowledge that Diana's life gave so many people so much can now be balanced by the hope that, in death, her legacy will be immortal. Thank you all very, very much for your kindness.'

As to the funeral oration, Charles wrote it himself, says Claircourt, so ignore any and all of the stories about various public figures either helping him construct it in the first place or tidying up his first draft in some way afterwards. Rumours were widespread about whose hand had guided Spencer's to produce so elegantly crafted an oration. Among the more frequently mentioned were Jeffrey Archer, millionaire novelist and former deputy chairman of the Conservative Party; Geordie Grieg, literary editor of the *Sunday Times* and whose sister, Laura Lonsdale, was once a lady-in-waiting to the Princess; Boris Johnson, a contemporary of the Earl's at Eton and Oxford, and now a respected right-wing journalist and commentator on the *Daily Telegraph* in London; and Lord Attenborough, the highly regarded actor, film director and close friend of Diana.

In a characteristically courteous response to the suggestion that he'd helped her younger brother in writing his speech, Attenborough praised its content while categorically denying any part in its construction. 'The Address was courageous, considered, compassionate and determined,' he said. He was also clearly deeply moved by the public reaction to Charles's words. 'The applause was extraordinary. All the way down the nave of Westminster Abbey, the congregation were applauding with such affection and respect. It was a unique occasion. It would have been heartbreaking if Lord Spencer had not been as outspoken as he was.' The Princes William and Harry, according to observers, joined in with the general applause. Prince Charles was seen to tap his thigh with his hand – whether in muted applause, or irritation, remains unclear – before, apparently, composing himself. The Queen, sphinx-like as ever, displayed no outward emotion, however much she may have been seething inside. Prince Philip's face remained a mask throughout. The Queen Mother looked merely bewildered by so unexpected a broadside.

Two days later, Prime Minister Tony Blair – the man who had played such a pivotal role in communicating to the Queen and, consequently, to the rest of the royals, the mood of the country following Diana's death, and the increasingly urgent need for her to return to the capital from Balmoral – was also the man who mounted a spirited defence of the Windsors in the week immediately after the Princess's funeral. 'The Royal Family has been through a very hard time,' he said, 'and I think criticism of them is very unfair. It has been a tremendously difficult situation for them and they have coped in a way that I think is very much to their credit.'

Blair is not on record as to his opinion of Charles Spencer's funeral Address. 'But whatever anyone may think of what he said,' says Shelley-Anne Claircourt, 'the truth is that those were Charles's words and his alone.' He did, however, show the speech to two personal friends, neither of them in the public eye, to test their reaction.

Sir Nicholas Lloyd, editor of the *Daily Express* from 1986 to 1996 and, latterly, co-founder of Brown Lloyd James, a media communications consultancy based in London and New York, viewed proceedings from a rather different perspective. 'When I arrived at the *Daily Express* in the mid-eighties,' recalls Lloyd, 'the royal fairy-tale was still in place, more or less, even if, quite quickly, rumours began to circulate that all was not well with the marriage, stories the media knew about but which they didn't print for some considerable time. In the ensuing ten years, the fairy-tale degenerated into pantomime, farce and, ultimately, tragedy.'

Lloyd regarded Earl Spencer's funeral Address as unfortunate; 'ill-judged', in his estimation. 'This was not the appropriate moment for him to talk about blood relatives or to issue what amounted to a school report on the behaviour of the Royal Family *to* the Royal Family. I felt the funeral should have been entirely about remembering the Princess of Wales; not an occasion to pick a very public family fight. Charles seemed to have decided he would go to war – and to declare as much in the Abbey – with those people he regarded as the opposition, people who had done his sister down, people who had not valued her in the way he felt she should have been valued. To my mind, the Address should have been to do with the caring and the humanity and the beauty and the glamour of the woman we all felt we had lost.

'I'm no blinkered fan of the Royal Family any more than I'm a strident republican. But to use the occasion to remind the royals that the Spencers had been around a long time, and that, anyway, in his family's view, the Windsors had mistreated Diana, was just plain shabby. I'm the first to acknowledge that the Windsors are far from being the ideal family, the set-up to which we should all aspire. They are undeniably dysfunctional: three out of the Queen's four children have failed marriages behind them. Her own long-running marriage to Prince Philip, were it to be put under the spotlight, might well reveal certain shortcomings.

'Even so, I found it very difficult to stomach Charles Althorp delivering a sermon to the rest of us – the Royal Family included – on family life. He comes from an appallingly fractured family where the parents parted acrimoniously with who knows what effect on their children? The splintering of her parents' marriage may explain to some extent the Princess of Wales's behaviour, her pronounced need to give and receive love. But then I believe it may explain a lot about her brother, too. He cannot be blamed for any of this but, coming from that background, and with his own failed marriage behind him, wouldn't you think he'd be a little more aware than to berate the Royal Family for their own failures and sadnesses? Charles's mistress, Josie Borain, attended Diana's funeral, for heaven's sake, not his wife. It was the mistress who went by train up to Althorp following the service to be with him. Is he incapable of seeing himself as others might see him? A little bit of humility wouldn't go amiss, would it?'

On the other hand, look at the public reaction to Charles's words in Westminster Abbey. Ah, but that, says Lloyd, is because the Princess of Wales was seen, somewhat through rose-tinted spectacles, as a great humanitarian, almost as a sister of mercy. 'And, given her work with the sick and the suffering, her declared wish to be known – or, at least, thought of – as the Queen of Hearts has some merit. I am not, however, aware of Earl Spencer filling his life with the pursuit of good works.

'The spontaneous applause that rolled like a tidal wave through the Abbey was in response to the way in which he'd summed up a national guilt that all of us – journalists, in particular – undoubtedly felt. We had lived not only *with* Diana but *off* her. We needed her every day to provide a glamorous picture for our newspapers and that's what we got.' It's more than that, though. 'She appeared,' says Lloyd, 'to be the classic Wronged Woman, a good mother to whom her much older husband found it hard to relate and whom he betrayed with another woman.'

Lloyd's interpretation could scarcely be at greater odds with that of Stephanie Schutte, executive director of Lifeline/ ChildLine in Cape Town. The Earl accepted her invitation to become the charity's patron in the autumn of 1997, a gesture that grew precisely out of his funeral Address. 'Charles's words didn't come across as angry,' Schutte told listeners to Cape Talk Radio. 'All the feelings in his speech were absolutely true. He didn't try to pretend anything; he said what he felt. I also got the feeling he had the ability to stand back from his experience. It was a crafted speech; he used words really exquisitely. That ability to feel the feelings and make something really good out of them was what I was moved by and why I wrote to him to ask whether he would consider being our patron. What struck me about Charles's funeral Address was that he had quite clearly come to grips with a whole lot of things and that he'd obviously done so long before his sister's death. I felt that he was brave to do what he did and say what he said and that he was really in touch with his emotions at a very deep level. It's why I responded to what he was saying. It didn't occur to me to approach him as Princess Diana's brother but as the person who made that speech.'

The distinguished psychologist and writer, Dorothy Rowe, agrees with Stephanie Schutte on the genuineness of the Earl's chosen words but parts company with her on their motivation. 'I thought Charles was very warm and genuine,' says Dr Rowe, 'but in the way that a small child is genuine. There was no artifice about him. There are a lot of people nowadays who get offended with the press but who wouldn't take them on publicly because, by and large, it's better not to court disaster. If you attack the press, they'll get you. So Charles was rather brave, wasn't he, to stand up in Westminster Abbey in front of the Royal Family and the rest of the world and give that eulogy to his sister? Was he also foolish? Maybe, but a lot less so than if he'd said what he said four hundred years earlier. He'd probably have been beheaded on the spot had it been 1597.

'I would imagine that, although he was deprived in many ways as a child, the fact that he was heir to the title and estate, and the fact his father became so ill and frail when Charles was still a teenager, combined to give him the idea that you can say what you like and people will put up with it. You give orders and they're carried out. So when it came to him standing up before his godmother, the Queen, and saying what he did, his attitude would have been, "Why shouldn't I say this? I can speak my mind. I always have done." He was well used to having people around him who would support him although, on that occasion, the reaction of the crowd outside the Abbey and the congregation within it must have reinforced his feelings of having got it right. I was amazed, when he sat down after giving his oration, that he managed to stop himself punching the air in triumph.

'I feel very strongly that he would imagine he'd done the right thing – and would continue to think so to this day. If you're being hammered by the press, you can cheer yourself up by thinking, "Well, at least I did *that* right." The alternative is to take the martyr's stance: "I am a moral person. These people have tried to crucify me. But I wouldn't be shaken. I spoke my mind." '

So, what, finally, of the man himself? Speaking with some dignity – although surprisingly dispassionately, barely two months after the death of his sister – on Cape Talk radio station in his adopted South Africa, Charles managed to get in a dig at the media before considering his funeral Address, and the reaction to it. 'Of course, the tabloid press in Britain have had fun down the years playing around with caricatures and trying to make out that I was some kind of spoiled brat just because they assumed Diana's brother *had* to be a spoiled brat. So it was a relief in a way to reclaim my own identity in that speech. I've since had letters from people saying how extraordinary they thought it was that I could speak in that way but that was just me being myself. I wasn't trying to present myself in any different, or artificial, light.

'It was a very easy speech to write, I must say. I was flying back to London on the day that Diana died and I was trying to busy myself with practical things to think about in connection with being head of her family. I was wondering to myself who could make the Address at her funeral and it was difficult. I just couldn't see anyone who was a consistent theme in her life. Then I suddenly realized it had to be me.

'But that went on the back burner for a few days because I had so many other things to deal with as soon as I reached London. Then I woke up very early in the morning – at about 4.30 – on the Wednesday between her death and the funeral. I sat down at my computer and I'd finished the speech by six o'clock; it had taken just an hour and a half to write. That was it. I didn't change anything except the removal of one paragraph that was incredibly strong against the press and was unnecessary. I hope I got my point across without it. The speech just stood. It was something that came from my heart. I don't analyse it now. I said it and I meant it and I don't take a word back. I had no agenda. I was just speaking as a brother to a sister – and on behalf of a sister. Simple as that.'

2

THE CHILDHOOD

It was the wedding of the year, some said the decade. Viscount Althorp, the 30-year-old equerry to the Queen, married the Hon Frances Roche, younger daughter of Lord and Lady Fermoy, on 1 June 1954. They did so in front of the Queen, Prince Philip, the Queen Mother, Princess Margaret and 1,700 or so assorted guests – everyone from the highest born in the land to the lowliest employee from the Althorp estate, ancestral seat of the Spencers since the beginning of the sixteenth century. At 18, the beautiful new Lady Althorp – she of the handspan waist and showgirl legs – was the youngest Westminster Abbey bride of the century. The subsequent reception was held at St James's Palace, loaned for the occasion by the grateful monarch, lately returned from a triumphant tour of Australia and New Zealand, during which a lovelorn Viscount Althorp had acted as Master of the Royal Household. Indeed, so besotted had he been with the charms of his débutante fiancée that Johnnie had commissioned artist Nicholas Egon to paint a life-sized portrait of Frances, completed in twenty-four hours flat and rushed to the quayside just before the liner, *Gothic*, set sail on the Royal Tour.

Following the honeymoon in Italy and Austria, Lord Althorp relinquished his court duties – working for the royals, he told a friend, made it almost impossible for courtiers to have lives of their own – and embarked on a course in farming and estate management at Cirencester in Gloucestershire. Nine months after the wedding, Frances gave birth to 'a honeymoon baby', Sarah. The young couple moved to Orchard Manor on the Althorp estate in Northamptonshire but not for long. With the death of Lord Fermoy in 1955, his widow insisted that her daughter and family should move into Park House on the Sandringham estate. Frances was delighted, happily back home in the house in which she had been raised. Johnnie, meanwhile, quickly found his stride as a traditional British landowner, although putting almost a hundred miles between himself and his father, the cantankerous seventh Earl Spencer, was felt to be an additional persuasive factor.

When a second daughter, Jane, arrived in 1957, Johnnie Althorp was proud if a little concerned. He needed a son and heir. Frances was duly despatched to a Harley Street gynaecologist, presumably in the vain hope he might be able to affect the gender of their next child.

In the spring of 1959, Frances found herself pregnant once more. 'Everything was completely normal,' she told *Hello!* magazine more than thirty-five years later. 'That pregnancy was the easiest of the lot. I decided that, as I'd already had Sarah and Jane in hospital, I'd have this baby at home.' But the moment the child, a boy, was born, it was clear something was very wrong. The baby was unable to breathe; he died eleven hours later. In an exclusive interview with journalist Fidelma Cook for the *Mail on Sunday* in March 1997, Frances spoke with heartbreaking poignancy about her third child. 'Medical opinion was different in those days. Babies were taken away and you were told they would be back. But I never saw him, never held him. I was told he needed help and I could see him later on. But he never came back. I lost that close association with a wee soul who grew within me, side by side. I gave him nourishment and my arms still ache for the wanting to have held him.

'This has been compounded by what I have read over the years, authoritatively stated in books, that he was horribly deformed. He wasn't. John was an 8lb baby boy who had a lung malfunction which meant he couldn't survive. I often think I'm the only one who remembers his anniversary. Things have changed now. It is recognized that, whatever happens, the mother can see and hold the baby. In those days, one had to keep a stiff upper lip and get on with it. I was crying about what had happened and I was told, "You'll have another child." That next child is not a replacement, though, and the soul of the lost child remains. The child who came next – Diana – was a different soul and it is so wrong that she should ever have been considered a replacement.' In a postscript in *Hello!*, Frances added, 'Even now, I still look at young men who were born at the same time and wonder what John would have been like. It is something that will always live with me.'

While the sex of Diana may have been an initial disappointment to her father, who had been convinced, for no very good reason, that she would be a boy, she became the very apple of his eye – the last of the Three Graces, as he nicknamed his daughters, and, by common consent, his favourite. Yet still the long line of Spencers looked as if it might come to a full stop with Johnnie, himself an only son. And then, on 20 May 1964, at the London Clinic and weighing in at a healthy 8lbs, Charles Edward Maurice Spencer entered the world. Flags flew at Althorp and a grand christening was held in Westminster Abbey, the Queen graciously accepting the invitation to act as the child's principal godparent. (Diana, by contrast, had been born at home and christened at the local Sandringham church, St Mary Magdalene.) The longed-for son must have seemed for all the world like a new beginning for one of Britain's oldest families; in fact, his arrival more or less heralded the end of his parents' now shaky marriage.

Frances had built up a busy social whirl in London, often leaving her husband, twelve years her senior and happy enough with the more predictable pleasures of rural Norfolk, to his own devices. She was still only 31 when she met the handsome, debonair Peter Shand Kydd – only a year younger than her husband, he had made a fortune from the family wallpaper business. Newly returned with his wife, Janet, and their three children, from running a sheep farm in Australia, Shand Kydd carried about him just that whiff of bohemian *joie de vivre*

Frances found irresistible. He made her laugh, and vice versa. Johnnie was with his wife the night she met Shand Kydd but failed to notice any danger signals. Within months, the two couples were on a skiing holiday together in Courcheval, southeast France. 'That's when we realized there was a strong attraction,' Frances was later to reveal. Back in England, they embarked on an affair. By September 1967, Shand Kydd had left his wife and Frances had asked Johnnie for a trial separation. The ensuing scandal broke new ground in society circles: affairs were tolerated, indeed enthusiastically picked over, albeit in hushed voices behind closed drawing-room doors; divorce, or the possibility of it, was, on the other hand, as unthinkable as it was unforgivable.

Lady Althorp was breaking rank in an alarming way. Clearly, she was risking the possibility of placing desire before duty. But what about the children? Did she discuss with them her decision to separate from their father? 'Of course I did,' she told *Hello!* indignantly in the March 1997 interview, said to have caused a rift between herself and Diana. 'It was something I put a lot of thought into. I discussed it then and always. As they got older, there were relevant questions according to their age. We still talk openly and discuss it. I feel it's terribly important to be honest; you can be economical with the truth but you must be straight.' Nor did she attempt to belittle the effect of the parents' failed marriage on their children. One of Charles's first memories, he has disclosed, was of seeing his mother cry. 'There were tears, on both sides, from all my children,' says Frances. 'It would be ridiculous to suggest that it was anything other than traumatic.'

But, understandably perhaps, she still finds it hard to contemplate the real effects of the separation and subsequent divorce on Sarah, Jane, Diana and Charles. 'You can't, can you? I didn't come from a broken home so never experienced it. In the long term, I'm sure it was better for them that we separated as there was such an air of tension in the house. What I'm certain they realize is that they were top priority for both their parents.'

In the event, Sarah and Jane, the two older children, were already away at boarding school during term-time. And the younger two? Frances may be for ever dubbed the bolter for walking out on the marriage but the stubborn facts suggest she had no way of knowing at that stage that she would be faced with the possibility of losing custody of her children. When she and Johnnie seemed to have nothing left to give each other, Frances took Diana and Charles, six and three respectively, with her to her Cadogan Square flat in Knightsbridge, south-west London. For a term, the two children were enrolled at local schools, returning to see their father at Park House most weekends. In October 1967, the whole family was reunited in Norfolk during the half-term holiday.

Six weeks later, they were back with their father in Norfolk for the Christmas holidays. 'And that was it,' says Frances. 'Without telling me, he had booked Diana and Charles into new schools and the lawyers stepped in. I was devastated but there was nothing I could do about it.' The hitherto rather easy-going Johnnie had been galvanized – uncharacteristically, it is said – into unstoppable action: he simply refused to allow his estranged wife to take their younger children back to London, insisting that they stay with him and attend school in King's Lynn. Frances, presented with little choice, returned to Cadogan Square after the grim festivities, desolate but confident at bedrock that she would win custody of her offspring.

Events moved swiftly, and inexorably, through 1968. In the spring, Frances was cited as 'the other woman' in the uncontested divorce case of Peter and Janet Shand Kydd. By June, Lord and Lady Althorp had embarked upon a bitter custody battle behind closed doors in the Family Division of the High Court. A pivotal role in the proceedings was played by Frances's mother, Ruth, Lady Fermoy, a Woman of the Bedchamber – or lady-in-waiting, in contemporary parlance – and a close friend of the Queen Mother. She sided with her son-in-law against her own daughter, preferring to see her grandchildren raised as Spencers within the orbit of the Royal Family than as stepchildren of a wallpaper tycoon. To this day, Frances remains tight-lipped on

30

what must have seemed to her the ultimate betrayal. 'You can imagine how much it hurt,' she told *Hello!*, adding, 'but I simply will not talk about people who are dead and cannot defend themselves.' (Lady Fermoy died on 6 July 1993.) Johnnie, against what must have seemed the prevailing odds, was awarded custody of his four children.

And yet, much counted against Frances. Fourteen years after the divorce, former newscaster and author Gordon Honeycombe, while writing his book, *The Year of the Princess*, was invited by the first Lady Althorp to her Scottish island home to hear her side of the custody battle. 'Several factors had worked against her,' Honeycombe subsequently wrote. 'The weight of aristocratic opinion was against her as was her own mother; and Norfolk, where the children had spent nearly all their lives, was a better place to bring them up than London. The law itself favoured the father who happened to be the son and heir of an earl. Custody of children involved in a divorce case is invariably given to the mother unless she is mentally deranged, a drug addict – or married to a nobleman. His rank and title give him prior claims. [This last] is unwritten and it would probably be denied if actually put to a lawyer but it reflects the aristocracy's view of women.'

Frances, emerging from her corner after fourteen years' dignified silence, and after so many one-sided reports that seemed to confirm her as the bolter, opened wounds in her relationship with her ex-husband that had never properly healed. Johnnie was said to be shocked to read details in the tabloid press, taken from Honeycombe's book, about the break-up of his first marriage. (In the meantime, he had married romantic novelist Barbara Cartland's daughter, the formidable Raine Dartmouth.) 'It is very unkind of her to speak in that way about our separation,' he told reporters in August 1982. 'I was totally surprised that she should bring it up in public. I don't know why my ex-wife felt she had to do such a thing. She should have thought about the children. It doesn't matter about my feelings but she should have thought about them. I feel sure it will upset them deeply.'

*

Fourteen years earlier, back in December 1968, divorce proceedings began in the High Court in the case of Althorp vs. Althorp. In a desperate attempt to reverse the earlier custody decision, Frances alleged cruelty. Reluctantly, it is said, Johnnie cross-petitioned on the grounds of her admitted adultery. 'Lord Althorp entered upon this course with hesitation and reluctance,' claimed his QC, Mr Geoffrey Crispin. 'He would much rather have his wife back but recognizes now that this marriage has broken down completely.' Frances stood little or no chance. On 15 April the following year, Viscount Althorp was granted a decree nisi on the grounds of his wife's adultery with Peter Shand Kydd. The judge, Mr Justice Wrangham, ordered Lady Althorp and Peter Shand Kydd to pay £3,000 towards Johnnie's costs. Frances was granted access to her children and allowed to have them with her in London at weekends. One month later, on 2 May 1969, she married Shand Kydd and the couple moved to West Itchenor on the Sussex coast. In 1972, they bought a farm on the Isle of Seil in Argyllshire where she bred Shetland ponies and ran a gift shop in Oban. In 1988, nineteen years later, the marriage collapsed and Peter has since married (and separated from) another woman.

History has pigeon-holed Frances Shand Kydd as a scarlet woman and, clearly, she feels aggrieved by so one-dimensional a judgement. Sir Nicholas Lloyd had numerous dealings with her in his ten-year reign as *Daily Express* editor. 'In the late eighties and early nineties,' recalls Lloyd, 'the *Express* was the largest-selling English newspaper in Scotland – and the one Frances Shand Kydd read every day. She'd ring me up quite often, usually after lunch, and tell me I'd got things wrong. Our conversations would be amusing but not especially enlightening. Since she never really told me anything I could get my teeth into, there was little I could do to set the record straight.'

His judgement on her ultimate action is, nonetheless, uncompromising. 'In the normal course of events, mothers never leave their children. Frances Shand Kydd was branded a bolter although it's only fair to point out that everybody – and, incredibly enough, that included her own mother, Lady Fermoy –

sided with the father (and the money) in a pretty disgusting way. The upshot was that she lost control of her children. But driven out or not, she still behaved, in my experience, in a way that most women – and, particularly, most mothers – would find incomprehensible. Even driven out, most women wouldn't stay out, then or now. When Diana was killed, for instance, Frances didn't come to London until the following Wednesday, four days after her daughter's death. Most mothers I know would have trampled over anyone and everyone to get to Paris to be with their child. Not that she could have done anything; but it would have been an understandable, a primeval, reaction. In the event, she has led a distant life and, to my mind, was not all that close to her daughter as a result.'

Her children's upbringing, and Charles's in particular, says Lloyd, must have been very odd indeed. 'Johnnie Spencer, however lovely he may have been, was, nonetheless, something of a throwback father, even by contemporary standards; and no mother was present during Charles's formative years except, as he said in his funeral Address, at the end of long train journeys.'

Johnnie seemed to have won a pyrrhic victory. In the aftermath of the divorce, he was desolate, his bewilderment plain even to his young son. 'He was really miserable after the divorce, basic-ally shell-shocked,' Charles confided in Andrew Morton. 'He used to sit in his study the whole time. I remember occasionally, very occasionally, he used to play cricket with me on the lawn. That was a great treat.' According to Johnnie's aunt, Lady Margaret Douglas-Home, her nephew couldn't believe what had happened. 'It was all absolutely unexpected and he was devast-ated. I don't think he ever mended. The children were very badly affected. He tried to put everything right but of course it was never possible.' Some years later, talking to a local East Anglian newspaper reporter, Johnnie Spencer reinforced his aunt's recollection of events. 'The divorce couldn't have happened at a worse possible time,' he said. 'We got some girls in to help look after the children but they were still very young.

It was quite an unusual household but we developed a system and it worked out quite well.'

Charles recalls this succession of nannies from his rather different perspective. 'Some of them were very tough indeed,' he told *Hello!* in 1992. 'My mother had to sack one because, every time my two eldest sisters were naughty, she used to give them strong doses of laxatives, and it was really harming their health.' Another, apparently, would bang together the heads of the two younger children if they misbehaved or, if one of them did something wrong, she would bang that child's head against the wall. 'As children, we accepted this as quite normal but now it seems so frightening.'

It is clear, though, that their charges certainly gave the nannies a run for their money. 'If my brother and I didn't like them,' Diana told Andrew Morton, 'we used to stick pins in their chair and throw their clothes out of the window. We always thought they were a threat because they tried to take mother's position. They were all rather young and pretty. They were chosen by my father. It was terribly disruptive to come back from school one day to find a new nanny.' In fairness, Charles told *Hello!*, 'I did have some very nice nannies during those years although we got through quite a few so I can imagine we must have been a bit of a handful.'

One of the most successful, in terms of both kindness and capability, was Mary Clarke, the last 'girl' Earl Spencer hired to look after his children. When she accepted the job, Diana (like her sisters) was already away at boarding school, Charles the only one still at home. 'For the next nineteen months,' says Mary, 'until he himself went off to Maidwell as a boarder, I was the one person, perhaps above all others, who was the most constant factor in Charles's life. The divorce had already happened by the time I arrived. There had been a tremendous amount of upheaval, of course, but most of that was in the past.

'Lord Althorp was looking for someone to provide a steady influence for his children. He had seen sixty-four people in London, I was later told, before I spotted his advertisement in *The Lady* magazine. Because I was based in Norfolk, Lord

Althorp agreed to see me. I was still only 20 and I had no experience as a nanny. He wanted someone who could establish a good secure base for Diana when she came home for the school holidays. Charles, at that time, wasn't so much shy as very self-contained and introverted; he was a quiet, serious little boy and his father was rather concerned how he would cope when he was sent away to prep school. He wanted someone who would make Charles a little more boisterous, more outgoing, someone who would prepare him for boarding school.

'During my interview, the woman who was then looking after Charles brought him down to meet me. He was six at the time. There was still quite a divide between the children's quarters and the adult part of the house so I think it was all a bit overwhelming for the lad. But he was extremely polite. He shook my hand and I tried to put him at his ease with a few small jokes. I told him he must have much better things to do upstairs and, with a swift sidelong look at his father to check that it would be all right, he left the room as quickly as he could.

'I grew up in the sixties and I suppose that gave me the confidence to feel I could do anything I set my mind to. I'd taught a few children to ride but, beyond that, I knew next to nothing about them. But I'd seen the advertisement – Lord Althorp was looking for someone who could ride, swim and drive. And I'd get paid! The fact that I'd have to look after children didn't cross my mind as any sort of impediment. My twin brother and I had been brought up to be quietly confident.'

Lord Althorp told Mary he would contact her within the week after their initial interview. 'Then my father took a phone call from him a few days later saying that he would be visiting friends near where we lived and that he'd like to meet my parents. I hadn't told them about applying for the job so I think they were quite surprised that Lord Althorp was going to drop in. But I was impressed – and so were they – that he'd taken the trouble to see for himself my home environment. At the end of the visit, I was offered the job. Two weeks later, when I was 21, I started work.' It was February 1971.

'Once at Sandringham, I didn't see much of Lord Althorp; he

was often away or caught up in his own affairs. I like to think he established early on that I was doing a capable job and left me to get on with it. It's better, of course, for children to be with two happy parents although, in these particular circumstances, the Spencer children spent more quality time with each parent so perhaps the divorce wasn't all that harmful for them.

'I have read numerous accounts of Charles crying himself to sleep and Diana comforting him. I am perfectly certain he did miss his mother – it would be strange if he hadn't – but I got to know the old retainers who had been at Park House throughout the bitterness of the divorce and they never mentioned Charles being wretchedly unhappy. Certainly, I never saw it.

'It saddens me when I read negative reports about Diana and Charles's father. Maybe he hadn't been all that nice to Frances – I wouldn't know – but what couple is nice to one another when they're on the point of parting? I can only speak as I found him and as everyone I knew at the time found him. He was an extremely kind, thoughtful man. I can't believe we were all wrong about him. I only met his father, the seventh Earl, on a handful of occasions. He was a very, very difficult man. He and Johnnie had a pretty strained relationship, to say the least. But Johnnie's mother, Cynthia, was adored by everyone, the most enchanting woman imaginable. A lot of those qualities were to be found in her son.

'When Johnnie was at home, he was very good with his children. He went out most evenings but he'd always make sure that he was there when Charles went to bed and Diana, too, during the holidays. He would read them bedtime stories. Charles was a very clever boy, the brightest of all the Spencer children. He was an avid, fluent reader by the time he went to Silfield aged 4 but, like all children, he used to like being read to at night. His father often chose historical themes which Charles always showed great interest in. One of his favourite pastimes was playing with his toy soldiers. He knew all the battles and the details of where his lead soldiers should stand. His father must have taught him all of that. He was at pains to imbue in Charles a sense of his heritage. The Spencers had been around much longer than the Windsors, for instance: a good five hundred years. I think the eighth Earl wanted his children to grow up aware of their place in history. But although his father had a beautiful scaled-down gun made for him, Charles shared with Diana an aversion to killing animals. My solution was to line up tin cans so Charles could get used to a little target practice without doing any harm to a living creature.

'During my time at Park House, the Earl met Raine Dartmouth, as she then was, and he was away from home a great deal. But I have a vivid memory of him sitting in his study writing to all three of his daughters so that they had regular news from home while they were at boarding school. He never missed a week. And he was very kind to Charles when the two of them were at home together. I can only think that Charles has happy memories of his father. They got closer when I suggested that Charles and I ought to eat with Lord Althorp rather than him being in the main dining-room and Charles and me eating in the nursery. Sarah and Jane, the older two, were already eating meals with their father when they were home from school; but it made it much more of a family unit from the time Diana and Charles joined them for meals.

'Perhaps Lord Althorp wasn't at home as much as he should have been or would have liked to have been. But he had his various business pursuits – the responsibilities that came with running a farm, for instance – as well as his life in London. It's hard to imagine that he could have spent much more time with Charles than he did; in other words, he was no different from many men of his generation. Indeed, because he was divorced and he had custody of the children, I believe he made more time for them than he might otherwise have done. The Spencer children may not have had the parental influence felt in many households but then they didn't have to suffer the bickering and rows some children witness. We didn't have rows at Park House; and never once, in all my time there, did I hear Johnnie run down Frances in front of their children – or, indeed, in front of anyone else.

'I'm sure, deep down, Charles did have thoughts about his

mother when he returned to Sandringham from having seen her. But other than saying what he'd done when he'd been with her, he never said too much about what he was feeling. Children don't. They talk about facts, not feelings. They're very black and white.'

Unsurprisingly, Mary Clarke's relationship with Frances was, at best, little more than courteous. 'But I never felt any antagonism towards her,' she says. 'To begin with, I'd take the children on the train to stay with her, kiss them goodbye and hand them over. She was perfectly civil to me. But all that changed, of course, when, in 1971, she renewed her bid to win back custody of them on the grounds that I wasn't a fit and proper person to be bringing up Diana and Charles. She became very cool to me then. I'll never forget standing in Court 21 – I was the key witness – just thinking how incredibly sad the whole situation had become. I still find it impossible to understand how Frances's mother, Lady Fermoy, could have testified against her own daughter in the original divorce case. For me, blood always runs thicker than water.'

But Mary Clarke does little to disguise the enjoyment she derived from her remarkably carefree existence in Viscount Althorp's employment. 'The holidays were bedlam. The life I had with Charles during the term was very quiet. We spent nearly all our time at Park House. I didn't have to worry about housework or cooking; other people were responsible for those things. I was purely there for the children or for Charles when Diana was away at school. I was living a wonderful life for a 21-year-old. I think my friends were rather envious. I remember the occasion when my brother came to visit and Lord Althorp – another example of his kindness – allowed him to drive his XJS Jaguar.

'Charles was very lovable and very easy to grow fond of. He was so affable. He wasn't a clinging child but he was affectionate. I used to have to drag him outside; he wasn't so keen on the great outdoors. I taught him to ride. We just did everything together. I'd try to instil in him a sense of adventure, of a world outside his experience. He wasn't in the least spoilt but then none of them were. All right, there was an outdoor heated pool, one of the first to be built in Britain, but those rumours that the Spencer children were each given a catalogue from Hamley's toy shop and told to tick any item they'd like are completely untrue. I'm sure they ticked all sorts of things but that didn't inevitably mean they'd be given them all. I remember doing exactly the same thing as a child, an opportunity to dream and hope.

'Charles's greatest treat, I remember, when we went into King's Lynn, was to go into a big stationer's to buy crayons, just like any child. I used to say to Lord Althorp, and he readily agreed, that it was more important for the children to have friends over to play. We'd go to the beach or go on special outings. That was how they derived their greatest pleasure; certainly not from material things. I don't ever remember Diana or Charles asking for anything; if they'd been spoilt children, they had ample opportunity to play one parent off against the other. But I never saw one example of that.'

Mary Clarke is an honest witness, palpably a sensible woman who did what she felt was right by her charges. It was not her fault, indeed it was self-evidently outside her control, that she inherited for her nineteen-month tenure of the post of Park House nanny, children who were, to a greater or lesser extent, damaged goods. 'I have very few memories of my mother and father together,' Charles told *Hello!*. 'The clearest is of my mother in tears and my father nearly in tears so I don't have any happy memories of them together at all. And, really, between their divorce and my father's death, they hardly spoke so I've never really thought of them as a unit in any way.

'I can remember [finding out that my parents wouldn't be living together any more] very clearly. I must have been three or four at the time. My mother went away and I can remember asking where she was and being told that she'd gone away on holiday; then asking every day and sensing that something was very wrong but not understanding at all really. I can remember that, and I can remember, too, that, as a child, you know if some-one's lying to you.

'My childhood wasn't especially sad. To any outsider, it looks immensely privileged. We grew up in a wonderful house, beau-tiful grounds, the setting for an ideal childhood. But I suppose not seeing much of one's mother does slightly put a dampener on that. It wasn't a sob story; it just wasn't a particularly happy time in my life. I have a very good memory but a lot of my child-hood is a blank. I've been told that, when my mother left, I used to cry the whole time, sob all night . . . But I have to say I can't remember it.'

Perhaps not. But the psychologist Dorothy Rowe is in no doubt as to the effects of this fractured childhood on the current Earl Spencer. Nor does she claim any special insight: the child, she says, has ever been father to the man.'Right from birth, every child needs to have one figure, one person – although not neces-sarily their biological mother or father – to provide consistency and to let them know that the adult thinks they're wonderful. Having two adults as a source of unconditional love is even better but one is enough to give the child the firm foundation which will equip him or her for dealing with most difficulties later on.

'Diana and Charles didn't have that solid centre. They had an absentee mother and a father who, however much he said he loved them, seems to have been rather a remote figure, albeit living under the same roof, caught up in his own problems. The children were left in the care of a succession of nannies. Children have to feel that their parents are available for them; it isn't enough just being there. Nor is it enough to parrot every so often in a rather sentimental way that you adore them. Love is not enough. Then, of course, at no age at all, Diana and Charles were packed off to boarding schools. The result was that they would have been dealing with a whole lot of unmet needs which, in turn, inspires children to dream up ways to get themselves noticed, to get those needs met.

'What happens in a lot of families is that children discover that, by being good, they get nothing. For instance, parents may threaten children that, if they're not good, Santa Claus won't bring them anything at Christmas whereas, in reality, what happens is that, if they're good – in other words, quiet and amenable – the adults take little or no notice of them. As soon as you start to kick up a fuss, parents start to listen. And once you learn a way of behaving that produces the kind of results you want, you go on using it. You only modify your behaviour when you grow older because your situation has changed. That is why there are lots of people who, when they don't get what they want, continue to throw adult versions of their childhood tantrums.

'The people who are really effective with tantrums are those who surround themselves with anyone who will take their tantrums seriously. One of the problems for Diana when she got married was that her methods of being upset didn't mean anything to the Royal Family. These are people who cry when an old ship like *Britannia* is being decommissioned but who don't shed a tear – in public, at any rate – at the early death of a daughter-in-law.

'If you've been born into a family where no one notices your tantrums or, alternatively, punishes you for them, you develop other ways to get your needs met. Children have to come up with something that utilizes what little power they possess. Diana, when her needs were overlooked, attracted attention by being ill or by being very distressed. With more power in the first place because he was the heir, her brother Charles's tantrums would have taken the form of bald demands and they are likely to have been met for no better reason than that he was valued more for being the only boy: he must be listened to more.

'I was very struck by the reported conversation he had with Victoria when he was lying in the bath and announcing to her that not only was the marriage over but that she'd never been any good as a wife. That is exactly the equivalent of what an imperious little boy would say. A 4-year-old's rage is total: he says exactly and only what he feels. As we get older, we should develop a way of understanding the effects of our words and

actions. The needy small child doesn't understand the importance of taking into account the other person's needs.
Unchecked, that lack of comprehension carries over into adult-
hood.

'A child who has been overlooked, a child who has been
made to feel – very often by omission – that he or she is rather
less than wonderful, then begins to believe it. The adults seem to
be saying that the child is bad and unacceptable so it must be
true. Small children will say, "If I'd been really good, my mother
wouldn't have left me." They blame themselves and there's little
wonder: adults do blame children for all sorts of things. Like
clumsiness, for instance. But the fact is that small children *are*
clumsy which is hardly surprising since they haven't yet got fine
movement worked out; and parents often don't take the time to
accept what has happened as an accident.

'Many terrible things flow from not thinking much of yourself and one of them is that it makes you completely self-
absorbed. You're always frightened of other people; you're
scared that you'll upset them and they'll reject you or hurt you
or criticize you. You're convinced you'll never be able to do
things right. The result is that all your attentions are focused on
yourself; you become a selfish person oblivious to what is going
on in the world around you and unaware of the needs of other
people and of what makes them tick. It means you go on and on
making mistakes with other people because you've never taken
the time to work out how the rest of the world might think and
feel. The cycle is self-perpetuating.

'From the evidence of Charles's behaviour and actions, he
would appear not to have attempted to understand why he feels
and acts as he does. Speaking as a therapist, the essence of ther-
apy, in my opinion, should be to address this central issue of
how you feel about yourself. It isn't necessary to go back to
uncover every hideous event in your childhood. What *is* necessary is to come to understand that this feeling of essential inad-
equacy and unacceptability isn't so much a part of you like the
colour of your eyes or your gender; it's a way of feeling that has
developed from the conclusions you drew from your childhood

experiences. We can't change the past but we can change our ideas about the past.'

So has Charles Spencer begun to change *his* ideas about the past? On the evidence of his recent behaviour, says Dr Rowe, the answer must be emphatically in the negative.

3

THE HISTORY

In an exchange subsequently repeated in every bar and club-house in the land, Diana's father, the eighth Earl Spencer, when asked by some impertinent reporter whether his lord-ship felt his daughter was good enough to marry into the Royal Family, is said to have replied – his tongue some distance from his cheek – that the question, rather, was whether the Windsors were good enough for Diana.

Behind the querulous response could be heard the distant echoes of generations of Spencers: as powerful a family as any in post-fifteenth century Britain (although some considerable ground has been lost since the Industrial Revolution) and invested with the unassailable confidence – or right, as individual members might claim – to meet the monarch of the day eyeball to eyeball. This, as his last nanny Mary Clarke points out, is why it would never have crossed the ninth Earl's mind to be nervous about saying what he wanted to say, what he felt *should* be said, in front of the Queen in his funeral Address in Westminster Abbey. To fully understand the evolution of Charles Spencer's psyche it is necessary to trace the history of the rich and powerful Spencer dynasty.

With the exception of Lord Robert Spencer – universally referred to as the Trimmer and described in the *Dictionary of National Biography* (though doubtless not in the official Althorp guidebook) as 'the craftiest, most rapacious and most unscrupulous of all the politicians of the second half of the seventeenth century' – successive Spencer heirs seem to have been rather a commendable breed. Liberal(ish) entrepreneurs with, in some instances, a marked desire to patronize the arts, they have been men who danced only to the beat of their own drums.

Sir John Spencer (1533–99) was the first of the 'modern' line and as typical as any: he bought the Wormleighton estate in Warwickshire and Althorp in Northamptonshire, on which to graze his sheep. A shrewd businessman, he hit upon the age-old wheeze of bypassing the middle man – in this case, the local markets – preferring to sell his produce directly to wool merchants and butchers in the capital, and became one of the great Elizabethan 'sheep masters', as they were known. He authorized the construction of a less than distinguished red-brick manor house to be built at Althorp. Sir John may have been one of the richest men in England but he was not one to squander his wealth.

Sir John's son Robert (1570–1627), having bought a barony from James I, was in 1622 to be found reflecting on bygone days in the upper chamber. His lordship was interrupted by Lord Arundel. 'When these things were doing,' said Arundel, 'the noble Lord's ancestors were keeping sheep.' To which Spencer retorted, 'When my ancestors were keeping sheep, the noble Lord's ancestors were plotting treason.' Collapse of stout party as all assembled knew full well that Arundel's father and grandfather had both been beheaded as traitors. Robert Spencer was savvy enough to negotiate a safe passage between the Scylla and Charybdis of opposing court factions, smart enough to marry a wealthy woman – Katherine Kitson, daughter of a fabulously rich merchant, Sir Robert Kitson – and every bit silver-tongued enough to deflect any criticism in the House of Lords.

This unwillingness to toe the party line was inherited by Robert's son William (1591–1636), who resolutely refused the royal offer of an earldom and who gave a wide berth to the mixed pleasures of court life. His son Henry, the third Baron Spencer (1620–43) was made Earl of Sunderland after lending Charles I £10,000 (add on three noughts for today's value) during the Civil War. A matter of weeks later, on 23 September 1643, he was beheaded at the Battle of Newbury by Oliver Cromwell's Roundheads and interred at the battle site –

although his heart was taken back to be buried at the Spencer grave at Great Brington in Northamptonshire.

And so it was that Lord Robert Spencer (1641–1702), although only little more than a toddler at the time, became the second Earl of Sunderland. In time a brilliant if unscrupulous statesman, he earned his nickname, the Trimmer, by making himself indispensable to Charles II, James II and William III in swift succession. But, for all the latter-day vilification, his lordship was a man of unswerving good taste, the chatelain who converted Althorp from a respectable, if dull, red-brick manor house into a magnificent mansion. Having authorized its reconstruction, Lord Spencer filled it with all manner of treasures: priceless paintings by Rubens and Van Dyck, French silver, beautiful furniture and a fabulous library to rival the best in the land. He was also fleet of foot when it came to finding suitable brides for his heir, Charles (1675–1722): first, the daughter of the Earl of Devonshire, who died in 1698; and then, Anne Churchill, younger daughter of the Duke of Marlborough – the hero who had defeated the French at Blenheim, Ramillies and Malplaquet, and direct ancestor of Sir Winston Churchill.

Two years after the Trimmer's death, and through a complicated quirk of fate involving premature deaths in other branches of the family, two of his five children – Charles and John – were able to carve up both the titles and the wealth of the Spencer and Marlborough dynasties. Charles (1706–58) got the titles and became both Earl of Sunderland and Duke of Marlborough; while his younger brother John (1708–46), favourite of his wealthy, widowed grandmother, the Duchess of Marlborough, got the money. The inheritance was huge, including not only estates in Northampton and Warwickshire but Holywell House in St Albans, Hertfordshire, and a villa, Park House, attached to a sizeable slab of Wimbledon Common in south-west London. This was the point when the families, although inextricably linked, split and became two hugely wealthy branches of the same family tree.

*

It was John Spencer's son, also called John (1734–83), who was to become the first Earl Spencer in 1765, ennobled by Prime Minister William Pitt, who was anxious for the political support of one of Britain's grandest and most influential families. Spencer secretly married Georgiana Poyntz, his childhood sweetheart, at his coming of age party; the bride, a dazzling beauty, was only 18. So wealthy was the groom, the buckles that adorned the shoes he wore on his honeymoon were valued at £30,000. Not content with the stately pile in Northamptonshire and the country house on Wimbledon Common, Spencer built a magnificent Palladian townhouse in London overlooking Green Park. Begun in 1756, Spencer House was initially designed by architect John Vardy (a pupil of William Kent), who was superseded by James Stuart two years later. One of the most ambitious private palaces ever to be built in the capital, it was filled with treasures. It remains open to the public today.

John and Georgiana had three children including their son and heir, yet another John, the second Earl Spencer (1758–1834), who became First Lord of the Admiralty during the time of Lord Nelson. Their daughter, also Georgiana, was widely held to be the most talked about and envied woman of her age, her celebrated good looks matched by an equally agile mind. She was just 17 when the Duke of Devonshire made her his bride – a cynical move since he was said never to have loved her and to have maintained a mistress before and during their marriage. Undaunted, Georgiana, never short of slavish admirers, took a succession of high-ranking lovers including the future Prime Minister, Lord Grey.

Devonshire House, meanwhile, became the epicentre of what was dubbed 'grand Whiggery', a reference to the political movement dedicated to subordinating the power of the Crown to that of Parliament and the upper classes. Georgiana used her abundant assets to champion the cause of Charles James Fox, even resorting, it is said, to exchanging kisses for votes in the 1744 Westminster by-election in which Fox was a candidate.

When she died in 1806, so, too, did the golden years of the Spencers.

The political life of one of Charles Spencer's ancestors, however, draws interesting parallels with the man who spoke from the pulpit in September 1997. John Charles, the third Earl Spencer (1782–1845), was universally known as Honest Jack Althorp and embodied the new moral earnestness of the nineteenth-century Spencers. Chancellor of the Exchequer and Leader of the Commons in the Lord Grey government of the early 1830s, Spencer was a radical Whig who helped steer the great Reform Act of 1832 on to the statute book. Away from politics, his abiding passion was farming and he is now perhaps best remembered for his successful breeding of Shorthorn cattle as well as for founding the Royal Agricultural Society of England.

One episode in his early political career serves to illustrate the courage required to stand up to the Crown and the lack of concern apparently felt by male Spencers in speaking their mind to royalty. As Georgina Battiscombe details in her book, *The Spencers of Althorp*, the third Earl became spokesman for a group known as the Young Whigs who united to expose a particularly unpleasant piece of royal corruption.

'George III's son, Frederick Duke of York,' writes Battiscombe, 'was Commander-in-Chief of the Army. His mistress, Mrs Clarke, was accused of taking bribes from officers seeking appointments of promotion. Mrs Clarke's dealings were proved beyond a shadow of doubt and her lover's complicity in them seemed almost certain; nevertheless, the House of Commons was inclined to deal leniently with him, much to the fury of the Radicals. Althorp and his friends were particularly horrified, believing, as they did, in the importance of maintaining moral principles both in public and private life, and inheriting all the Whig mistrust of the Royal Family.

'They were joined by other young men of similar views and Althorp was chosen as their spokesman in spite of the fact that, although he had been in the House of Commons for five years, he had never yet made his maiden speech. Now, he had at last found a cause which roused and interested him, a subject which could vie with hunting in its claim on his attention; in his sister Sarah, Lady Lyttelton's opinion, "He was all eagerness to hunt down both the foxes and the Duke of York." His speech was described as "totally devoid of affectation and full of ability". The motion of censure was defeated but public indignation was so great that the Duke was forced to resign. In thus attacking a royal personage, Althorp had acted contrary to the judgement of those older men whom he regarded as his political leaders, and of his father in particular.'

His brother, Frederick, the fourth Earl Spencer (1798–1857), began his career in the Navy and played a leading role in the Battle of Navarino. Later, he became Lord Chamberlain of the Queen's Household and was awarded the Order of the Garter. But it was *his* son, the Red Earl, who was probably the most famous of them all. John Poyntz, the fifth Earl (1835–1910), acquired the nickname because of his voluminous beard in the inherited Spencer shade of rich red – a shade which can be traced to our current Prince Harry.

A successful politician, he looked forward to the coming Liberals rather than back to the departing Whigs. He was a great friend and ally of Gladstone's and, like his uncle the third Earl before him, was widely liked and respected, narrowly missing becoming Prime Minister. From 1859 to 1861, he assumed the arcane mantle of Groom of the Stole to the Prince Consort and then, reluctantly, accepted the same post in the household of the Prince of Wales until 1866 when he resigned.

After the Red Earl had made a name for himself in the Lords and proved an excellent chairman of an important commission, Gladstone appointed him Viceroy – or Lord Lieutenant – of Ireland in 1869. When the Liberals lost power five years later, the Earl returned to England having established a reputation for firmness and courage combined with a sympathy for Irish grievances.

The Liberals were returned to power in 1880 and Spencer was given a cabinet post as Lord President of the Council, the minister responsible for education and agriculture. He never lost his interest in Irish affairs, though, and served a second term as Viceroy from 1882. The new Chief Secretary was Lord Frederick Cavendish, linked to the Red Earl by blood as well as friendship. ('The ramifications of the great Whig cousinry,' according to Georgina Battiscombe, 'were immense and its hold on political office extraordinary. Spencer, Granville and the two Cavendish brothers – Hartington and Lord Frederick – were all descended from the first Earl Spencer; and Frederick Cavendish had married another cousin, Lucy Lyttelton, niece to the Gladstones through her mother, Mary Glynne.')

On his return to southern Ireland, Earl Spencer was lucky to escape with his life. Accompanied from Dublin Castle to Viceregal Lodge by Frederick Cavendish and Permanent Under-secretary Thomas Burke, Spencer rode ahead through Phoenix Park and reached the Lodge without mishap. His companions, however, were set upon by a group called the Invincibles and murdered in the park. The Red Earl's name was clearly next on the group's hit-list but he remained undaunted despite being obliged to live a beleaguered garrison life at the Castle and Lodge. The following September, he toured through some of the most lawless and disaffected parts of Ireland surrounded by military police, soldiers and detectives.

Reaction to the Phoenix Park murders drove the British government to a policy of coercion. Spencer instructed the suppression of crime and disorder with vim and vigour, a programme that earned him considerable unpopularity in Ireland but which enhanced his reputation back home, where he returned in June 1885 when the Liberals again lost power. At the end of that year, with the party split over Home Rule for Ireland, the Red Earl sided with Gladstone in favour of it. Spencer was quoted as saying, 'I consider our old methods of government in Ireland quite useless.' A contemporary commentator described him as 'hardly of less weight than Mr Gladstone himself'.

Six years later, in December 1891, five leading Liberals – Gladstone, Rosebery, Harcourt, John Morley and Spencer – convened an informal conference at Althorp in the candlelit library. Within months, the party was back in power and the Red Earl was made First Lord of the Admiralty, a post he held until 1895. During his tenure, the 'Spencer programme' provided new fighting ships for the Navy. Such was his determination to see through this programme that Spencer clashed swords with his Prime Minister, a stand-off that brought about Gladstone's resignation. Small wonder then that Charles Spencer inherited a sense of his family's power to affect government and public opinion.

As a backdrop to this high-profile public life, the Red Earl was feeling the financial pinch. A depression in agricultural sales had forced him to raise money by other means: in this case, the sale of treasures from Althorp's impressive library, replete with first editions from William Caxton's printing press, that realized £220,000 – a considerable fortune at the time – and what was to prove the nucleus of a public library in Manchester.

The Red Earl died following a stroke in 1910. The great, great grandfather of Diana and Charles was a superlative shot, a mad-keen cricketer, being both President of Northamptonshire Cricket Club and the MCC, a superb horseman and the last Spencer to be Master of the Pytchley Hunt. As an editorial in the *Daily Chronicle* pointed out at the time, 'No one recalls a bitter speech or an envious action in the whole of his career, lived though it was for the most part in the fierce light of publicity.' Sadly, he and his wife Charlotte were childless, so that the title passed to his nephew, Charles Robert, the sixth Earl (1857–1922). At just 22, he had entered Parliament as the Liberal member for north Northamptonshire and, six years later, had been appointed groom-in-waiting to Queen Victoria. Vice-chamberlain from 1895, the sixth Earl was Lord Chamberlain of the Household from 1905, often accompanying Edward VII when he travelled abroad.

His wife Margaret died in childbirth, and 'Bobby' Spencer cut himself off from his children and society in general. At the point of his death in 1922, the Spencers, like the aristocracy as a whole, appeared to be economically and socially in retreat. It may explain why his successor, Albert Edward, the seventh Earl (1892–1975), sought comprehensive refuge in the past, having been wounded in action during the First World War. Jack, as he was popularly known, loved Althorp absolutely and became its most enthusiastic champion. Indeed, he was sometimes referred to as the Curator Earl for the enthusiasm with which he collated every treasure under its roof. An abiding friend of Queen Mary – she shared his unlikely passion for embroidery – he was something of a sociopath, so gruff was his demeanour, so unforgiving his behaviour. Legend has it that, on one occasion, he seized the cigar butt from the clenched teeth of Sir Winston Churchill with one swift action at the precise moment he believed the great man's ash might fall on to the carpet of Althorp's library.

But he did have the good sense to marry Cynthia, the blameless and beautiful daughter of the third Duke of Abercorn. Lady of the Bedchamber to Elizabeth, both as Queen and Queen Mother, Cynthia was once described as one of those 'rare women of whom people speak only in superlatives of praise'. And so her son, yet another John, understandably adored his mother but found it difficult to stay in the same room and remain civil to his short-tempered father.

Johnnie, perhaps because of this antagonism, came to hate Althorp, referring to it as 'the mausoleum'. And an echo is to be found in his son, Charles, the ninth and current Earl Spencer, who told Andrew Morton, 'When I was young, it was like an old man's club with lots of clocks ticking away. For an impressionable child, it was a nightmarish place.' It is a verdict that seems to have been inherited by the ninth Earl's offspring. 'My own children would prefer not to live at Althorp,' he said as he headed south to Cape Town at the end of 1995. 'There is the fun of space but the children like it when we go away and have a quieter, more intimate time. Whenever I take my eldest daughter, Kitty, back, she says, "I hate it here".'

But it was to there that Charles and his sisters were destined to move on the seventh Earl's death in 1975. And for that, the blame – or otherwise – can be laid more or less fair and square at the door of Ruth, Lady Fermoy – mother of Frances, mother-in-law of Johnnie, inseparable friend of the Queen Mother and royal prestidigitator *par excellence*. Having successfully, if that is the apposite word, seen her younger daughter married off to the future Earl Spencer, and having become permanent lady-in-waiting to the Queen Mother on the death of Lord Fermoy, Ruth had sided with her son-in-law over Frances's defection into the arms of Peter Shand Kydd. The result was Johnnie keeping the children and the entire ménage moving, when he acceded to the title, from Park House on the Sandringham Estate to Althorp Park in Northamptonshire. (Charles is said to have bidden farewell to each room in Park House when the move from Norfolk became inevitable.)

In the fullness of time, Ruth fell to fretting about Frances's third daughter. Sarah had married Neil McCorquodale, a former Coldstream Guards officer. Jane had long since become the wife of Sir Robert Fellowes, the Queen's private secretary. But what of Diana? And what, indeed, of Prince Charles, an equal source of concern to the Queen Mother whose eldest grandson was also her favourite? It did not take long for the two formidable widows to put one and one together. At 32, Prince Charles, a string of mistresses behind him, was becoming prematurely crusty and needed to produce an heir (and, if possible, a spare), preferably with a partner devoid of any sexual past that might return to haunt them both.

Sure enough, on 29 July 1981, Diana Frances married Charles Philip Arthur George amid much pomp and ceremony at St Paul's Cathedral in London. The couple – as Lady Fermoy, among others in the charmed circle, and then the rest of the world in time, came to know – lived increasingly unhappily ever after. When the marriage finally disintegrated, the Princess of Wales's maternal grandmother, in an eerie echo of earlier tactics, sided with the husband (and the Royal Family). Divorce, Dodi Fayed and a shocking and premature death were to be Diana's destiny.

But what of the fate of her younger brother: a man who, however much he might dislike the observation, became – and remains – famous by default? And what, too, of little Louis Frederick John, the Viscount Althorp, and one day, all things being equal, the tenth Earl Spencer? What might be his inheritance – and his bequest?

4

THE EDUCATION

Of all four Spencer children, Charles is, by common accord, the brightest – something Diana acknowledged when she spoke to Andrew Morton for what was, effectively, her autobiography. 'I've always seen him as the brains of the family,' she said. 'I still see that. He's got S-levels and things like that. I think that my brother, being the youngest and the only boy, was quite precious because Althorp is a big place. Remember, I was the girl who was supposed to be a boy. Being third in line was a very good position to be in – I got away with murder. I was my father's favourite; there's no doubt about that. I longed to be as good as Charles in the schoolroom but I was never jealous of him.'

Indeed, there is plenty of evidence to suggest that Diana mothered her younger brother, both at home and in the classroom, in the immediate aftermath of their parents' difficult divorce – as Jean Lowe can testify.

A nursery school already existed on the current site of Silfield School in King's Lynn when Miss Lowe, along with her sister and brother-in-law, took it over in 1953 and opened a companion school – with just nine pupils initially – for the over-fives. They bought the school at the end of the fifties. Jean Lowe remained there for thirty years, retiring in 1983. She remembers the young Charles Spencer clearly. 'He was a very affectionate and lovable little boy,' she says, 'and *very* bright. That was noticeable from an early age. He joined the nursery at 4 and then, as with all the other children, moved up into the main school at 5 where boys remained until they were ready to go to their next school at around 8. The girls could stay at Silfield, though, until they were 11.'

Diana and her younger brother came to the school, from their home on the Sandringham estate, at the beginning of 1968 when their parents had separated but not yet divorced. Among the other pupils were Charles and Alexandra Loyd, children of the Queen's land agent, as well as William and Annabel Fox whose mother, Carol, was Diana's godmother. 'Both Spencer children were quite quiet at first but then it was a difficult time for them. They were devoted to each other. Their older sisters, Sarah and Jane, were both away at boarding school. I particularly remember Diana worrying about whether or not Charles was settling into the nursery happily on his first day. She kept saying to me, "Do you think Charles is all right?" Then, a few minutes later, up would go her hand again. "Do you think Charles is all right?" Finally, I said, "Well, I think you'd better go and see." So, off she trotted to the nursery class and then came back and announced, "Yes, he's fine." She felt a keen sense of wanting to protect him right from the very beginning.'

Diana was an instinctively loving child, says Jean Lowe, but someone who needed to be loved in return. 'As a little girl, when she used to come up to read for me, she always lent against me. Even at that age, she craved to be touched. Her father was of the generation that didn't kiss and cuddle their children. Diana – and Charles, too – rather lost out on all of that at home.'

Nonetheless, in her experience, Earl Spencer was a caring father who was proud of his two younger children. 'He would often come into the schoolroom to see their work and talk to their friends. When he was able to do the school run, he was most careful to ensure they both had their homework, games clothes and so on.' Certainly, the two younger Spencer children behaved in much the same way as their classmates. 'They were popular and friendly; they went to parties at the houses of other children, just like anyone else. I never thought of them as in any way different. But then one didn't know what was going to happen, of course.'

Clearly, this sense of not being special had been instilled at

Charles and Diana, 1967.

© MSI

The young Spencer family, 1967.

An adolescent Charles.

Disguised but recognised, Charles as Santa Claus.   © ALAN DAVIDSON/ALPHA

Right: Charles hits
Cannes in his
presenter's shades,
1987.

© Duncan Raban/Alpha

Left and below:
Viscount Althorp
interviews Rupert
Everett and Bo Derek,
May 1987.

© Universal Pictoral Press

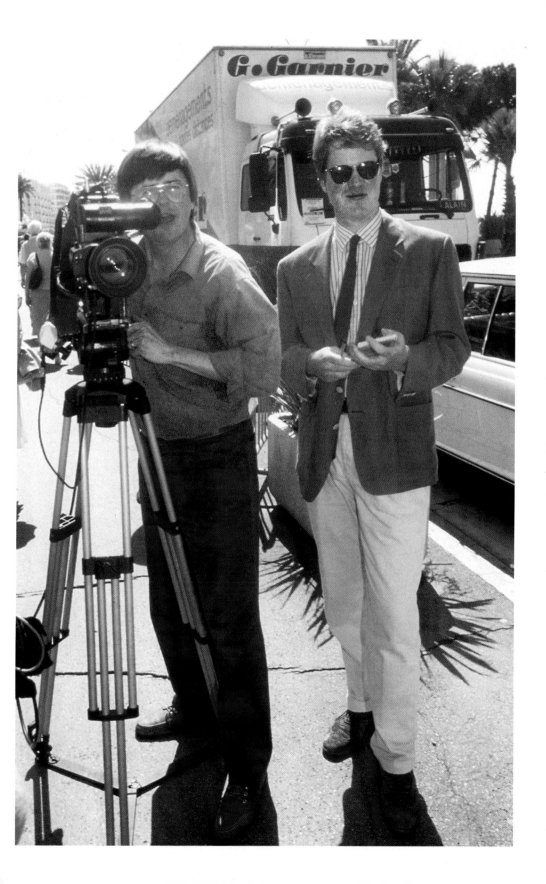

Charles and Diana at the Red and Gold Birthright Ball, Royal Albert Hall, 1985. © MSI

Earl Spencer – an energetic fundraiser.   © ALPHA

The funeral of Johnny Spencer, 8th Earl Spencer – the end of an era, April 1992.
(Left to right; Raine, Diana, Victoria and Charles)
© UNIVERSAL PICTORAL PRESS

With his mother Frances Shand Kydd at Lady Fermoy's funeral, Kings Lynn, July 1993.
© STEVE DANIELS/ALPHA

home. Jean Lowe recalls overhearing one exchange between Charles, then aged 7, and a friend. 'The other boy must have heard some adults discussing the Spencer family because he turned to Charles one day and announced, apropos of absolutely nothing, "I'm not going to call you 'Lord' when I grow up." To which Charles replied, "Oh, I'll only be an ordinary lord, not a Jesus Lord, silly." I remember telling Charles's father about that; he thought it was very funny.'

The only thing that set the younger Spencers apart from their schoolmates, says Jean Lowe, was the fact of their parents' divorce. 'They were the only children at Silfield at that time with divorced parents. They would go up to London for the weekend to see their mother. In fact, they'd have to leave a little early on a Friday to catch the London train. The other children would often ask where Diana and Charles were going – and why. I'd always say it was because their mummy lived in London just now. I think those trips were quite traumatic for them. Obviously, they'd be accompanied by a nanny but it was a long journey for children of their age.'

When Charles Spencer left Silfield, Jean Lowe didn't see him again for over twenty years – at the funeral of his maternal grandmother Ruth, Lady Fermoy. 'He was there with his wife,' she recalls. 'I was sitting at the side of the church where the choirstalls had been. I saw Charles's sister, Lady Jane, who knew me by sight, turn to her husband, Sir Robert Fellowes, and whisper that I was there. I then watched this information being relayed all the way down the pew. Charles couldn't see me because there was a pillar blocking his view. But when he was told, he obviously left his seat because I suddenly saw him striding towards me. He gave me a great big hug. And then, before he went to live with his family in South Africa, he'd always get in touch at Christmas. He'd send a card and tell me what he'd been doing and bring me up to date with news about his children.'

Jean Lowe is mildly surprised, she says, at the adult Charles Spencer. 'To be honest, he hasn't grown into the man I would have predicted. He's much more forceful than I thought he would become. That quality never showed up when he was a child but then his Address at Diana's funeral demonstrated how very angry he was.' Not that she is criticizing him for what he said. 'On the contrary, I agreed with him entirely. I think it was something that needed saying whether it upset the royals or not.'

Soon after hearing the news of Diana's death, Jean Lowe wrote to Charles. 'Obviously, I wanted to say how very saddened I was but I also decided to tell him the little story of Diana worrying about him when he first went into the nursery at Silfield. I assumed the letter would be acknowledged by one of his secretaries. But not at all. I had a handwritten letter – and the envelope, too. I thought that was quite extraordinary. He must have had hundreds, perhaps thousands of letters from people offering their commiserations. On the other hand, I suppose he would write personally to those people who could address him as "Dear Charles" rather than "Dear Earl Spencer". He thanked me warmly for sharing my recollection following, and I quote, "Diana's brutal death". It was so good of him. But then I think they were brought up like that; certainly, Diana and Charles always had beautiful manners as young children.'

For all the backdrop of sadness at home, Charles consistently shone at school. At 8, he left Silfield and was enrolled at Maidwell Hall Preparatory School in Northamptonshire as a boarder. Many years later, in 1992, he confessed to *Hello!* magazine his feelings of loneliness when his father would drop him off there and return alone to Norfolk. 'I must say that I was fairly miserable at the beginning of each term,' he said, 'because it's just too young to be sent away. I would hope that my daughters wouldn't go away to boarding school until they were 11 at the earliest; and then, if they didn't want to go, I'd never force them. I think it's one of the sadnesses of the British middle and upper classes that they have sent their children away so often. I think it does inevitably alter the relationship between child and parent. If you feel, even subconsciously, that you were sent away, rejected, at an early age, then that has to be with you all your life.'

He felt that the Duke of Westminster had made a good point when he'd said that he wouldn't want to entrust his children to people he didn't know and, if he did, probably wouldn't like. 'I'm sure that's absolutely right. I look back at some of the schoolmasters I had and my blood chills.' John Paul, headmaster of Maidwell at the time of these remarks, told the London *Evening Standard* that he was unsurprised by Charles's comments. 'I came here in 1978,' said Paul, 'some two years after Earl Spencer left. There was almost a complete change of staff after his time. They weren't masters I appointed and some I wouldn't have been happy to have. I don't know which masters he was referring to, but there are a couple I do have in mind.'

For all that, Charles's time at Maidwell cannot have been unremittingly grim. 'He's been in constant touch with the school ever since,' according to Paul, 'so I don't think he could have been that unhappy.' Indeed, it is said he is considering the school for his own son, Louis. Either way, it seemed to have served him well in the classroom. Alec Porch, his headmaster, wrote to Jean Lowe soon after Charles arrived to tell her he was well advanced academically for his years. Then, when at 13 he won a place at Eton, his father told Miss Lowe that his son had scored one of the top marks of all the applicants taking that school's entrance examination.

Michael Wright (not his real name) first got to know Charles Althorp when they found themselves in the same house at the top boys' public school. 'I was in Penn House at Eton with Charles,' says Wright, 'although I was two years younger than him. And yet, despite the age difference which normally meant I wouldn't have known him that well, we did have quite a lot to do with each other via various drama productions, and the school magazine, the *Eton College Chronicle*. We were both bright although neither of us were scholars. Charlie had a top tutor in his sixth form years called Dr Tom Connor, a brilliant historian, who was in charge of his intellectual development. A small group of boys would visit him once or twice a week to discuss issues of moral importance. By the end of his career at Eton, Charlie was house captain and a member of Pop, the Eton Society to which the most popular boys of each year were elected. Looking back now, I can see he was a bit of a star, a natural leader.

'He was in the sixth form when Prince Charles announced his engagement to Lady Diana Spencer. I think that produced some problems for him. I remember one occasion when a press photographer walked into Charlie's room and took his picture, and then, later on, when some reporters were nosing around. There are twenty-five houses at Eton with fifty boys in each house; everyone had his own room but none of the doors had locks on them so anyone could wander in. Our quarters looked like a nineteenth-century prison, although the housemaster's wing was more civilized. It had a lovely garden at the back with a magnificent Lebanese cedar. Diana would visit her brother occasionally, driving herself down in the Mini Metro given to her by Prince Charles.

'Clearly, the announcement of the engagement between Charles and Diana had an effect on Charlie but I would say the defining event of his teenage years was the stroke his father suffered [in September 1978]. Johnnie Spencer very nearly died and that must have been a traumatic time for his only son who was after all only 14 when it happened. This was about the time I went to Eton so I only got to know about it afterwards. But I recall Charlie telling me that, although he didn't like his step-mother, Raine, the one thing he did respect her for was the way she had pulled his father through.'

There is little doubt that, although Charles's father had survived his cerebral haemorrhage, he would have been little more than a vegetable but for Raine's intervention. She insisted on getting a new 'wonder drug' called Aslocillin, at that point unlicensed in Britain, sent from Germany to the Brompton Hospital in South Kensington, where Johnnie had been transferred following a relapse in November of that year. Aslocillin was duly administered and, as Andrew Morton has chronicled, the Countess was sitting beside her husband's bed one winter's day, the stirring strains of *Madam Butterfly* playing in the background, when suddenly the eighth Earl opened his eyes. He was 'back'.

'Charlie was at a very vulnerable age when all that happened,' says Wright. 'I do know that Anthony Ray, our housemaster, was an invaluable support to him throughout that troubled time. But then so was the Dame [the name given to the matron of each of Eton's houses, the Dame of Penn House being Vera Arnold]. Charlie always said how incredibly kind she was to him and I'm sure that's right. My own mother was very ill when I was at Eton and I recall him telling me I should speak to the housemaster and the Dame because they'd both been so helpful to him.'

He might have been the heir apparent to one of England's oldest earldoms but 'Charlie Althorp' was how he was happy to be called throughout his career at Eton. Notwithstanding the spotlight trained upon him once it became known his sister was going to marry the Prince of Wales, the future ninth Earl Spencer never flaunted his title, says Wright, never lorded it. 'If there was any whiff of arrogance about him at that point, it was perhaps intellectual. He didn't suffer fools gladly. For instance, I remember writing a piece, at his invitation, for the *Eton College Chronicle*, which contained one particularly lazy sentence. Charlie really bollocked me. I was quite hurt, I must admit, while acknowledging he was absolutely right. He could be sharp, even at that stage and in that context.'

Charles began his 'career' on the *Chronicle* in May 1981 as arts editor, becoming joint editor (with Kabir Nath) in September of the same year. On 9 October 1981, and with edition no. 3,783, the two editors decided to take the publication tabloid although the price was to remain the same at 30p. In a front-page leader, headed 'The New Look', they wrote:

The transformation of the *Chronicle* into a more conventional size is long overdue. The reasons for this change are that we used to have to have our own paper produced at great expense; advertisers in the biannual special issues complained at having to enlarge their adverts to fit our pages. We hope that, committees permitting, we shall be able to increase our circulation to boys' houses so that even more of you can receive copies.

We realize that the more traditional of our readers will protest at a change that follows those that have overtaken Rowlands, Tap, the School Laundry and the Choir School. In anticipation of letters of complaint, we should like to point out that the *Chronicle* had only been in its previous form since 1973.

The year Prince Charles married Lady Diana Spencer was a busy one for her younger brother. In June 1981, just weeks before the royal wedding, both Michael Wright and Charlie Althorp acted in a production called *Prince Hal*, an adaptation of *Henry IV Parts I and II*. 'Charlie played a character called Poins whose sister, if you can believe it, is being wooed by the then Prince of Wales.' By the time the production was fit to put before an audience, Britain was in the grip of royal fairy-tale fever. 'At one point,' recalls Wright, 'Prince Hal turns to his companion and says, "But do you use me thus, Ned? Must I marry your sister?" To which Charlie had to reply, "God send the wench no worse fortune!" It brought the house down. He took it all in good part, though. But then what can you do when your sister becomes the most photographed woman in the world? He was very self-effacing in that respect.' The following September, he allowed himself to be pelted with rotten tomatoes and eggs, for a modest 5p a throw, in one of the sideshows at Eton's community fair.

So it was no surprise to Wright when Charles was elected to Pop. The Eton Society, as it is sometimes called, is made up of the twenty-five most popular, most distinguished boys in each year. The self-elected body's principal role in the running of the school is as an independent and autonomous caucus of prefects, its president answering directly to the headmaster. Members of Pop can stop other boys in the street and fine them for chewing gum, say, or cycling along a forbidden road. They are also entitled to dress differently: they can wear checked trousers, flowery waist-coats and a buttonhole in their tailcoat. They are additionally allowed to roll up their umbrellas – an absurd privilege denied the common herd who must struggle as best they can through their school career, saddled with the wretched inconvenience of a permanently unfurled brolly.

'Becoming a member of Pop is a mark of self-congratulation,' says Wright, 'something that is very important to some people.' It is said that the writer Cyril Connolly never quite got over the fact he was never elected to Pop. 'Charlie was always on course for election. In his year, he was well-liked and generally consid-ered to be a good egg. He was bright without being a swot (an "A" not an "A+"), upright without being a goody-goody; and he was good company. In time, he became a well-respected house captain. There were no scandals at Penn when he was top of the heap, no drugs, nothing. I'd say he had a good career at Eton.' This is a view reinforced by Anthony Ray, his housemaster. 'Charles Spencer was a very hard-working boy,' he says, 'who contributed a lot to the house and the school and who, through his natural ability, earned his place at Oxford.'

But before he went up to Magdalen College in October 1983, he took a year out, during which he worked for a month as a quality controller in a Midlands factory supplying cooked foods to supermarkets and then as a 'blue button', or gofer, scurrying round London's Stock Exchange for the Queen's brokers, Rowe and Pitman. Finally, there was a brief stint in America learning the rudiments of Wall Street. (It had been widely reported – inaccurately, as it turned out – that Charles had wanted to use his 'gap' year travelling the world but that his father had thwarted his plans. 'On the contrary,' he told journalist Compton Miller, 'it was my idea to get some experience before I went up to Oxford.')

*

Life was not all work, though, and Charles showed a natural, though not overly pronounced, penchant for play. Very quickly, however, he was to discover the hard way that the younger brother of the Princess of Wales might have his fair share of disagreements in public places but, unlike his anonymous 19-year-old contemporaries, he could not expect to keep these out of the tabloid press. There was, for instance, the occasion when a couple of bouncers from Boodles nightclub in Oxford accused him of trying to leave the premises without paying for his champagne. In the event, another member of his party settled the bill but this small skirmish was enough to spawn the first of many stories that branded Viscount Althorp 'Champagne Charlie'.

He was outraged, granting an interview to the *Daily Star* to set the record straight. 'I object to being typecast as an arrogant, spoiled brat,' he said, 'when I'm totally defenceless. The implication is that here is Diana's brother. We all know she's wonderful – which she is – and now her brattish little brother lets her down.' He saw himself, he said, as a sitting target. 'Anyone my age wants to go out with friends. But they're not braying Old Etonians. That's not the sort I like. Now I'm worried I'll ruin their evening because of the attention from the press. I'm expected either to enjoy it all or grit my teeth and go through with it. I'll have to take the publicity as it comes.' But then came a warning, a taste of things to come. 'Every time people overstep a reasonable mark, I'll react accordingly. What will I do? I'll get my solicitor's advice.'

September 1983 proved to be a month of mixed fortunes for Charles. After the magnified problems of the nightclub débâcle, he landed a non-speaking part – at £200 a day – in the film of the hit stage play, *Another Country*, the story of homosexual spy and traitor, Guy Burgess. According to impresario Robert Fox, 'This is a holiday job for the Viscount before he goes up to university next month.' Just ten days later, Charles was back in the papers again when he admitted driving his Mini Metro at 94 mph on the M1 and was fined £80 by Northamptonshire magistrates. The reason for the excessive speed, he claimed in a letter to the court, was that he had been beaten up at the Toddington service station. 'I know I had no business to be going at that speed,' he explained in his letter, 'but at the time I had just been unexpectedly attacked by people getting out of a coach at a garage.' The incident, which had gone unreported to Charles Cedric, assistant catering manager at the service station – 'Everything is reported to me,' he said, 'and I certainly don't recall it' – was triggered, apparently, by Viscount Althorp's altercation with the coach earlier on a stretch of the motorway.

Then there were the girls. The tall, fresh-faced Charles, the next best thing to a full-blooded royal, was fast becoming one of Britain's most eligible bachelors, as he was all too well aware. If you believe the *News of the World*, 'Mothers always push their daughters at me,' he was quoted as having said, 'usually something fat that rides.'

Left to his own devices, though, he preferred a slim, sparky blonde – in this case, Lucy Stiles, daughter of a wealthy farmer with property in Surrey and the Isle of Wight. The two teenagers met at a party in London in January 1982 and were inseparable for the next sixteen months. 'I had a deep relationship with Lucy,' Charles later revealed. 'She was not my first girlfriend but the one I have been most serious about.' In November 1981, she told the London *Evening Standard*, 'I've been going out with Charlie for nearly a year and you can say we are very happy together but, as we are both quite young, it would be silly to talk about more permanent arrangements.'

By the following May, it was all over. 'We are still very much in love,' she said, 'but it became too involved. We are much too young to marry and had become too dependent on each other. Now we'll play it by ear. I don't know if we'll get back together.' A year later, Charles was telling *Sunday* magazine, 'It was rumoured that we broke off because we feared we were drifting towards marriage and felt too young. But that's totally untrue.' He declined to reveal the real reasons for the split.

In May 1985 – the month of Charles's high-profile 21st birthday party, an event to which Lucy was not invited – she spoke to the *News of the World*, in less than flattering terms, about her erstwhile boyfriend. 'The three words he must have used more than any others,' she was quoted as saying, 'were: "Am I handsome?" He spent hours in front of the mirror and he always wanted to know if he was good-looking. I always told him he was – just to keep him happy.' Nor, apparently, was he faithful to her during their romance. 'But I was so stupid and so in love with him,' said Lucy, 'that I thought it didn't matter. When I think about him now, I can't understand what all the fuss was about. He's got spots on his back and he never washes out the bath after he's used it.'

From heel to hero in one bound: Viscount Althorp was making headline news in February 1984 after giving chase to a suspected shoplifter who had made off with six cashmere coats from Harrods department store in Knightsbridge. When the case came up before magistrates at London's Horseferry Road court, it was revealed that Charles and another man had chased the accused for 150 yards. 'I play rugger regularly,' he told reporters after the man was fined £100, 'so I was fit and he wasn't. He backed up against a wall and we waited for the police to arrive. It wasn't that amazing. It was all over in a minute.' Said a Harrods spokesman: 'We are grateful to Lord Althorp. Our chairman has sent a letter of thanks and a small token of our appreciation.'

Just before his 20th birthday, Charles bought his own house in London's Notting Hill, a short step away from Kensington Palace, the home of his sister, Diana. It cost £200,000, money made available from the family trust fund. 'It's my first house,' he told the *Daily Mail*, 'and I'm very happy with it. It's a house typical of the area with three rooms on each floor and all quite narrow.' The dashing young Viscount was also said to be taking flying lessons in a Piper Cherokee and contemplating his first parachute jump to raise money for the International Centre for Child Studies.

But trouble was just around the corner. The very next month, at his birthday party in La Paesana, an Italian restaurant near his new home, some of his chums attempted to remove the trousers of – or 'debag' – a fellow diner, disc jockey Tony Blackburn. Despite a flurry of lurid headlines – 'Di's brother in birthday brawl', screamed one; 'How could Diana have a brother like this?' asked another – Charles remained unrepentant. 'I don't see why I should change my lifestyle just because of this sort of publicity,' he told one newspaperman. 'It depresses me when people publish lies about me. I've had no complaints about my behaviour from my family or the dean of my college.' Under a little pressure, he did acknowledge that he had perhaps occasionally got himself into situations which could be construed as embarrassing. 'But I feel I've got an answer to every one of these criticisms,' he countered. 'I'm a young person entitled to enjoy myself like anybody else,' adding, a touch naively, 'I don't feel any constraints should be imposed on me because of who I am.'

However long and loud his protestations of innocence, the popular press had made up its mind that young Charles Althorp was a champagne-guzzling roisterer. 'That always struck me as unfair,' says Michael Wright. 'It simply wasn't true, or no more true, at any rate, than of any red-blooded, single student aged 20. In my view, it was an easy tag lazily applied by the tabloids. From personal experience [Wright went up to Oxford at the beginning of Charles's final year there], I can say that Charlie's lifestyle was no more extravagant or expensive than any other student from his type of background.' The facts would appear to support this assessment. For example, he was offered membership of the Bullingdon, an exclusive drinking club with precisely the sort of reputation that reinforced the stereotype of Bollinger-sozzled, bun-hurling Hooray Henrys. Viscount Althorp politely but firmly declined the invitation.

One area, it seems, in which Charles Spencer did fail to come up to scratch was in his dealings with the opposite sex. 'It was always said,' says Wright, 'and one heard this, of course, only from women, that he was bad at handling his romantic attachments. The suspicion with Charlie was that he liked his women to be compliant but that he would then tire of them quickly. Any who answered back, who gave as good as she got, didn't last long, either.' Wright remembers one fellow student who now works in the property field in London. 'She was a very nice girl,' he says, 'friendly, lively, full of fun. Her relationship with Charlie was tempestuous from the start. They were always arguing. She'd go around saying that he didn't know how to handle a woman properly.'

In fairness, this view was not universal. One young woman who knows him well, but who preferred to remain anonymous when talking to *Sunday* magazine, recalled the first time she met Charles. 'We were all having something to eat before going to a party. As we were about to leave, looking a bit embarrassed, Charlie said to the girls: "Do you mind if I arrive at the party alone in case there's a photographer? Any girl I'm seen with is immediately thought to be my girlfriend and gets hassled." Then he explained that Lucy Stiles had once been knocked off her bike so that someone could get a picture of her. I was expecting him to be rude and arrogant but I felt he was a very caring person.'

By the time of his 21st birthday party, Charles was living, during term-time, in what one newspaper called 'a crumbling red-brick semi, hardly a spanner's throw from the Cowley motor works in unfashionable east Oxford'. Between studies, he had taken on the co-editorship of *Tributary*, the university's satirical magazine, known for its irreverent wit and unbridled gossip. As Charles could testify from first-hand experience: he had featured as the subject of a story when it was reported that a group of male undergraduates were attempting to ingratiate themselves with members of the opposite sex by pretending to be him. (Despite his profile in the national press, he was not instantly recognizable, apparently, in and around Oxford. One female undergraduate recalls the time she was propositioned in a town-centre pub, The Bear, by a slightly worse-for-wear Charles. She repeatedly resisted his advances until, with imperious exasperation, he asked if she knew who he was. She told him she had no idea. 'I'm Charlie Althorp,' he said, with a triumphant flourish. 'Oh, sure,' replied the object of his attentions, 'and I'm the Princess of Wales.')

His first course of action when he started work on *Tributary*, according to the *Mail on Sunday*, was to expose these impostors. He also let it be known that he would be reporting on the latest outrages perpetrated by a group of high-spirited students, members of something called the Assassins Club. 'It should be pretty steamy stuff,' promised his co-editor, Darius Guppy, a man who was to play an increasingly prominent role in the Viscount's life. 'Charlie knows a great deal about that sort of thing.'

He was certainly no slouch when it came to throwing a party. His 21st birthday bash, costing anything between £25,000 and £100,000 (depending on which publication you read), was nothing if not lavish. The setting was Spencer House, London's last surviving private mansion, with its sixty rooms overlooking Green Park, and said to be worth a contemporary £20 million. Dozens of workmen spent all day preparing the house, including putting up a 120-foot blue and white canopy along the balcony of the mansion and rigging floodlights on the 1,000-square-foot lawn at the back. Some 350 guests, including all the young royals, drank their way through 1,000 bottles of champagne and danced till dawn to Ronnie Scott's jazz band. American singer Phyllis Nelson provided a classy cabaret turn by live satellite link from Los Angeles, and a fashion show with nine scantily-clad dancers brought whoops of delight from the revellers.

First, though, the birthday boy was treated to dinner at the swish Mirabelle restaurant by his father and stepmother, Raine, along with the Prince and Princess of Wales and other close family members. Galette of duck in orange sauce was followed by consommé with celery, and then fillets of sole served in a cream sauce with lobster mousse, and was accompanied by a Chablis premier cru '83. Back in Oxford the following day, Charles pronounced himself satisfied with the events of Monday 20 May 1985. 'I think it all went very well,' he said. 'I was very happy with it. There didn't seem to be too many people looking bored.'

The same could be said of the spectacular Red and Gold Ball held in November 1985 in aid of Birthright, the mother and baby charity of which Princess Diana became patron. 'One of the best ways of raising money for Birthright,' says Vivienne Parry, national organizer of the charity at the time, 'was through high-profile film premières, balls and fashion shows. By the mid-eighties, Birthright's profile had reached its height because the Princess made herself available for all sorts of glamorous, fundraising events; this was at a point before she transferred her affections to more compassionate pursuits.

'The Red and Gold Ball at London's Royal Albert Hall, with both the Prince and Princess of Wales in attendance, was a very swanky affair sponsored by, among others, the society magazine *Harpers & Queen*, Cartier and Charles of the Ritz. The Albert Hall was decorated by Harvey Nichols, the top department store, in the appropriate colours, with red fruits and swags of gold material everywhere. It was fabulous, one of the most outstandingly successful fundraising events of the eighties. Everybody who was anybody was there, 1,800 people dancing the night away, bidding for a stunning collection of masks at auction, eating food prepared by the Roux brothers and enjoying a first-class cabaret.

'Charles Althorp, in his final year at Oxford, was chairman of the junior committee for the event. I was well used to knowing how to deal with the Princess but I was slightly apprehensive about her brother, a little unsure of myself. But he seemed very charming and, as we got to know each other better, I was impressed that someone still so young could display such confidence. Along with Anna Harvey, then deputy editor of *Vogue* magazine, Charles and I were in charge of the cabaret so the three of us went off to see the impresario, Harvey Goldsmith, who had promised to help us.

'It was widely reported at the time, whether rightly or wrongly, that the Prince of Wales's favourite band was the Three Degrees. Harvey said to us, "I've got this singer coming over at the beginning of November and she's going to be sensational." We'd vaguely heard of her but we still wanted the Three Degrees. "Look," said Harvey, "I'm confident that this girl's latest single will be Number One that very week." But Charles Althorp was adamant, with Anna and me backing him up, that it was to be the Three Degrees or no one. And so it proved – and very good they were, too. Mind you, Harvey clearly knew what he was talking about. The singer he had in mind was Whitney Houston who indeed topped the charts that November so much so that on any subsequent occasion I've seen Charles, I've only had to whisper "Whitney Houston" in his ear and he skulks away into a corner.

'I'll never forget the day of the Ball. You only get the Albert Hall for twenty-four hours so everyone was working furiously to transform it from somewhat faded glory to full-blown opulence in eight hours flat. Charles was there in jeans and T-shirt doing his bit, the main task, I recall, obliging him to visit every loo in the Albert Hall and replace the rather nasty, hard, shiny lavatory paper – quite unsuitable for all those expensive bottoms – with soft toilet tissue. Throughout it all, Charles was energetic, enthusiastic, sweet-natured, courteous and certainly not playing the ticket of being the Princess of Wales's brother. That evening, he turned up wearing a very fetching scarlet tunic and looking gorgeous. I liked him.'

Charles loved London life. Oxford, by contrast, had turned out to have confounded his expectations. 'I enjoy it,' he said. 'But I do find it a bit of an anti-climax. Maybe I was expecting too much.' Maybe. In August 1985, he opened his heart to the *Sunday Times* magazine for its Life In The Day Of series. 'When I went up to Oxford,' he said, 'I lived in college which was all right but a bit like being at school. Every day, I go into Magdalen to pick up my mail and use the library. I hardly ever go to lectures – not many people do – and anyway I prefer reading to listening. We have to do three essays a fortnight which you read out in front of four or five other people at tutorials.'

Initially, he said, he had found university life totally unstructured, 'and that was very difficult to come to terms with at first, especially after Eton where there wasn't a minute that wasn't

ordered.' Two of his friends, he revealed, had recently commit-
ted suicide by jumping under trains. Charles had his own explanation: 'I don't think it's the pressure of work. I think it's the lack
of pressure. You can get very lonely at Oxford. My first week
was awful. I was just wandering around wondering when something was going to happen. I was very pleased when the work
came along. I think you'd be sunk without it.'

There was an active social life, although he wouldn't have
dreamt, he said, of going to a party given by someone he hadn't
met. 'I was quite depressed during my first term at Oxford
because everyone thought I was going to be unbearable from
what they'd read about me and there was great hostility. I just
kept trying to be normal and do whatever I would have done if
it hadn't been like that. I can't help my upbringing but I can help
my outlook.'

In the forthcoming holidays, he was looking forward to
moving into the Falconry on the Althorp estate in
Northamptonshire. 'There's a heronry you can see from the
house,' he said, 'and a herd of black deer and fields and a beautiful garden. It's beautiful. When I'm in Northampton, my father
usually drops in on me – I don't often visit him in the main
house – and my sister, Jane, lives on the estate as well so I see her
quite often.' He also admitted to feeling frightened at night
when trying to get to sleep at Althorp. 'The windows are made
of tiny squares of glass which rattle in the wind. I find it quite
frightening in London by myself, too, but I've always been like
that. I keep a gun under my bed which I know how to use. The
one most predictable thing I do is shoot.'

This confession promptly brought a firearms warning in its
wake. 'There is no law against keeping a gun under your bed,'
said a Scotland Yard spokesman. 'But it is extremely unwise. If
you use a weapon in self-defence, you may have to justify it in
law. The law does say that undue force must not be used.' It was
also revealed that, following an earlier leaked story that the IRA
were planning to kidnap someone connected with the Royal
Family, Charles had had a panic button installed in his London
home connected to the local police station.

Touchingly, he concluded his *Sunday Times* interview by revealing that he said his prayers every night. 'I don't believe in God but I always say my prayers otherwise I can't sleep. I've said them every day since I was four. I'm not religious; I don't lead the sort of life God would approve of that much. When my father was ill, I prayed and prayed to God but usually I should think I say six prayers, five of which are routine and then there's one specific one for that day or the next.' (The interviewer for this piece was journalist Sally Ann Lasson. It was the first time the two had met but not, as it would turn out, the last.)

He never said as much but it seems likely that he would have sent up a prayer for poor Olivia Channon, the daughter of Industry Secretary Paul Channon, who died from an accidental drugs overdose. Charles had stood shoulder to shoulder with Olivia in the second week of June 1986 when both were waiting to take their seats in a Finals examination at the end of their three-year Oxford courses. 'She seemed absolutely fine,' Charles subsequently told the *Mail on Sunday*. 'We had a short conversation about nothing in particular. We were both going in for our last paper and chatting about it. After the exam, I left through the back door because the press were there and I didn't want to speak to them. I immediately got separated from the rest and didn't see Olivia again.'

A fierce opponent of drugs, Charles agreed to an interview on breakfast television station TV-am. He stated, not for the first time, his opposition to drugs in any form but he felt that undergraduate life at Oxford had been misrepresented in the wake of Olivia Channon's death. 'Most students are more worried about where their next cup of coffee is coming from,' he said. 'It's unreal the picture that has been painted over the last couple of days about Oxford. I've never been offered anything. There are a lot of pressures on Oxford students but drug-taking just doesn't enter into anyone's thinking. The press is keen on a particular image and there is anger at the way Oxford is being portrayed.' He had been nothing if not consistent. Five years earlier, while arts editor of the *Eton College Chronicle*, he had included the following poem in his pages: 'Blow out your mind on angel's dust/If brains were steel then you would rust/Your name they'll spell on granite rocks/And put you under in a box.'

In the summer of 1986, Charles Althorp graduated from Oxford with a 2.1 in Modern History having specialized in the French Revolution. 'He was a fine scholar,' said his tutor, Angus Macintyre (sadly, killed in a car accident in 1995), 'with a deep and genuine interest in modern history and his family's role in it.' An exotic footnote to his university days comes in the shape of the dazzling, if flawed, Darius Guppy. Son of the writer and explorer, Nicholas Guppy, and his Persian wife, Shusha (something of a star in the sixties, both as a celebrated beauty and as a singer of Middle Eastern folk songs), Darius is Charles's precise contemporary, arriving at Eton in the same year and simultaneously moving on to Oxford with him.

Regarded more for his style than his substance, Guppy nonetheless graduated with a double first in Modern History and French – no mean achievement given his attachment to dedicated eating and drinking societies like the Piers Gaveston and the Bullingdon. Nor was he assailed by any sense of modesty: a good-looking young man, he swaggered around the city of dreaming spires, his nose stuck so high in the air that, according to one female contemporary, it was a wonder – perhaps a shame, even – that he managed successfully to negotiate the lamp-posts.

One graduate friend of both described Guppy to the London *Evening Standard* as court jester to Althorp. 'Darius didn't fit in very well with Charlie's other friends, regular landowning types. He had never been on a shoot, for instance, before he went to Oxford but got into it to please Charlie. They used to drive around in a Land-Rover at night killing rabbits on Charlie's estate with Darius firing away like Rambo.' When the law finally caught up with Guppy over an insurance swindle he and a friend had perpetrated, it was Viscount Althorp who stood the £250,000 surety initially needed to keep him out of jail as he awaited trial.

It was not the first time Charles had weighed in on Darius's behalf. While at Oxford, Guppy had confronted five gate-crashers at a friend's party. 'I was always hot-tempered and impulsive,' Guppy confessed to the *News of the World* in 1996. 'I told them to get out or there'd be trouble. They refused to leave so, in a mad moment, I just started laying into them and tried to beat them up. There were five men and I was on my own. The odds were stacked against me. I looked around for help and all my friends seemed to have disappeared except for one. Charlie. He rolled up his sleeves and piled in with me. We saw off the five men with a good beating. Charlie had the guts to stand by me then.'

As he did when Darius was sent to jail for five years. 'I really believe he saved my life and my sanity,' said Guppy. 'If it wasn't for his unfailing support, not just for me but for my wife Patricia and daughter Isabella, I can't imagine what would have happened. I suppose everyone expected Charlie to disown me after the robbery. After all, he had the family to protect and I can imagine the establishment at the Palace were delighted with any new mud they could sling at the Spencer name. The two of us have a code. Right from the outset, he was very loyal and was prepared to accept any flak when a lot of people in his position would have run a mile. Like his sister, Charlie is exceptionally kind to people. He and Diana get it from their mother, an amazing woman. He has the common touch. I always say I liked Charlie not because he was an aristocrat but in spite of it. He's a man of honour.'

5

THE CAREER

He said it himself. 'If you're brought up with the knowledge that things are expected of you,' Charles told *Woman*'s Mary Fletcher, in a revealing interview at the beginning of 1987, 'there's more pressure than if you get lost in a crowd and find your own feet. If you know one day you're going to inherit a large estate, it's very easy just to do nothing until that happens. And maybe out of laziness, or because you don't have the financial worries to have to go out and get a job, the temptation is to do nothing. You sit around and go to parties the whole time and get in with a crowd of people who may be fun to be with but who are pretty superficial . . . [But] I don't believe you should just sit around and wait for your father to hand everything over to you.'

True to his word, Charles set his professional cap, not at the Army or the City, as had so many of his contemporaries, but at the media (a curious choice, you may feel, given his already well-developed hatred of the Fourth Estate). What started out as an advisory role for a filmed report on the financial demands of running a stately home in Britain was expanded by NBC, the commissioning company, into a presence in front of the camera. 'I am very worried about American tourists who have cancelled their visits to Britain and the subsequent loss to our tourist industry,' Charles declared at the time. 'I was asked to get involved [for a reported fee of £2,000] on behalf of British Heritage and, as I'm waiting for my exam results, I was very happy to help out.'

NBC were obviously impressed, subsequently offering the cub reporter the opportunity to cover the upcoming wedding of

76

Prince Andrew and Sarah Ferguson on 23 July 1986. Broadcasting live from a specially constructed studio outside Buckingham Palace – and for a fee of £10,000 – Charles had clearly done some careful research in advance. 'I didn't have a script,' he later revealed, 'but I had walked the whole length from Buckingham Palace to Westminster Abbey just looking at things of interest to comment on when the carriages went by. And I'd assumed Prince Andrew *would* be made Duke of York so I'd done my homework on that.' Not that the assignment was without its testing moments. 'When the two of them didn't come out on to the balcony on time, there was about forty minutes of ad-libbing – and I know that if I'd done badly that would have been the end of it.'

In fact, it was the beginning. NBC European producer Karen Curry professed herself thrilled with the Viscount. 'We wanted him because of his expertise at such weddings and his terrific inside knowledge.' The bonus, she said, was that Charles 'is a natural in front of the camera. He can talk to it as if he was talking personally to you. He learned to do almost immediately what it takes others years to learn.' The upshot was that NBC began wooing him to become their London-based reporter for the top-rated 'Today' programme – a flirtation that was consummated in October when Charles signed a one-year contract for a reputed salary of £30,000. 'I shall be responsible,' he said, 'for bringing my expertise to various projects, in areas of traditional and cultural interest, and introducing American audiences to places and people I know. It's very exciting.'

He was refreshingly candid in answer to the late Jean Rook's observation that his surname and his siblings could not be described exactly as drawbacks in his vertical assault on the medium. 'I'm not so naive,' he said, 'as to be unaware that there must be people high up in NBC who wanted me for the wrong reasons when they asked me to do the royal wedding. Of course I wouldn't have got that assignment if I hadn't been who I am. But if I'd made a poor job of it, they wouldn't have offered me further work. Look, what upsets me is that I'm 22, I've just left Oxford with a good degree and all Fleet Street is interested in is

my "wild past", which they themselves invented, and in insinu-
ating that NBC wants me for only one reason – my social situation. But NBC aren't interested in the nine-day wonder of getting
Lord Althorp on TV. They're only interested in their ratings.'
Charles then cited Maria Shriver reporting on the royal
wedding. 'She's the daughter of a Kennedy, she's married to
Arnold Schwarzenegger, she's beautiful, she looked like a
natural on television but the monitor told them that people were
switching off when she came on. So she went. In America, if they
had the Pope doing a Sunday morning slot and his ratings went
down, he'd go.'

Charles Althorp, television reporter, was beginning to hit his
stride. 'I am very ambitious,' he told *Woman* magazine, 'but I
hope not in a purely financial sense. I want to maintain and, if
possible, improve my family's house and estate when it comes to
me. And to do that, I have to have a successful career which pays
well. At the moment, television fits the bill. I've always believed
that if you've got any sort of talent, there's no point in pretending you haven't. Now I just feel that everything has come
together quite well and I hope I can make a go of this. When I
take over at home, then the way I approach television may have
to change. But I hope I will always be involved in it because I
think it's not only interesting, it's also worthwhile.'

From a mixed bag of assignments over the next couple of years,
some proved a little more worthwhile than others. His interview
with actress Bo Derek at the 1987 Cannes Film Festival never
caught fire. ('She's not exactly the most intelligent woman in the
world,' he was heard to mutter after their lacklustre encounter.)
His report on an apparent racket run by Asian hoteliers for
London's homeless turned out to be considerably more sparky –
his camera crew were attacked as Charles beat a hasty retreat.
His job also included a fair measure of globetrotting – to Tonga
in the Pacific, for instance, in the late summer of 1988, and to
New Zealand, Singapore, Malaysia and Hong Kong after that.

Little wonder that Charles confided in journalist Compton

Miller in October of the same year that he found his job 'very satisfying'. He had begun, he said, by covering soft stories, the better to cut his teeth. 'I reported from Wimbledon, the Berkeley Dress Show and the Cannes Film Festival. I did short news features on the House of Lords and the Sandhurst Military Academy, and a profile of Jeffrey Archer. I was then given more serious assignments like examining the special relationship between Britain and America since the First World War, and an investigation into the victims of the Thalidomide tragedy.'

At that point, he was recording his six-part series on the British Empire with a five-week trip to India, his next port of call. 'I'm delighted with the way the company is giving me increasing independence to do interesting features,' he said. 'I now produce as well as report which means I travel with just a cameraman and sound-recordist. I've already been to twenty different countries this year, including doing a three-part series on great European familes – the Mussolinis, the Bismarcks and the Hapsburgs. I've been to Sweden to cover the world 12-metre yacht final, and I've just returned from reporting on the Greek island of Patmos.'

'We think he's terrific,' gushed New York-based 'Today' producer Marty Ryan. 'He's a bright reporter with a good eye for a story. He's proved very popular with the viewers,' adding, disingenuously, 'and I imagine few of them know that he's the brother of the future Queen of England.' What is more, apparently, Charles was developing into 'a wonderful interviewer. He's very intelligent and hard-working and has what I call television charisma. I'm very proud of him. Right now, I'm discussing with NBC for him perhaps to become a full-time correspondent not tied to the "Today" programme. No question he has all the qualifications necessary to become a top talk-show host or anchor man. He's very popular in America.'

Such seamless success! Such glowing testimonials! And yet, by March 1991, it had all unravelled. 'I wasn't fired,' he said. 'I resigned. I had always decided to leave after three years but got to four because I didn't want to leave when I had just got married. I didn't want a second upheaval in my life. I have several things lined up in British television,' he added, 'all of which are just prior to the signing stage. I cannot say what they are.'

When asked whether the recent revelation of his brief extra-marital fling with former girlfriend, Sally Ann Lasson, might have counted against him, he disagreed. 'I do not think people in New York read that sort of thing,' he told the *News of the World*. 'I don't think they even knew about it. Their only interest is in my ability to do my work.' Karen Curry, NBC producer in London, summed up the situation when she said, 'Charles had decided to go into British television after over four years with NBC. At the same time, the economic pressures on the company meant they were deciding to cut back. I'm sorry to see him go because he was a wonderful addition. He contributed a lot to the show. He would not have stayed on as long as he did if he was just flavour of the month.'

Less than a month later, it was announced that Charles Althorp had landed a £40,000-a-year job with ITV for a new afternoon show. His first interview was with Elizabeth Glaser, the Aids-infected wife of 'Starsky and Hutch' star, Paul Michael Glaser. Granada producer Liz Warner was full of praise for Charles's sensitive handling of this human tragedy. 'He was not given the job because of his royal connections,' she said. 'He was taken on because he is a thoroughly competent professional. There are no airs and graces about him and he definitely knows what he's doing.'

In fact, the ITV show that employed Charles turned out to be 'This Morning', hosted by husband-and-wife team Richard Madeley and Judy Finnigan. His brief was wide-ranging. There was the filmed report on Russian girls being trained in Moscow to become strippers. It triggered a complaint to the Broadcasting Standards Authority which was asked to censure Granada for running such an item at midday, shortly before a programme for toddlers. But a spokesman for the network was unmoved. 'The film showed nothing more,' he said, 'than you can see in any popular tabloid.' Then there was Charles's coverage of the plight of stricken Bosnian families living through a savage winter in primitive housing with little or no food.

Clearly, it made quite an impact on him. Five years later, talking to radio interviewer Lisa Chait, he referred to, among other harrowing assignments, his experiences in the former Yugoslavia. But first he set his chosen career in what he felt was its proper context. The past seventeen years – from the time, therefore, that his sister became a public figure – had been spent, to a greater or lesser degree, he said, dealing with people's pre-judgements. 'But, throughout it all, I've just tried to get on with my life. I've been a war correspondent in Yugoslavia. I've been a radio presenter. I went straight from reading Modern History at Oxford to the American network, NBC, as a television reporter; I worked in forty countries as a roving reporter, mainly doing features on the stories behind the news. That lasted five years. Then I did two years for a British network when I concentrated mainly on Eastern Europe and Bosnia.'

His work had not been without its life-endangering moments. He recalled particularly the time he was in a hospital in Slavonsky Brod under continual mortar fire. 'On occasions, in Eastern Europe, it was pretty clear that one side wasn't particularly keen on us surviving; we were continually being sent to incredibly dangerous places. My most abiding memory of Yugoslavia, though, was of two children in a refugee camp. One was a boy of about 12, the senior male left in the village when all the men went off to fight. He'd been left with a rifle. He was to stand guard at night and look after the women and the younger children. When I came across him in a refugee camp, he was completely silent; he'd gone to pieces. One night, he'd seen a man try to crawl in the window of his house and he'd shot him dead. It was his father, returning early from the war.

'There was another child who was totally uncontrollable and violent and who had to be kept away from sharp objects. That child had been made to watch while his pregnant mother had been gutted in front of him. These horrors, so far beyond the experience of anything in my life, had produced a level of trauma I'll never forget.' But it was more than that. 'What you also saw was the hatred cascading down the generations. That Croatian boy was only going to want to kill Serbs when he grew up. It just goes on. Those children never regain any innocence. Their eyes have been opened. It is the loss of childhood, something from which they can never recover.

'The most harrowing assignment elsewhere was having to cover a hotel fire in Egypt while it was still going on and people were dying. That was desperate. It was just appalling having to witness the carnage. But then I had such a variety of assignments. I was lucky enough to report on every aspect of human nature over a nine-year period.'

His final major commission from NBC was a twelve-part series of half-hour documentaries on great houses of the world, one of them near Somerset West in Cape Town. 'We were filming a particularly beautiful sunset and I remember turning to the cameraman and saying, "You know, I'm going to come and live here one day." I don't think he believed me but, when it came to it, my children were young enough to make the move. My wife was happy, too; she had personal contacts there. So we did it.'

By then, of course, Charles was married and a father four times over. But that's another story.

6

HURRICANE RAINE

However successfully his career in television might prove to be, Viscount Althorp could never forget that one day, assuming the natural order, he would become the ninth Earl Spencer, and chatelain of Althorp House and its 8,500 acres. As a schoolboy at Eton, of course, there was no reason for Charles to suppose that his father, a hale and hearty man in his early fifties, would be making way for him in the foreseeable future. This ease of mind lasted until intimations of Johnnie's mortality were brought forcibly, and quite unexpectedly, to bear in September 1978, when he suffered a cerebral haemorrhage. The stroke very nearly killed him and might well have left him in a permanently disorientated, semi-vegetative state had it not been for the iron will of one woman.

It was as Raine Dartmouth, daughter of the romantic novelist Barbara Cartland, and wife of the Earl of Dartmouth, that she first met Johnnie Spencer, some years after his emotionally debilitating divorce from his first wife. They found themselves working together on a book for the Greater London Council called *What Is Our Heritage?* (something of an irony, given what was to follow), and got along famously from the off. Raine had four children from her twenty-eight-year marriage, the youngest two, Charlotte and Henry, only 12 and 7 respectively at the time of the divorce (granted to her husband on the uncontested grounds of his wife's adultery with Johnnie Spencer). She hadn't fought the court decision that awarded custody of those children to her ex-husband.

Still only in her mid-forties (she had married at 18), the formidable Countess of Dartmouth enthralled the eighth Earl Spencer, a man who, like so many of his generation, and many more since, seemed to function at only half his capacity without a capable woman at his side. Wherever the fault had lain for the tempestuous demise of his first marriage, no one begrudged Johnnie the prospect of getting it right second time around. What people did question – and principal among them were his four children – was his choice of consort. Almost from the moment Sarah, Jane, Diana and Charles caught sight of the woman with the fussy printed frocks and hurricane-proof hairdo, they became implacably opposed to her.

After a get-to-know-you dinner in King's Lynn at the Duke's Head hotel, Diana and Charles pooled their opinions. 'We didn't like her one bit,' he recalled for Andrew Morton's book on his sister; so much so, in fact, that the Spencer children announced to their father that they'd have nothing to do with him if he married Raine. To underline this point, Charles, only 12 and still at Maidwell Hall Preparatory School, sent his prospective stepmother a letter he himself subsequently described as 'vile'. Diana, meanwhile, persuaded a schoolfriend to write Raine a poison-pen letter. 'The incident which prompted their behaviour,' as Morton has recorded, 'was the discovery, shortly before the death of the seventh Earl, of a letter Raine had sent to their father discussing her plans for Althorp. Her private opinions of the incumbent Earl did not match the way Diana and Charles saw her behave in public towards their grandfather.'

When Johnnie inherited the title on his father's death in 1975 and moved to Althorp, Raine became a regular visitor. His children, having cast her in the role of Wicked Stepmother (in waiting), took to marching through the corridors chanting, 'Raine, Raine, go away'. If she minded, and it is hard to imagine that even she was entirely impervious to this small, but determined, army of enemies, she certainly wasn't going to let it show. There was, as yet, no ring on her finger, whether of engagement or wedding, but Lady Dartmouth behaved, nonetheless, as though she were mistress of the manor. Nor did Althorp House ring with Johnnie's remonstrations; he was utterly bewitched. Raine's interior designer, David Laws, was duly summoned and a comprehensive programme of redecoration commenced.

Her decree nisi was granted on 29 May 1976, and Raine then graciously accepted Johnnie's proposal of marriage. The following July – Bastille Day, as it turned out – the two were married in a ten-minute ceremony at Caxton Hall Register Office in London. None of Earl Spencer's children had been told in advance of the nuptials. His heir was informed that he had acquired a stepmother during his final term at Maidwell prep school by the headmaster, Alec Porch. With the possible exception of Lady Jane, Johnnie's children continued to cold-shoulder their new stepmother. According to Angela Levin, in her book *Raine and Johnnie*, 'There was open hostility not just to her as a person. [The children] also disliked the way she dominated and became so possessive of their father which made them feel they had to compete with her for his attention.' 'My father believes himself to be happy,' Charles once observed when asked about the state of Johnnie's relationship with Raine.

Johnnie's aunt, Lady Margaret Douglas-Home, had her own ideas. 'I don't think Raine went about it in the right way,' she later said. 'I don't think she is made to be a stepmother. She hasn't the right temperament. She must be the only pebble on the beach and wasn't willing to take second place to Johnnie's children. She used to claim all of him the whole time and didn't like them interfering in her life with Johnnie. The children never liked it and they were old enough to know. I was very sorry for them. They looked so miserable.'

Within weeks of the Earl's remarriage, John Edwards, estate manager for the previous fourteen years, had been given three months' notice to quit the house where he lived with his wife, Jenny, and their two children. There had been no clash, apparently, between boss and employee. Three months earlier, there had been a foretaste of what was to come as part of the Spencers' plan for dealing with the seventh Earl's swingeing death duties. A Stradivarius dating from 1720 was to be put up for auction at Christie's; its estimated sale price was said to be £50,000 although almost all of that would pass directly to the taxman. 'I don't think my father ever played the instrument,' Johnnie told the local paper, the *Chronicle and Echo*. 'In fact, I don't think it has ever been played since my grandmother, Margaret Spencer, died. We have to raise so much money to pay these taxes,' he added, 'so the violin just had to go. It is very sad but we have no choice. I think probably about eighty per cent of all the money that will be raised through the sale of our possessions will go straight to the Treasury.'

It was the thin end of a wedge: soon lorry-loads of prized pieces were heading out of the grounds of Althorp and down the M1 to London showrooms and auction houses. Nobody disputes that Johnnie was acting in good faith (albeit with Raine's spread-eagled hands applied firmly to the small of his back) but there was less than universal consensus about the inevitability of those actions. 'Experts point out,' according to James Dalrymple writing in the *Sunday Times* in September 1991, 'that schemes exist to cushion certain works of art of national importance from death duties, and, although the Althorp estates and their London home, Spencer House, were not exempt, old Jack [the seventh Earl] had vested them in a series of tax-efficient trusts for the benefit of Charles, the grandson and ultimate heir.' But Johnnie and Raine had elected to pay the tax in full, leaving them free to sell anything they chose.

And sell they did. With a growing sense of barely concealed outrage, the art sales correspondents of the broadsheets filled their columns with details of yet more Althorp treasures being put up for sale, often at bargain basement prices; and, in some instances, being allowed to leave Britain to join foreign collections. A portrait of the Swiss artist, Angelica Kauffmann, painted by Sir Joshua Reynolds around 1770, was sold in the middle of 1980, for instance, for £100,000 to Artemis Fine Arts in London who shared ownership with an American partner. A double portrait masterpiece by Van Dyck had been bought by the

National Gallery in 1977; three other paintings by the same artist were also sold. In the end, all but three of the fifteen works by the Dutch master were eventually 'let go'.

There were said originally to have been some 700 paintings of merit in the family including works by Rubens and Poussin, and portraits by Gainsborough, Reynolds and Lely, as well as fine pieces of antique furniture, porcelain and the Marlborough silver collection. But an attempt by Earl Spencer to sell two Italian old masters – *Liberality and Modesty* by Guido Reni, and *Apollo Crowning the Singer Pasqualini* by Andrea Saachi – was thwarted by the then Minister for the Arts, Norman St John Stevas, who turned down his request for an export licence. The young Viscount Althorp, meanwhile, had been pressed into service by his father as a tour guide during his school holidays, showing his family's treasures to parties of visitors. 'He's as good as any professional,' said Johnnie, proudly.

The announcement, at the beginning of 1982, that two 22-carat gold, seventeenth-century wine coolers, weighing 25lbs and part of the Marlborough plate collection, were to be bought by the British Museum for around £250,000 caused further comment. The sale was to raise money to begin a maintenance fund, in accordance with the previous year's Finance Act, to contribute towards the upkeep of the stately home; the fund would not be liable to tax. Clearly, the Earl had been unsettled by the audible groundswell of critical voices. 'The wine coolers have been in a bank in Fleet Street for the last hundred years,' he said, a touch defensively, to the *Sunday Telegraph*. 'There was no income from them and no one could see them.'

But that, he said, was that. 'We have nothing else in mind at the moment; and everything we have sold we have offered to the nation first. The trouble is that the nation is rather poor.' Althorp's annual running costs, maintenance apart, were around £70,000, he said. 'We also have to renew the library ceiling because the plaster has come away from the joists.' This was due partly to age and partly to visitors, many more of whom had flocked to the house and its grounds since Diana had married Prince Charles the previous June. 'We are spending all the extra revenue – about £50,000 – on doing up the house. We're getting new curtains and carpets, cleaning the paintings, renewing the frames, and doing some redecorating.'

One major problem on the seventh Earl's death, it seems, was the condition of the farms on the estate. 'They were very run down,' revealed Johnnie. 'The estate should support the house but the house has had to support the estate. I have to spend £2,000 per acre across 300 acres on drainage and other works. I've built a new grain store. Do you realize,' he added, 'that it took three men two days just to clear the snow off the roof of Althorp?'

None of this helped to staunch the flow of criticism. Just before Christmas of that year, more dissenting voices claimed Earl Spencer was selling off the family treasures to pay for decorations and restoration that many believed reflected the taste and demands of Raine. Much of the work was sneered at by both purists and those people who felt that the often-quoted 'noble intimacy' of the magnificent Althorp House was unlikely to benefit from the Countess's particular vision. There had been an openly hostile report in *The Times*, taking the Earl to task for selling £2 million worth of heirlooms. 'The rate at which art treasures are being sold from the historic Spencer collection at Althorp,' wrote art room correspondent Geraldine Norman, 'and the lack of reliable information on what has been sold, is causing consternation in heritage circles. The present Lady Spencer has had charge of the sales since her marriage to the Earl in 1976. Virtually every main London dealer has been down to Althorp for confidential discussions usually followed by purchases.'

Scholars had pointed out that the catalogue of paintings at Althorp, published in the year of Johnnie's remarriage, listed 717 pictures; some 200 now appeared to be missing. 'The object is for Spencers to go on living at Althorp,' the Earl told *The Times*. 'The house is now in better condition than it has ever been, I think.' Others, Norman reported, did not agree. 'It looks like the inside of a summer pudding,' grumbled one heritage veteran. Lord Spencer was clearly stung. 'When my father died,' he retaliated, 'I was left with debts in excess of £2 million. I decided to keep the house running and to refurbish. That meant something had to go. Paintings and furniture have been sold from the Althorp collection, sometimes to buyers abroad. I hate selling anything that belongs to the family but what am I supposed to do?'

He also bridled at the suggestion that Raine was the prime mover in Althorp's upheaval. 'People imply that I have very little to do with the running of the house and that my wife runs everything. In fact, everything we have chosen for the house has been done together. People have said nasty things about the restoration but many of them have not been to see it. It is the best restored house in England and my wife and I believe it has been done beautifully.

'I was ill a few years ago but my mind is perfectly sound.' No one doubted it, but Timothy Clifford, Director of the Manchester City Art Gallery, was by no means a lone voice when he articulated his disquiet about the insidious inroads being made into the family's collection. How much better, he argued, to retain the Van Dycks than sell them and spend the money on the house. 'I am very much afraid for the Spencer collection,' he said. 'There is also another family property, Spencer House in London. It contains superb furniture and paintings, and that is to be sold and that unique collection dispersed.'

By 1991, cottages on the family estate were said to be up for sale, its tenants fearful for their future, Viscount Althorp declaring, 'It has nothing to do with me.' The sixty properties were put on the market for around £60,000 each, their occupants being given the first option to buy in a letter received from the Earl's solicitors. 'We understand that your short-holding tenancy has expired,' it was explained, 'and Lord Spencer would like to offer you the opportunity to purchase the freehold of the cottage.' Enquiries were being fielded by Pauline Shaw, a member of Raine's personal staff. Many of the cottages, it was claimed by their occupants, had leaking roofs and required damp-proofing. Repair costs on individual properties could amount to as much as £15,000.

In August, the volcano erupted. Staff subsequently told of a blazing row between Earl Spencer and Charles in the library of Althorp House. 'We could hear Lord Althorp accusing his father and Raine of destroying 500 years of family heritage,' one source revealed to the *Daily Mail*. 'He [Charles] said that in the past fifteen years more damage had been done than in the last four centuries. He reminded his father that his role should be to look after the house during his lifetime.' The confrontation was clearly bitter: Charles would no longer enter the house while his stepmother was there and, if she turned up unexpectedly, would not sit down at the same dinner table as her. Diana, too, was appalled at her stepmother's sweeping programme of renovation and redecoration.

'If it were not so tragic, what has happened at Althorp would be, of course, high comedy.' So began a damning piece in *Harpers & Queen*, written in the late eighties by Alexandra Artley and Thomas Dibdin. If you managed to slalom successfully through the rampant snobbery (Raine was dismissed at one point as 'the sharp lady from Haute Suburbia . . . tripping about like a corn dolly wearing hats in her own house'), there were some revealing insights. People who knew the extent of the seventh Earl's restoration work, according to the authors, 'cannot understand Raine's oft-repeated remark that the house was an uncomfortable ruin when she took it over'. They recoiled, too, from what they saw as the 'astonishingly overt commercialism' of the new Althorp. 'The whole place is run like Aristocracy plc. She gets into the air-conditioned Roller in her hat,' they sniffed, 'and drives 300 yards to The Shop, a place of unmatched tawdriness.'

More substantially, Artley and Dibdin summed up the legacy of the Countess ('Raine damage', according to another observer) bequeathed to one of England's finest stately homes. 'The seventeenth- and eighteenth-century lacquer chests in the Long Gallery (now close-carpeted like a country house hotel) have been more or less rebuilt and all their brass mounts gilded, even though they had never been gilded before. A tremendous amount of gilding seems to have gone on. The set of chairs from the Spencer House Great Room has been given the same treatment. Originally white and gold with green brocade seats, they are now brightly gilded all over and re-upholstered in astonishing mango stamped velvet.' The set was then broken up and some were sold.

Artley and Dibdin continued, 'This transaction neatly encapsulates the general view of Raine's reign at Althorp – the unnecessary and vulgar "restoration" (done without Listed Building consent), the profits made by Bond Street dealers at the expense of one of England's great historic family collections, and the sheer useless turmoil of it all. Even the famous Whig sculpture joke in the entrance hall (the Nollekens bust of Pitt used to look at Fox while Fox looked out of the window) has been spoiled by unnecessary rearrangement.

'One sad day, when Raine sits at Tradewinds [one of three seaside homes she and Johnnie bought in Bognor for half a million pounds], perhaps continuing to let the other two "luxury" Spencer villas (Hacienda and Water's Edge House), Charles, the ninth Earl Spencer, will wander across acres of strange carpet, looking at photographic records of the house, wondering if gilding can be undone but knowing that the papers, letters, drawings, music, silver, furniture and pictures of his own family are very unlikely ever to come home again.'

In September 1991, Raine and Johnnie, happy to escape the encircling row over Operation Althorp, flew to the south of France for a welcome break. On board the flight to Nice, they were 'ambushed' by journalist Brian Vine who secured a revealing interview with the captive couple, Lady Spencer for once going on the record. 'Yes, I've heard myself called "wicked stepmother",' she acknowledged, 'but all the names go over my head. I'm only interested in my love for John and for what he is trying to do for posterity. He loves Althorp and everything we have done with it. Do you think that for one minute, if I didn't love Lord Spencer, I would put up with all this hassle and bad blood? I don't need it. I have money, all the money I'll ever need. I've even lent some of it to John when the interest rate has looked too high on loans. So some of me is in the house. Not many people know that but it's a fact.

'I have a fascinating job as a director of the British Tourist Authority. I own my own home still and I have my health. People are so ungrateful. John has been very generous with all his children. I know that for a fact. But people never seem very grateful, whatever you do. However, no one can hurt me now. I've been through all sorts of hurt: John's stroke and nursing him, a career in politics [at the old Greater London Council] and a step-family.' She was at a loss, she said, to understand why people felt she was the driving force behind the upheavals at Althorp. 'I don't make those decisions to sell paintings or cottages. I get my orders from my husband. He tells me what to do and I do it. This idea that I have some great influence is not right. These possessions are his to do what he likes with.' It is just the same, she felt, a trifle bewilderingly to the outside observer, as if someone passes down a silver bracelet or a teapot to you. 'They should be happy for you to sell it.'

Lord Spencer was a vigorous supporter of what his wife had achieved at Althorp, he said. 'I think Raine has done a magnificent job. No one could have done it better. She's a natural interior decorator. All the pictures have been cleaned and re-lined and the furniture has been re-covered. I love it.' And the reaction of his children? 'Of course I haven't stopped speaking to Diana or Charles,' he said, reacting to stories in some papers. 'I think my son's a little immature but he'll get over it all; just you wait and see.' It was, interjected Raine, absolutely unrealistic to imagine that people didn't sell certain of their possessions during their lifetime. 'It's ridiculous when other people get dismayed,' she concluded. Her husband was unshakable in his view that he and his wife were doing the right thing. 'Raine is here to stay,' he said, 'and so is her decor. And they say I've got twenty more years,' he added cheerfully, though inaccurately, as it turned out. (In fact, he had less than seven months.)

It had been widely rumoured that the publicity around the Spencer children's alarm over the dispersal of Althorp's treasures had been carefully orchestrated by them, meeting in emergency session at Kensington Palace; a trusted friend, apparently, had been chosen to leak the story to the national press. Whatever the gung-ho attitude subsequently displayed by the eighth Earl and his wife, the public outcry – it even caused mutterings, it was said, at Buckingham Palace – had hit home. That, surely, was the end of the affair. In fact, it very swiftly proved to have been a false dawn. Within days of the furore first being reported, new depths of questionable commercialism had been plumbed.

From Japan, where Johnnie and Raine were due to travel at the end of the month, came the news that replicas of Princess Diana's wedding dress were to be sold in Japanese chain stores – a licensing arrangement concluded with the apparent blessing of the Earl. This announcement followed hard on the heels of the revelation that the Spencer name and family crest were to be licensed to a new golf club in the same country. The Royal Spencer Golf Club (although he had no right to sanction the use of the 'royal' tag) at Kushiro, on Japan's northern island of Hokkaido, was said to be offering membership for fees of £26,000 to the first 400 signed-up members. Subsequent members would be expected to pay £80,000 for the privilege of playing at a club that was to be given a 'British air', as well as at two clubs in Britain, one at Althorp.

Johnnie was said, perhaps understandably, to have been deeply embarrassed when confronting his son and heir with the latest scheme of capitalizing on Diana's bridal gown. But then, as every visitor to The Shop, or browser through the Althorp catalogue, would have known, a replica of Diana's sapphire and diamond engagement ring was available at a knock-down £17.99. For a mere £1 there were, additionally, signed colour postcards of the Earl and Countess. The Queen, it was said, was aghast at the actions of her former equerry. 'Earl Spencer,' according to a Palace insider, 'has ruined a lifetime's friendship by his foolish behaviour.'

In the middle of March 1992, Johnnie was unexpectedly admitted to the Wellington Hospital in London with suspected pneumonia. For the next twelve days, he seemed to be bearing up well. Then, without warning, on 29 March, he suffered a massive heart attack. At 68, the eighth Earl Spencer was dead. Diana, on holiday with her family in Switzerland (she had been assured before she'd flown out of Britain that her father would soon be released from hospital), flew home to RAF Northolt.

The eighth Earl – assured an indelible niche in the national consciousness for the sweet and courageous way he had led his third daughter down the long aisle of St Paul's Cathedral on her wedding day – had never flinched from acknowledging the incalculable debt he owed his second wife. 'Without Raine,' he once said, 'I would never have lived to see Diana marry the Prince of Wales. Raine saved my life by sheer will-power. The doctors had me on the death list eight times. They said I'd need a miracle to survive. Raine was my miracle. It's entirely due to her – her love for me, her determination not to let me go – that I stayed around.'

Charles inherited an estate subsequently valued at £89,251,441. It was an awesome mantle. As he paced the corridors of the stately pile that had been reduced, in some places, as he later famously remarked, 'to the wedding cake vulgarity of a five-star hotel in Monaco', his mind must have been a swirl of emotions. '[Raine] tried to create a corner of Mayfair in Northamptonshire,' he was reported subsequently to reflect. His father had died at four o'clock in the afternoon; from one minute past four, he announced, Raine Spencer was no longer welcome in Althorp House or its grounds.

He began to eradicate all traces of her from the family seat: Barbara Cartland's novels and signed postcards of his step-mother were removed from The Shop, as were all photographs of Raine and the gaudy portrait of her which hung overlooking the main stairwell of the house. When Raine's maid arrived to collect the last of her clothes, Charles insisted they be packed in black binliners instead of the expensive Louis Vuitton suitcases which, he maintained, had belonged to his father. At the last moment, his temper got the better of him and he hurled the bulging binliners down the stairs of Althorp House as it moved seamlessly into its new phase of being home to the ninth Earl Spencer.

7

LOVE AND MARRIAGE

Like it or not – and there are, after all, worse fates – Charles Althorp entered his twenties as one of Britain's most eligible bachelors. What, wondered *Woman* magazine in 1987, would constitute his ideal partner? 'I really don't mind about background unless *she* was worried about it,' he replied, 'because that could lead to friction. I'd also like someone with a highly developed sense of humour which she would probably need being married to me. And I'd like her to be able to get on with people well because in my life I'll always be meeting lots of new people and I don't want a wife who's going to be shy and hate every moment. It would be a bonus if she were beautiful,' he concluded, adding, 'I obviously wouldn't want somebody who was beautiful and then didn't want children because I'd like several.'

Before he was to meet the person he believed to be his ultimate soulmate, Charles enjoyed squiring a succession of good-looking, well-bred young women round his favourite haunts. His first serious affair – with Oxford secretarial college student Lucy Stiles – gave way, after almost a year and a half, to a brief fling with Marianna Lewis who was with him when he had the motorway service station altercation that led to a speeding fine. Industrialist's daughter, Rachel Kelly – who now works on the property pages of *The Times* – ended her romance with Lady Antonia Fraser's son, Damien, in favour of Charles's charms when both were at Magdalen College. Their stormy affair lasted less than a year, ending a week before they were due to return from a holiday together in America and the Far East. Two days before Rachel's 21st birthday, Charles confided in gossip columnist Nigel Dempster that the bust-up had resulted in the two of them flying home to Britain separately.

It was the demands of his roving brief as an NBC correspondent that finally put paid to his affair with Rachel's successor, art student Katie Braine. (She it was, when she took up sculpting, who once used Charles's good friend, Darius Guppy, as a life model. The work completed, Katie is said to have asked Guppy to suggest a title. 'Sheer Perfection' was his considered response.) The 23-year-old Viscount Althorp was reported as being 'in a continually tearful state' about the loss of his latest love but then his simultaneous dalliance with journalist and cartoonist Sally Ann Lasson had, apparently, hardened Katie's heart. Mentioned briefly in despatches thereafter were Lucy Lane Fox and Janet Astor, daughter of Bronwen, Viscountess Astor. But the ambitious young television reporter was increasingly more intent on pursuing his career, it seemed, than in tracking down a suitable wife. For all that, though, he had revealed, in a prescient remark reported in *Sunday* magazine on the eve of his 20th birthday, 'I am very impetuous when it comes to matters of the heart. I'm a romantic and can fall head-over-heels in love very easily.'

So he should have been unsurprised when, just ten days after meeting international model Victoria Lockwood, at the beginning of June 1989, he found himself falling to one knee and proposing marriage. In the elegant Georgian house of Charles's Old Etonian school chum, Nick Weslowski – the photographer son of a former Polish army officer – Britain's nearly royal, most eligible bachelor had been introduced to the daughter of the Civil Aviation Authority's personnel director and his magistrate wife. Although Victoria was there at the time with reformed drug addict boyfriend Martin Fraser, she later acknowledged that, 'As soon as we spoke, I felt something quite unusual and extraordinary. We both did. I always knew that, if I got married, it would be like this. Instantaneous.'

Her smitten fiancé clearly felt just as bowled over. 'I didn't think it would be like this at all,' he told *Daily Mail* royal correspondent, Richard Kay. 'I assumed you saw someone for years and then stumbled into marriage. What has happened has surprised me as much as everyone else. People have suggested that things have gone a little too fast but I never had a moment's doubt.' To Nigel Dempster, he confessed, 'When I met Victoria, it was love at first sight. I didn't think such things happened but they obviously do. I just knew she was the one for me and luckily she felt the same. We are both dead certain.'

The same could not be said of Dempster who, when asked about Charles's choice of bride, is reported to have dismissed her as 'an extraordinary girl – and totally unsuitable'. If the judgment was harsh, it was no less prophetic for that. Victoria Lockwood may have been beautiful but many factors weighed against her as a suitable consort for the man who would one day succeed to the title of the ninth Earl Spencer. She was firmly middle-class and quite unused to the peculiar and particular demands of what used to be called the ruling class. Nor was she her future husband's intellectual equal; indeed, her elder brother Christopher, a journalist currently working on the *Daily Telegraph*, once remarked to a colleague that of the two children, he got the brains, his sister the beauty.

What she also got was an addictive personality and a strong streak of vulnerability. It was to prove a potent mix. Her modelling career had taken off, almost vertically, from the moment she was spotted by a talent scout while out shopping as a 17-year-old in Chelsea. But the demands of jetting round the world and remaining fashionably thin – as was later to be revealed during the Spencers' divorce case – took an unforgiving toll. At one stage, Victoria's habitual intake appeared to be confined to alcohol and ice cream. In times, drugs, too, were on the menu. So Charles's arrival on the scene represented, to some extent, her chance of salvation. What it did not do – perhaps could not do – was erase her dependent personality at a stroke: the 'extraordinary, totally unsuitable' Victoria Lockwood may have metamorphosed, in time, into the Countess Spencer but the splendid outer trappings of her new life could not mask for long the fact that she was bringing to the marriage a certain amount of emotional baggage. Baggage that was to prove dangerously destabilising. Less than two years after Charles and Victoria's wedding, there was a charity cricket match at Althorp followed by an auction in the evening. A top table guest on that occasion recalls being shocked at the appearance and behaviour of the Countess at what should have been, for her, an uncomplicatedly happy event. 'It was very clear that Victoria was in a terrible state,' remembers the guest. 'Everyone was quite dressed up while she was dressed down, to put it mildly, in a little cotton dress, bare legs and sandals. She looked divine – she is, after all, very beautiful. But she kicked off her shoes, tucked her legs up underneath her and sat for most of the evening holding the hand of a girlfriend sitting next to her. She hardly ate a thing; she barely spoke.

'She was like a child. I wanted to hug her. It was very sad. She seemed so frail, so vulnerable and so unbelievably thin. It wasn't that grand an event and it was rather jolly. Peter O'Toole said grace. Ronnie Wood of the Rolling Stones was there, I remember. But Victoria just didn't seem able to cope. I tried talking to her – she was sitting two people away from me – but without much success. Charles, on the other hand, was quite chatty and nice, if rather intense. But then I think he was obviously concerned about his wife. He had spent much of the day trying to shore her up.

'I kept thinking that here was this ravishing girl, well used to the high life, now married to a rich and glamorous man and with a new baby on whom she doted who, nonetheless, seemed swamped by proceedings. She was like a little waif at the banquet. I've never forgotten the sight of someone clearly cracking up before my eyes. Something was obviously very wrong. I just felt that this was a sad, lost soul.'

Back in the summer of '89, though, love was in the air. The young woman once described by American designer Ralph Lauren as 'the most beautiful girl in the world' now had to adjust to becoming one of the most famous. How was she contemplating the prospect of having the Princess of Wales as a sister-in-law? 'Having met Diana,' she replied, 'I am thrilled to become part of her family.' The feeling, apparently, was reciprocated. 'Two of my sisters, including Diana, have met her already,' said Charles, 'and they very much approve.' The former pupil at Frances Holland School in Regent's Park had, until recently, been modelling in New York and Paris. 'But she's definitely not a bimbo,' said her future husband. So what of Victoria's future? 'I am certainly not going into hibernation,' she said, 'particularly with Charles being away a lot in his job. He would hate me to stay at home. We are both young with plenty we want to do. We are very much alike which is wonderful. I hope there will be children but possibly not for a couple of years yet.'

On 11 July 1989, *The Times* ran the engagement of, 'Charles, only son of the Earl Spencer and the Hon Mrs Shand Kydd, of the Isle of Seil, Argyll, and Catherine Victoria, only daughter of Mr and Mrs John Lockwood, of Barnes, London'. Speaking from the family seat, the eighth Earl said that he and his (second) wife were very pleased. 'Charles deserves this,' he said. The Lockwoods told reporters outside their Thames-side house, 'We are naturally delighted and very happy for Victoria and Charles who are very much in love. We knew from the start. It was quite obvious that this was clearly something very special.'

Charles's choice of an antique Victorian heart-shaped engagement ring of rubies and diamonds was made in 1850 and supplied by Bond Street jewellers, S J Phillips. It was said to have cost around £10,000. 'I rang them up and asked to see a selection,' he later revealed. The jewellers sent round a tray. 'I really had no predetermined idea of exactly what I wanted except that it had to be a little different and that it must contain rubies because they perfectly suit Victoria's colouring.' He obviously chose well. 'It's absolutely beautiful,' cooed Victoria. 'I love it.' (In time, though, she took to leaving it off on the grounds that she felt it to be too ostentatious.)

With the wedding fixed for Saturday, 16 September 1989, at the twelfth-century St Mary the Virgin at Great Brington – the church nearest to the Althorp estate – details were released of the outfits to be worn by the page boys and bridesmaids. Prince Harry, celebrating his 5th birthday the day before the ceremony, and Alexander Fellowes, 6-year-old son of Charles's sister, Lady Jane, were each to be decked out in white breeches and black felt hat, their shirts trimmed with ruffled lace collars and cuffs, the whole ensemble finished off with a large blue cummerbund tied in a bow at the side. The inspiration came, apparently, from a portrait of the third Earl Spencer, painted by Joshua Reynolds in 1779. The bridesmaids – 6-year-old Emily McCorquodale, Lady Sarah's daughter, and 4-year-old Eleanor Fellowes – were to be attired in white dresses trimmed with pink satin and topped off with a cap decorated with pink roses (Thomas Gainsborough's 1763 portrait of Lady Georgiana Spencer being the inspiration).

The world had to wait for the big day to see what Polish-born designer Tomasz Starzewski had dreamed up for the bride. In the event, her £16,000 dress of gold silk crêpe and lace – 15 metres of silk, 10 metres of lace, 70 hours in the making – and trimmed with sable fur, drew a mixed reaction. Fashion writer Newby Hands revealed that the unusual shade of champagne had been achieved with a little help from a bottle of domestic bleach. Victoria, it was said, had wanted, like so many brides before and since, to add her own personal touches to the outfit she would wear just once. A blue medallion blessed by the Pope was stitched on to the right cuff of the dress, above the hand that would rest on the Bible during the wedding ceremony. A tooth from her pet cat was hidden under the left arm. 'We even embroidered little gold whiskers round it for a bit of fun,' said Starzewski. Like Diana, and her two older sisters before her, Victoria wore the Spencer family tiara, an arc of diamond leaves, in her shoulder-length, undressed hair. Los Angeles-based fashion critic Richard Blackwell remained unimpressed. 'The bride,' he declared, 'looked like Anne Boleyn going to her execution. She must have been in a terrible state of depression to have chosen such a colour [for her bridal gown].'

The bride arrived for the ceremony a fashionable seventeen minutes late, beneath torrential rain, in an eighteenth-century coach – which had drawn the eighth Earl Spencer's parents to the Coronation of King George VI and Queen Elizabeth in 1937 – attended, on this occasion, by four outriders dressed as hunting cavaliers. The day before the wedding, the groom had confessed to a rush of last-minute nerves. 'I had amazed myself,' he said, 'at how cool I felt and how smoothly everything was going. But today I'm getting twitchy. I think it's getting to me at last.' But then Victoria, he revealed, was also beginning to feel nervous. 'Up to now, she has been marvellous, taking everything in her stride.'

She had also born the brunt of all the many demands of so high-profile an event. 'I think I should have stopped a little earlier,' said Charles, referring to the fact he had continued working for NBC until the Wednesday before the Saturday ceremony. 'I should have given her more of a hand. She's had to dash around all over the place. It has been such a rush with so much to organize that there has scarcely been any time to sit back and think.'

He had been surprised, he told the *Daily Mail*'s Richard Kay, at the media reaction to the engagement. 'I suppose we thought that, after the announcement, all the interest would die down but it certainly didn't.' This turned out to be a coded way of saying how very fed up he was at the constant hounding by the tabloids prior to the wedding. Three months after they were married, Lord and Lady Althorp spoke in a television interview for Channel 4's *Hard News* of their individual and shared harassment in the run-up to the big day. 'I think they [the tabloid press] are really totally insensitive, evil, evil people,' declared Victoria. 'I don't know how they go home to their wives and children and talk about their day with a clear conscience and have any self-esteem or self-respect.'

Her husband was fully behind her. 'They were not content with the story as it stood,' he said. 'They wanted to make it juicier, nastier. They didn't want somebody they saw as a privileged young man having the happy time that he deserved. They wanted to get back, to bring me down.' He went on to allege that one national newspaper had hired private detectives to follow him and his fiancée, and that he had even found a photographer buried in the bushes in the grounds of Althorp Park. 'We were having a drink on the lawn,' he said, 'and I suddenly heard this clicking sound from a bush at the end of the garden. So I raced down there and hauled out a photographer weighed down with cameras.'

The forty-five-minute marriage service was conducted by the Archbishop of Canterbury, Robert Runcie, an old friend of Charles's father. The traditional ceremony was taken from the 1662 Book of Common Prayer, the bride agreeing to 'love, honour *and* obey' her husband. The choir, from Charles's old Oxford college, Magdalen, was accompanied by a chamber orchestra; unusually, one of the two chosen hymns was the childhood favourite, 'All Things Bright and Beautiful'. Victoria, clutching a bouquet of deep red roses, walked back down the aisle on her husband's arm, to the ringing strains of Elgar's 'Nimrod'.

The 250 guests who had squeezed into the church were swelled by a further 200 for the reception in Althorp House. Curiously, and it has never been satisfactorily explained to this day, best man Darius Guppy, whether through nerves, the sudden onset of illness or by prior arrangement, failed to deliver the traditional speech. In the event, it was left to Old Harrovian Dan Wiggin to propose the toast to the bride and groom and to thank their attendants. The only moment of humour – or embarrassment, depending on which report you believe – came in Charles's short speech when, seeking to comfort his new father-in-law, he reassured him that he hadn't lost a daughter so much as 'gained Raine'.

The single serious blot on proceedings – the dismal weather apart – came when Lady Jane Fellowes left the £100,000 reception with her children and failed to negotiate a corner on a wet road at Badby in Northamptonshire, her F-registration Ford Montego flipping over and landing upside down in a ditch. Happily, Lady Jane and her three children had all been wearing seatbelts and no one was injured. The bride and groom, meanwhile, left for their honeymoon: a night in Paris followed by a two-week holiday in the Seychelles in the Indian Ocean.

Back home, the newlyweds settled down to married life in the Falconry, a five-bedroom Gothic house on the Althorp estate. 'Our immediate task is to fix things up around here,' Charles told one reporter on the eve of his wedding. 'This place is, I'm afraid, a typical bachelor's pad. Victoria intends to start doing it up when we come back from our honeymoon.' And she did, somewhat to the surprise of her friends who found it hard to imagine the jet-setting model swapping the high life for domesticity, albeit comfortably upholstered. 'I want to make a home for my husband,' she revealed to Richard Kay in a curiously old-fashioned turn of phrase. 'That will be my new job. All I want to do is look after Charles.'

According to her father, John Lockwood, 'Victoria is very style conscious. Interior design has always been very important to her.' She had her work cut out in the rather forbidding, yellowstone Victorian house. Echoing her husband, she declared that their home was 'badly in need of a woman's touch'. There was also the question of when to start a family: although both were keen to become parents, Victoria had speculated at the time of her wedding that they might wait a year or two. As it turned out, Lady Kitty Eleanor Spencer entered the world, by Caesarean section, at St Mary's hospital in Paddington, west London, on 30 December 1990, weighing in at 6lb 2oz.

A couple of months later, the proud father, rocking his daughter in his arms as he fed her from a bottle, spoke of the joys of parenthood. 'You don't realize so many of the responsibilities,' he said, 'until you become a parent and how much they're going to hit you. But I'm enjoying fatherhood very much – even at three in the morning. Nappies are the only duty I'm excused.' His wife was full of praise for the new father. 'Charles does much more than I ever expected him to,' she said.

Shusha Guppy, mother of Darius and prospective godmother to Lady Kitty, also spoke up for the happiness of Charles and Victoria Althorp. 'They're very much looking forward to the christening of their daughter,' she said, 'and to the other children they will have in the future. It will be a lovely chance for everyone to see how happy they are. They are wonderful parents and Kitty is an angel. I'm completely confident her future will be as part of a happy family. Victoria still implicitly trusts Charlie,' concluded Mrs Guppy. 'She knows it's impossible for people never to make mistakes. They feel their marriage will be much stronger after this. They have got closer in the last few days.'

The need for Shusha Guppy to break rank and agree to be wheeled out for this carefully controlled exercise in damage limitation had been occasioned by an unfortunate blip in the seemingly happy union: just six months into his marriage, in a Parisian hotel, Charles Althorp had resumed his affair, however fleetingly, with journalist and cartoonist, Sally Ann Lasson.

8

THE SALLY ANN LASSON AFFAIR

The facts are these. In 1985, journalist and cartoonist Sally Ann Lasson was despatched by the *Sunday Times* newspaper to interview Charles Spencer for a piece in its award-winning magazine. Clearly, the two found each other amusing – attractive, even – though she was married at the time to successful songwriter Dominic King. The two met intermittently over the next year, consummating their relationship in September 1986 at Charles's ancestral home, with Sally Ann confiding subsequently to a national tabloid, 'We spent a smashing time together and finally got around to sex. I couldn't help saying, "I don't know what took you so long." Charles said that he had never met a woman who sent out such distant and remote signals. I can only suppose I had been transmitting the opposite to what I felt.'

Pressure of work on each of them, apparently, made their ensuing 'romance' something of a stuttering affair and meant they didn't meet again until 1988 when she moved to a new flat (her marriage to Dominic now irretrievably over) and sent Charles a change of address card. He responded instantly. Over a smart, if discreet, dinner *à deux* at top central London hotel Claridges, the 24-year-old Viscount Althorp asked the 28-year-old Sally Ann – or so she is reported as saying – if she would embark on an affair with him. 'I gave him ten out of ten for cheek,' she recalled, 'but I told him we weren't very good at all of that last time around so perhaps we should avoid it.' They lunched next on New Year's Eve but it was not until the following March, according to Sally Ann, that the couple again had sex. 'I decided I was ready,' she says. 'We had a lovely evening together and then went back to my flat and made love.'

Their hectic work schedules precluded regular trysts but nothing had prepared Sally Ann, she says, for what followed. 'In the middle of one night in May, Charles got out of my bed because he said he didn't like the fact that my cat, Blackie, had jumped on him. I simply thought him childish at the time.' A week or so later, there was a message on her answering machine from Charles asking her to call him. She rang back but he was out. The next morning, she opened her daily newspaper. To her astonishment, she read the announcement that Charles Spencer, the Viscount Althorp, was to marry top model Victoria Lockwood. 'My heart leapt into my mouth. I couldn't believe it,' Sally Ann was reported as saying. 'As far as I was concerned, *we* were having a relationship.'

But Charles and Victoria, after a whirlwind romance, it seemed, were hopelessly in love. Indeed, in September of that same year, they were settling down to a life of wedded bliss. Though, sadly, not for long. Just six months later, Sally Ann received a call from the recently wed Charles Spencer to the effect that his marriage was in disarray – he described it subsequently as having hit 'a particularly messy patch' – and asking her whether she would care to accompany him to Paris. Five minutes later, he called back: he'd pick her up in half an hour. 'I was as happy as a person can be without exploding,' gushed Sally Ann subsequently.

Her happiness was again to prove shortlived. The trip – it amounted to little more than one dinner in a Parisian restaurant, one night together in the Hotel Balzac and one lunch the following day – was brought to an abrupt halt when Charles announced that he was going back to England to sort out his tangled private life. In a statement released the following February, his rather less than chivalrous explanation for his sudden return home from the French capital ran in part as follows: 'The experience so sickened me that I did not stay the second night in Paris but returned to London, eager to patch up my marriage. This my wife and I were able to do to such an extent that today ... we are deeply in love. Our marriage is the most important thing in both our lives.' History was to prove otherwise.

Back in England in the spring of 1990, Sally Ann truly believed, she says, that Charles was discussing divorce with Victoria. A matter of weeks later, he telephoned her with a fresh bombshell: his wife was pregnant. Angry and hurt as she was, that might have been the end of the affair had it not been for Sally Ann's financial plight. In December, weeks before the arrival of the Spencers' first child, Kitty, Sally Ann rang Charles to say that some workmen had run off with her money. As he later revealed to the *Daily Mail*'s veteran gossip columnist, Nigel Dempster, 'She was desperate for £5,000 immediately. She wondered if I could help raise it. But I was totally unreceptive to the idea.' Sally Ann's financial position did not improve and her father's health began to cause concern. At the end of January 1991, she contacted the *News of the World*, Britain's biggest-selling newspaper. She was prepared to sell her story for £5,000 – paltry by today's standards. Would they be interested?

On the Thursday before planned publication of the first instalment of Sally Ann's on-off affair with Charles Spencer – the lurid front-page headline subsequently read: 'Di's Brother Used Me As His Sex Toy' – she forewarned him in a telephone conversation of what she had done. She was speaking out, she said, because she wanted him, and the world, to know he couldn't go around behaving in what she felt was an irresponsible fashion. 'He shouldn't have played games. He should have made a decision – and stuck to it.' But she had reckoned without his reaction to her planned revelations; not that, in the event, Charles's chosen course of action did much more than merely authenticate her story. On the grounds that the best form of defence is attack, Charles rang his old friend Nigel Dempster and gave him a gleefully received scoop.

Thus it was that on the Saturday before the *News of the World* published its no longer exclusive story, the front page of the *Daily Mail* – followed pretty rapidly by later editions of the rest of the daily tabloids – revealed Charles Spencer's admission of an affair with Sally Ann Lasson before and after his marriage to Victoria Lockwood. 'I have caused my wife more grief than I would wish her to have in a lifetime,' he told Dempster, 'and I accept full responsibility for the folly of my actions. Now, a month after the birth of our baby, we are deeply in love and our marriage is the most important thing in our lives. Victoria is profoundly upset but has asked me to say that our marriage will not be destroyed by a woman who belonged to our unhappy past.'

There was more to come. Not content with spilling the beans in advance, Charles issued a further statement, printed in loving detail in the next day's *News of the World*, claiming it to be 'a correct record of events'.

In September 1986, I had a one-night stand with Ms Lasson but did not see her for 18 months after that. During this time, she on several occasions telephoned me with obsessive messages. In late 1988, I saw Ms Lasson again twice but no further physical relations took place. Once or twice, we spoke on the telephone but it was not until May 1989 that I saw her again, just prior to meeting my wife. Ms Lasson was extremely jealous when I got engaged to Victoria in a whirlwind romance and she made it clear that she had always wanted to be my wife – a thought that had never occurred to me.

In February and March 1990, my wife and I went through an extremely messy patch in our marriage, and a separation seemed possible. I talked to Ms Lasson about my marital problems – a foolish move in retrospect but, with a failed marriage behind her, I thought she might be in a position to give advice. On the afternoon of March 28, after a particularly unpleasant series of quarrels with my wife, I rang up Ms Lasson and asked if she would come to Paris with me for two days. I sincerely thought at the time that my marriage was over. We went to Paris and had our second one-night stand, four years after the first. The experience so sickened me that I did not stay the second night in Paris but returned to London, eager to patch up my marriage. This my wife and I were able to do to such an extent that today, a month after the birth of our first child, we are deeply in love. Our marriage is the most important thing in our lives.

Ms Lasson began behaving in an irrational way. She demanded at the beginning of July 1990 that I go round to her flat to discuss the whole matter. I went and explained how my marriage was increasingly happy. She was furious, demanding that she be my mistress and that I keep her, as her funds were, according to her, running low.

If Charles Spencer felt his pre-emptive strike had effectively spiked Sally Ann's guns, he had not reckoned with the justifiable – as she saw it – wrath of a woman scorned. Despite the lengthy interview she had already given to the *News of the World*, she issued a further statement countering Charles's version of events.

I don't know what he means by saying the experience of a night with me in Paris so sickened him that he returned to London. I won't be tacky and go into the detail of sex but I will say that when we made love in Paris, he was more romantic and sensual than I had ever known him. How can making love in Paris *not* be romantic?

But, as his sombre wedding pictures show, he's not the most demonstrative of men. He has a problem with being tactile, sensual and touchy. Sickened is a tacky word to use about a weekend you arrange with another woman in Paris – unless he means that's how his wife felt when he confessed to her two days ago. The first time we made love was not a one-night stand. It was at the end of a long friendship. I deny ever leaving obsessive messages on his answering machine. He has rung me far more than I have ever called him.

We had lunch together on New Year's Eve 1988, which is hardly the time when you meet a casual girlfriend, and we had been speaking on and off since November. I never said I wanted to be his wife. When he was droning on about his marriage problems in October of last year, I said: "If you're so unhappy with her, why didn't you marry me?" And he said: "Because I would have made you unhappy." I wanted him to use his title, wealth and position to spread a little philanthropy. I wanted to make him into a cross between the Earl of Shaftesbury – the peer who saved little boys from being sent up chimneys – and the stylish Cary Grant.

In the immediate fall-out of all the crossfire, one unexpected casualty was the regular column Sally Ann contributed to *Tatler*, a monthly style magazine bought by precisely the type of people who moved in the same circles as she and Charles. The 'Not So Innocent Bystander' column, as it was called, had been running for just three issues when the storm broke over her affair. Editor Jane Procter announced that *Tatler* had 'ended its association' with Sally Ann, adding that no other contributions would be appearing. Sally Ann was livid. This diary of a single society girl living in London was, she claimed, entirely fictional. She couldn't be held responsible for what people read into it. 'I know an awful lot of people,' she said. 'Why jump to the conclusion that Charles Althorp is my only source of material? It's ridiculous to say that I based it on my relationship with him although,' she had the grace to add, 'there are certain parallels.'

You can say that again. Take the brief (as it transpired) appearance of a character she called Harry. 'Harry is not being convenient at the moment,' she wrote in one of her columns. 'In fact, this being-married business is really most *inconvenient* to me and rather selfish of him. If he remains married to That Dreary Piece, then the least he can do is not mention it to me at every opportunity. Take last night. We went out for a lovely dinner at Joe's Café and Harry spends half the evening hunched over the table trying to pretend he's not there. He was so frantically worried in case any of his wife's friends spotted him, he refused to go to the loo.

'So there I was lumbered with a hunched man with a twitching bladder. Anyway, I told him that firstly his wife is such a bore that she probably doesn't have any friends and secondly I refuse to eat fishcakes with a man with bad posture. We've already sacrificed the trip to Paris on the altar of That Woman's egomania. Honestly, what more can she possibly want from us? Things picked up at bedtime . . . they usually do.' As a final flourish, she treated *Tatler* readers to the following observations: 'Aristocrats are only good at one thing and that's being pompous . . . Viscounts are cruel but at least they are intelligent in a condescending sort of way.'

Whatever the depth of her falling out with the magazine in 1991, it didn't last. A *rapprochement* of sorts had clearly occurred by the mid-nineties. These days, Sally Ann is a regular contributor again to the magazine. Take the May 1997 issue when she was invited to begin a debate in print about men's egos. Beneath the heading, 'The Ego Friendly Guide', came the rationale for the feature. 'We love men with big egos,' trilled *Tatler*. 'An ego the size of Wales is more often appealing than a brain of the same dimensions. Let's face it. Confidence equals egotism equals success in the sack.'

Now it was Sally Ann's turn. After some general chit-chat about egotism, she divested herself of the view that 'a motivated man has something to prove. It could be virility. It could be conquest. It doesn't matter so long as he proves it to his satisfaction – and to ours. This is the problem for so many aristocrats. Their ancestors did all the proving and now there's nothing left for them but dissipation. Their egos are merely empty husks, arrogant rather than self-confident and more prone to destroying a woman's self-esteem than to celebrating their own. And they're crap at sex.'

So, who is Sally Ann Lasson and how did she get to ensnare, albeit intermittently, the brother-in-law of the future King of

England? The daughter of an art dealer and a mother who used to run the gift shop at the Natural History Museum, she quickly acquired the reputation for being a good-looking young woman with a laser wit.

Here's Dominic King, the man she married just ten days after they first met (whirlwind romances seem to be quite the thing): 'Sally Ann is an extremely unusual girl. She can hold her own at any party even when she is outrageous. The thing that would strike you about her is that she would be the girl doing all the talking – almost holding court – with all the men fascinated by her mind.'

Ross Benson, a gossip columnist with the *Daily Express* when her affair with Charles Spencer became public knowledge, knew Sally Ann socially. 'Gaunt and highly strung,' opined Benson, 'she is a difficult woman to get along with. She holds the most radical of opinions and she insists on sharing them with you. If she doesn't like someone, she makes no effort whatsoever to hide the fact. Men, she used to say, are for the convenience and pleasure of women. She professed to despise such boyish [her word] pastimes as competitive horse riding and motor racing, even though racing drivers were among her closest male friends' – a less than oblique reference to Sally Ann's dalliances with both the late James Hunt, a dashing Formula One racing driver, and Alain de Cadenet (father of the emerging, Hollywood-based actress, Amanda), a man with a penchant for fast cars (he came third at Le Mans in 1976).

'The aristocracy,' according to Benson, 'also bore the brunt of Sally Ann's tongue, a strange hypocrisy, given her relationship with the heir [at the time] to one of the grandest of earldoms.' The upper classes, in her estimation, were spongers and wastrels – views, as she very well knew, that provoked a series of unnecessary rows at the weekend house parties where she invariably, and pointedly, chose to express them. Unsurprisingly, she was nicknamed Sally Anarchy, a sobriquet in which she took particular delight though it turned out not to be her favourite. Despite being lambasted by almost every newspaper columnist in Britain, it was all worth it, she said, to be dubbed by one, 'the

Violet Elizabeth Bott of the one-night stand' – a reference to the highly strung girl in Richmal Crompton's *Just William* stories, who threatened to 'thcweam and thcweam' if she didn't get her own way.

Yet, says Benson, it was difficult not to like this sophisticated, if sometimes spiky, woman. 'Underneath the vitriol, a rather amusing person was struggling to be heard. Her wit is sharp and abrasive but she can be very funny. It is reflected in her writing and cartoons.' She was a graduate from London's prestigious St Martin's School of Art and used to contribute to the *Independent*. Still, in Ross Benson's opinion, Sally Ann's humour could sometimes turn cruel. 'Certainly, Althorp must have squirmed when he read her "Not So Innocent Bystander" column in *Tatler* [in the February 1991 edition]. Her acerbic observations might raise a wry smile at a sophisticated house party. With the name of Viscount Althorp added and then plastered all over the yellow press, they can only cause heartbreak and despair.'

Sally Ann, in telling all to the gutter press, had done the unforgivable according to many people who knew her, however superficially: she had broken rank and dumped on one of her own circle. 'I always regarded her as something of a trouble-maker,' declared Benson, in a signed and exclusive column in the *Daily Express*, just after the news broke. 'But I had no inkling, and nor did anyone else, Charles included, of just how much trouble she could cause when, forsaking all her feminist values, she became the Woman Scorned.'

Certainly, no one who read Sally Ann's account of the affair in the *News of the World* could have emerged unaware of the details of the rollercoaster ride they enjoyed together. According to the newspaper's breathless version of events, 'Di's kid brother, "the boy" who took her to the peaks of ecstasy', was Sally Ann's perfect partner.

'He's the boy with everything,' she was reported as saying, 'the whole package. He's young, handsome, intelligent – possibly the most intelligent boy I know – and perceptive with all the material extras like a great house and paintings that a sophisticated girl could ever want. In my experience, you get some of those things together but rarely all of them in one boy. He was just too good to be true.'

When Sally Ann picked up the phone to Charles, a call he made in response to her change of address card, she was unprepared, she revealed, for the invitation to join him for lunch. 'But I was deeply, deeply excited about that first date.' Nor did he disappoint, it seems. 'Charles was lovely,' Sally Ann told the *News of the World*, 'but then he can be lovely,' adding, mysteriously, 'he has the technology for lovely.' That first date confirmed her opinion of Althorp as 'the boy with everything. I felt between his privilege and his brain power, he could have the world at his feet.' For all that, she quite determinedly kept him at arm's length. 'I wanted to get to know him before anything romantic happened. My life had been a boy-free zone for a long while and I wouldn't be rushed into bed.'

Charles appeared to accept this state of affairs – if, in truth, he was aware of it at all – content with seeing Sally Ann over restaurant meals on and off over many months. She, however, continued to work to her own agenda. 'I wanted him to make grand gestures and, as he could afford it, it seemed a shame not to. I wanted to be his finishing school. I wanted him to have polish. I wanted to make him good enough for me. He was after all going to inherit all those lovely paintings, for example, and I thought he should learn to appreciate them.'

When Charles returned from Paris after their aborted and illicit trip, Sally Ann decided to stay on with a friend who lived and worked there, not unduly perturbed that their tryst had been prematurely terminated. He'd gone back to England, she told herself, to talk divorce with Victoria. 'It wasn't until a couple of weeks later that we met again. He came round to my flat for lunch. At that stage, I believed Charles really intended to leave his wife. I certainly wasn't prepared to be his mistress even if he had wanted me to. I hated the idea of us making love in a sordid, sneaky way.

'But we did talk and I told Charles I was in love with him. He looked surprised.' He called Sally Ann a couple of weeks later and suggested, she says, that they should meet again. She floated the idea of a return trip to the French capital but he felt it was too risky. 'But we started seeing each other again and I presumed he was sorting out his marriage. I was coping with the secrecy and the partings because I thought Charles was in the process of ending his marriage.'

Despite her intermittent lapses into sophistry, there is nonetheless no reason to quarrel with Sally Ann's declaration that she has only ever loved two men in her life: her husband and Charles Spencer. Clearly, too, she has her own set of principles to which she would seem to adhere. 'I'm interested in *what* people are,' she told the *News of the World*, 'not *who* they are. I've got friends from all classes; and I'd date a milkman if I thought he was fab.

'I'm very proud of my nickname Sally Anarchy because I'm a non-conformist. I'm totally disinterested in royalty and I never asked Charles a single question about Diana. I don't ask most of my friends about their sisters so why should I ask him?' Nor was she ever happy to entertain the role of mistress. 'I started off being number one in Charles's life and I wasn't prepared for a demotion. The role of mistress is a job no self-respecting woman would want. With Charles, I could only look forward to secrecy, deception, loneliness and unhappiness.'

The subsequent revelation of Victoria's pregnancy – and all that ensued – meant that Charles Spencer and Sally Ann Lasson were never to meet again. It was the end of the affair. And the start of Sally Ann's potential ostracization from the very social circles that were her lifeblood, both personally and professionally. Anna Pasternak – later the author of a heavily criticized book in which Princess Diana's sometime lover James Hewitt told all – nevertheless wasted no time in denouncing Sally Ann for being 'so frightfully tacky'.

Her crime was not in consenting to a resumption of her affair with Charles Spencer after his marriage; it was in telling the world about it. 'What everyone from the countesses to the confidantes were condemning,' according to Pasternak, 'was not what a naughty boy Charlie had been but how *could* Sally Ann have told all? Nice girls, you see, do *not* kiss and tell. Well, they may kiss but tell ... never. In the charmed circles that make up money, style and, frequently, titles, there is a silent law. You turn a blind eye to your husband's indiscretions and you certainly don't expose your lover.'

It was a point echoed by John Rendall, social editor of *Hello!* magazine. 'People are very aware of the pressure to be discreet at a level so close to the Royal Family,' he said. 'When the families are important, there is a greater sense of responsibility and a greater tendency for a façade. As long as scandals like these are never discussed, the family can stick together – and usually do.' Unsurprisingly, this was not a viewpoint that washed with Sally Ann. Defending her decision to speak out, she said, 'I don't remember seeing Thou Shalt Not Kiss And Tell in the Ten Commandments. But I do remember seeing Thou Shalt Not Commit Adultery.'

Her ex-husband also went on the record to denounce Sally Ann's decision: 'I do not condone what she has done,' Dominic King told David Wigg, long-time showbusiness editor of the *Daily Express*. 'It's caused me a lot of discomfort by association but I can't say that I regret our five fascinating and unrepeatable years together. The marriage was stormy in bursts but no one sticks around something that is relentlessly miserable. The whole thing was an adventure which ran its course. But that adventure was never dull. I really loved her.'

He first fell for the woman he married on 26 July 1980 at a party given by the Dunhill tobacco family. 'The first time I saw her, she looked like an angel. She was 21, standing on a balcony at a party dressed all in white. She looked totally pure.' Looks, as he swiftly discovered, can be deceptive. 'She amazed me by coming up and asking me why I was so full of myself.' No shrinking violet himself, King replied, 'Too much success too young?' Sally Ann scoffed although, with 30 million records sold to his credit – including two hits he wrote for the Three Degrees, Prince Charles's favourite pop group of the seventies – Dominic was perhaps entitled, at 27, to feel that the world had so far treated him pretty well.

Although their marriage ultimately foundered, he remained chivalrous about his ex-wife even while disapproving of her actions. 'She's been depicted as a sort of crazy sex maniac,' he told David Wigg, 'which is a completely distorted view of an incredibly bright, witty, intelligent but wilful woman who has a talent to amuse.'

He remembered meeting Charles Spencer for the first time when he called at the couple's Knightsbridge house. 'We had a drink and a chat. He was polite but slightly on the shy side and spoke very quietly. I had no idea at that time this was the beginning of anything other than a professionally-based friendship. Sally Ann had lots of male friends with whom there was no romantic attachment. We weren't separated by then but we were starting to lead separate lives. I am convinced that nothing happened at that time.'

As the couple's divorce drew nearer, Dominic became aware that Sally Ann was seeing more and more of Charles. 'She never spoke about the substance of her relationship with the Viscount. She never talked about what they'd done or anything. She treated it almost as if she had a treasure in a box. She wasn't going to tell me about her relationship with him. She was very discreet. It was obviously something special to her. But I was pleased they got on. He read English at Oxford [though later switched to Modern History] and Sally Ann was reading all the time so they had plenty in common.'

Once, during a row about their impending divorce, Sally Ann rounded on Dominic. 'She said to me, "You don't think you're special, do you? There's Charlie Althorp, the man with everything. He's got good looks, he's clever, he's worth a fortune – and you're sounding just like him when he talks to me about how sad his family complications have been for him." At that moment, I realized she was at least a confidante and that their friendship seemed to have a special meaning.' Whatever the truth of how her relationship with Charles finally hit the rocks, it did not, in her ex-husband's estimation, exonerate Sally Ann for baring her soul to a Sunday newspaper. 'She went too far. If she had called me about Althorp, I would have said, "Don't do it." But she still would have done it. Sally Ann was her own woman and still is.'

Proof, if it were needed, that Sally Ann was unrepentant over her decision to kiss and tell, came in a self-penned piece – determinedly defiant – published in the *Mail on Sunday* three weeks to the day after her revelations first appeared in the *News of the World*. Having poured scorn on Charles (she referred to him throughout as Himself), she fell to pondering why anyone should have supposed she would have kept her mouth shut. 'Now, the tiresome thing about men,' she wrote, 'is that they don't have much sense of responsibility and the combination of a young male ego and a semi-royal ego is pretty lethal. The upshot is what someone less kind than myself might call astonishing arrogance.

'It is assumed by all men that The Other Woman will never reveal anything to anyone, thus preserving the status quo and allowing them To Get Away With It. It is particularly assumed by a semi-royal man because an association with the House of Windsor is meant to be like having Disney dust sprinkled on you from on high. Your co-operation in the conspiracy of silence is assured because who would want to forfeit the magic? Himself certainly always believed that he was beyond the concerns of the rest of us. In fact, he once referred to himself as "a living god". Mind you, with the kind of spiritual guidance he got from his local vicar, who can be surprised? This is what the Reverend Norman Knibbs – and yes, that really is his name – had to say on the subject of Himself's affair: "I'm not going to say Good Old Charlie, go and have some more. But these things happen to young people. And when you move in those kind of circles, the temptations are greater than for those further down the scale." So much for Christian theology.'

Sally Ann remained blasé to the end. 'I have acquired a racy past,' she wrote, 'without having to go to all the trouble of having to live one. And one day, when I am knitting my grandchildren things they do not want, I can get my scrapbook out and prove to them that one should always be a little preposterous. As Oscar Wilde said, "I am always astonishing myself. It is the only thing that makes life worth living." ' As a parting shot, she could not resist one final dig at her ex-husband, who claimed he had donated to charity the fee he received for talking to the *Daily Express*. 'The proceeds from this article,' concluded Sally Ann, 'are going to the Dominic King Appreciation Society.'

9

CHARLES TAKES CONTROL

Mrs Kathleen Hayes, of Nether Heyford, was puzzled. 'Have I been wrong all these years,' she wrote to the *Chronicle and Echo* in February 1981, 'in saying "Althorp"? The BBC newsreaders have been calling it "Althrup". I couldn't believe my ears. Surely they should be corrected – or should we?' The Northampton-based newspaper was only too happy to relieve Mrs Hayes' anguish. 'Members of the Spencer family,' it replied, 'have always called their ancestral home "Oltrop" not "Althorp". "Oltrop" is a derivation of the ancient name given in the Domesday Book where it is also referred to as Allethorp, Alidethorpe and Oldthorpe. The fifth Earl once said, "If my father had ever heard me refer to my home as Althorp instead of Oltrop, or to Daintree as Daventry, I think he would have kicked me out of the room."'

Throughout her marriage to Johnnie, Countess Spencer unerringly referred to her husband's ancestral home as Althorp. It was the least of Charles's problems. The death of his father on 29 March 1992, while being both sudden and sad, also instantly conferred an earldom on his young shoulders – he was still only 27 – and, with it, the never-ending headache that was the Big House. 'I see my title almost as a sort of job description,' he later told *Hello!* magazine. 'It means I am the owner here, the boss, so everyone on the estate does call me by my title. If I'm in London, I don't use it that much; in my television career, I'm just Charles Spencer. I think a title is relevant to the estate and to certain people in the country but probably to many others it's irrelevant.

'I suppose there have been restrictions in that I've always known I would inherit this house one day so my career options have been limited. In fact, television is one of the few things I could do because I can do it on a part-time basis. I couldn't if I was a lawyer or in another profession where you have to commit yourself one hundred per cent. I had to choose one that fitted in with my responsibilities but I've always been determined to have a career outside of my inheritance.' It was an inheritance, he admitted, that in some ways he had rather dreaded. 'When I was growing up, I was always quite frightened of taking over at Althorp because, as a little boy, it seemed very much an old man's house. It was my grandfather's and had the atmosphere of an old man about it. Now I've grown to love it. I know how much time and effort and love my family have put into this house over the generations. I feel enormous love for the house and for everything it stands for, and I really am prepared to devote my entire life to its upkeep and to making it a wonderful place for future generations of my family to grow up in and enjoy.'

None of which diminished the perpetual problems that came with the territory. 'From the outside,' said Charles, 'it must look like an incredible life and lifestyle. But, nowadays, living somewhere like this is an enormous effort really. I suppose I'd always thought that I'd come here in my late thirties, early forties. But my father's early death has obviously brought all that forward. If I have a regret, apart from the obvious one about my father dying, it would be that my wife and I didn't have more time in our house in the Park, a simple existence where we had fewer responsibilities and where we had more time for one another. Ideally, I would have liked to wait a few more years but, now it's here, it's a great challenge. It gives a purpose to your life looking after something like this. Yet, at the same time, I'm determined that my wife and I enjoy it. We have friends here and we have fun here, otherwise the whole thing can become a huge millstone around your neck. So I think we've got to keep trying as hard as possible to enjoy the house. One of the things we try and do is to use as many rooms as possible, otherwise the place just becomes a museum.'

Within three weeks of his father's death, the new Earl had reopened Althorp House to the public, hiking the entrance fee by nearly twenty per cent in the process, from £2.95 to £3.50. Everything was much as before minus, of course, any trace of the eighth Earl's second wife. While understanding, perhaps more acutely than ever, the need to find the money to pay the bills, Charles continued to be critical of Raine's solution to the problem. 'I think all owners of houses like this,' he said, 'face enormous pressures financially and, reluctantly, things are often sold. I think that in the past too much was sold in the wrong way because, if you're going to sell something that is part of a great collection, I think you are duty bound to get the best price for it so you don't have to sell something else. But the sales that were made were done in such a way that many dealers in Bond Street in London profited enormously at the expense of my family. It was all done on the quiet and I hope those dealers are ashamed of what they've done to a family collection like this.'

In another interview, with the magazine *Antique Collector*, he later came up with an altogether more highly coloured theory as to why some 200 artefacts had been put up for sale. 'I believe that my grandfather's compulsive devotion to the house [Jack Spencer was known as the Curator Earl] caused great resentment in my father,' said Charles. 'By selling off the art, my father may have derived pleasure in the knowledge that his father would be spinning in his grave. It was his revenge for not feeling loved as a child. Unlike my ancestors, my role as custodian of Althorp is a defensive one. My wife and I live a modest lifestyle with all resources earmarked for the perpetuation of the house. I would hate it if, 100 years from now, my great-grandson was sitting in a council flat cursing me. It is, therefore, very important for me that I leave Althorp in such a way that it is worth keeping and not a millstone around my successor's neck.'

He claimed, though, to feel no bitterness towards his father or stepmother. 'I think the real tragedy was that, in their futile attempts to avoid publicity, they were taken to the cleaners by art dealers. My family have always sold the wrong things. In 1937, my grandfather sold Holbein's superb portrait of Henry

VIII to Baron Thyssen for £10,000. Today, it is worth £55 million. My great-grand uncle was equally imprudent when he sold off three villages in the 1830s; they happened to be Clapham, Wandsworth and Wimbledon.'

When Charles inherited Althorp, he did so with a bill for death duties of £1.5 million although many of the surviving works of art were protected by a system of trusts and tax exemptions established by the seventh Earl. He soon discovered at first hand, though, the insatiable appetite of a major stately home: the annual maintenance bill currently eats up the better part of £500,000 a year. On top of that, Charles had his own vision of how the house should look. 'A lot of my aims,' he told the London *Evening Standard*, 'aren't really to go forward but to restore things to how they should be [in other words, before Raine set to work with her gilding brush]. This house hasn't had very young children living in it since my father and aunt grew up here in the twenties.'

All that was about to change. By June 1992, Charles had moved into a back part of the house while Victoria remained in London for the latter stages of her pregnancy. In July, the ninth Earl drove his wife home to the ancestral seat with two new additions to the family: Eliza Victoria (4lb 15oz) and Katya Amelia (5lb 4oz), born, like their older sister Kitty, in the Lindo Wing of St Mary's, Paddington, their sex known for some weeks before their birth. (Since the twins were born by Caesarean section, it was probably just as well they weren't male as it would have presented a ticklish problem to select which of the two was to become the tenth Earl Spencer.) Charles has always doted on his daughters but, he told *Hello!*, it would be wonderful to have a son. 'There aren't many men alive in my family at all. My father has one male first cousin who's now over 60 years old, unmarried and with no children. Then there's me. I don't know of any other male Spencers anywhere who are directly connected to the title. So, if I die and my cousin dies without an heir, then that's the end of the earldom.' But he remained philosophical. 'We have three daughters who are all wonderful. I suppose I have met the girl of my dreams. I've been extremely fortunate.'

The first half of 1993 culminated in Charles giving his maiden speech in the House of Lords but not before a couple of less edifying incidents, reported in loving detail in the tabloid press. Serena Scott Thomas, former-model-turned-actress sister of Kristin (star of *The English Patient* and *The Horse Whisperer*), was a member of Charles's inner circle courtesy of her long-term boyfriend, film student Andrew Conrad, godfather to the Spencer twins. For the film of Andrew Morton's book, *Diana: Her True Story*, a made-for-television mini-series shown on Sky in Britain, Serena was cast as the Princess. Charles, who had co-operated with Morton in the writing of the book and who went on the record subsequently to say that he stood by every word recorded in it, nonetheless blew a fuse. Serena was no longer welcome at Althorp, frozen out from that day to this. Then there was the ruckus over the Earl's tickets for the family box at the Royal Albert Hall turning up on the black market. It proved to be a storm in a teacup: Charles had been entirely unaware that the Pall Mall agency had bought the tickets from another agency for a particular client who then discovered he couldn't attend a performance by the Bolshoi Ballet. So Pall Mall had sent a 'messenger' to sell them outside the Albert Hall. 'If it's anyone's fault, it's ours,' said an agency spokesman subsequently. 'It certainly isn't Lord Spencer's.'

For his four-minute maiden speech, the ninth Earl chose as his theme the countryside, in general, and public access, in particular. After a brief introduction in which he recalled a speech in the same chamber by the newly ennobled second Earl Spencer in 1620, Charles continued:

My family's estate lies three miles from Northampton, at a place called Althorp. We are fortunate in having a block of coniferous woodland between us and the town. The town has grown from 130,000 inhabitants to, I believe, 180,000 in the past twenty years. People in the town of course want access to the countryside.

If one goes to that woodland on a Saturday or Sunday, one will see thousands of people exercising their children, their dogs or their more basic instincts in the woodland. Often, they will be using the public footpaths or bridle-ways. But we do not make them keep to the paths because we wish them to use the area as an amenity. As a family or as a farming unit, it does not affect us to have people using that piece of land. It does not invade our privacy; it does not affect our income. Therefore, they are welcome to use it.

Of course, with thousands of people using one piece of land, one has damage and vandalism. We have experienced everything from fences being pulled down and burned to animals being killed, devil worshipping, motor-bike racing and anything else that people might do in any area. However, we prefer to condense such activity in one easily reached area just outside a major town.

It works well for us to encourage people to go to one particular place. I am fortunate in having an area that I can almost hand over for public use and abuse in such a way. I appreciate that hill farmers and landowners with medium-sized or lesser-sized holdings may not have such an amenity to hand over.

However, I believe that there is a lesson to be learned from the example that I have given. If one allows and encourages people to use the bridleways and pathways to which they are entitled, one has them where one wants them and where they are legally entitled to be and not where one does not want them which is everywhere.

No one wants to be a park keeper, whether unpaid or receiving a few subsidies, but I think this arrangement is an effective compromise. I also think that, to make it more attractive to them so that their income and their privacy do not suffer, landowners should be encouraged, through grants, to make over more land in this way.

A final point I should like to make is that I believe that people who act in this responsible way are depriving the more politically zealous organizations – which sometimes seem to be more engrossed in pushing forwards their rights and powers than in doing anything for the delicate balance of the countryside – of their foot soldiers and adding respect for good stewards of the land.

These less than contentious views were overtaken, in July, by the Earl's revelation that he would be following Baroness Thatcher by voting for a referendum on the Maastricht Treaty; that is, giving the British electorate the opportunity to say whether or not they wished to become fully-fledged Europeans. 'People don't know what the Treaty is about,' he told listeners to Radio Northampton. 'I was not fully briefed before this vote [in the House of Lords] came up. It is only because I have seen both sides that I understand it is a dangerous thing. People do not understand that they will become citizens of the European state. The Queen will be a European citizen and will not be sovereign in the eyes of Europeans. The British people have not been given a chance to learn about the Treaty and its implications.'

Closer to home, the ninth Earl was doing his level best to dream up money-making schemes to pay for the upkeep of Althorp. He staged his first horse trials – dressage on Saturday, showjumping and cross-country on Sunday – with Virginia Leng and the then world champion, New Zealander Blyth Tait, among an Olympic-class field. There were performances of *Madam Butterfly*. There was a special concert by Spanish tenor José Carreras. The Bootleg Beatles sang a selection of songs made famous by the Fab Four. There was a country fair complete with Spanish stallions, and a display of scores of birds of prey. There were charity cricket matches with the likes of Allan Lamb and Rory Bremner turning out. Wheelchair users, it was announced, were welcome again at Althorp – the Dowager Countess, as Raine was now called, had not allowed wheelchairs inside the house on the grounds that they would damage the polished floors. The house was available for hire for meetings or corporate entertainment, a snip at £3,500 a day. Former hotelier (and long-time friend of Charles) David Horton-Fawkes was hired to run Althorp as a commercial enterprise.

British Telecom moved in for two weeks to entertain valued customers.

For all this ingenuity and industry, Earl Spencer was nonetheless forced to resort to the salerooms. Christie's sold an Axminster carpet on his behalf; 140 cases of port, brandy and wine – a sixth of Althorp's cellar and some of it dating from the Napoleonic Wars – went, too. 'I really don't see any shame,' he told Richard Kay, in August 1993, 'in selling things to pay tax. What I do see as indefensible is if I sold things to buy, say, an Aston Martin.' Two years later came the first rumblings of discontent from a band of homeowners when word got out that Charles might be about to do a deal with a property company for the construction of six houses on land he owned in the Bernard's Heath area of St Albans in Hertfordshire.

This was small beer compared to a scheme that emerged at the end of 1996. Earl Spencer, it was said, intended to sell off some 500 acres on the Althorp estate to developers planning to build 2,000 homes, a superstore, a school and a health centre. Local conservationists were horrified; as well as allowing building on farmland, Charles was thought to have agreed to the construction of a road through the edge of Harlestone Firs, one of the last tracts of recreational woodland on his estate. The woods are home to some of Northamptonshire's last breeding pairs of long-eared owl while the marshland contains its last six pairs of breeding snipe. Otters have been seen in the tributary which is also a haven for the Atlantic stream crayfish, an endangered species. Estate developers Saville's claimed that the proposed scheme in an area known as Dallington Heath would not unduly damage the woods.

At the beginning of 1997, there was yet more trouble over development plans, this time the conversion of three stone barns in the grounds of Yew Tree Farm on the estate into executive homes worth around half a million pounds between them. According to Edward Crookes, resident agent for Althorp, 'The objective of the proposed barn conversion is commercial and to preserve the barn buildings.' But Lynn Dyball, a parish councillor in Upper Harlestone, was unmoved. 'He was nice before he became Earl,' she told the *Daily Telegraph*, 'but all that has changed. He's become so selfish. He thinks he can do what he wants to make money for his estate.'

That ambition, if it is one that Charles Spencer acknowledges, looks set to be realized in spectacular fashion. The earlier plans to build a new town at Dallington Heath took a decisive step forward with the revelation in the *Sunday Times* in February 1998 that the Earl was about to sell 400 acres of Northamptonshire fields, woodland and heathland for that purpose. Trustees for Althorp were said already to have signed a legal agreement with a property consortium. Assuming planning permission is granted – and insiders believed it would not be opposed – the sale could net the estate as much as £50 million. A local resident whose home overlooks the proposed site was quoted as saying, 'This is a wonderful spot and it will be absolutely terrible if it's destroyed. Landowners like Earl Spencer have acquired the land through no efforts of their own and have a great responsibility. They should not just abdicate that when they decide they want a few more million in the bank.' The Earl was roundly defended by one of his advisers. 'This is not something that the Althorp estate has promoted,' he claimed. 'It has come through the town's expansion. The town has housing requirements and Earl Spencer is helping to meet those needs.'

Back in the early nineties, though, Charles had been more concerned about turning Althorp into a family home once more. His first complete year in residence had been a revelation, he said. 'I never thought this would ever be a happy family home because it never had been. I was talking the other day to one of my great aunts who lived here from 1906 to the 1930s and she said that, even in those days, it was very, very unhappy. In a way, my family have almost found it too much to cope with. It hasn't had happiness in it for ages, and no young children for seventy years. But it's not the house's fault, just the individuals'. Now, we've got dogs, babies, a happy staff [reduced, though, from fifteen in the eighth Earl's days to just five] and Victoria and I are coming to terms with living here. I feel the house has come to life again. It's a perfect place to bring up children and the staff treat them as the house mascots. Kitty roars around the galleries screaming to get echoes although I do worry that it might give her slightly grand ideas later in life. But it's important you give children a good start and I really can't think of a happier place for a child to grow up.'

Everything might well have been fine within his immediate family – indeed, Victoria was pregnant again with the couple's fourth child, due the following March – but a distressing row had broken out between Charles and his sister Diana. When it had become clear to the Princess that her marriage to the Prince of Wales had broken down irretrievably, she began to take stock of her life and consider how best she could manage her time with her beloved boys. 'She famously did not feel at home in the countryside,' says royal author Anthony Holden. 'She was a city rat. But William and Harry, she realized, were keen on country pursuits. She was smart enough to recognize that she'd have to go along with their interests because, unless she found some place in the country, they'd be with their father every weekend.'

So she turned to her brother to ask if she might have a house on the family estate to which she and her children could repair at weekends. Initially, Charles agreed, saying that the four-bedroom Garden House might be ideal and inviting Diana, and then her security team, to vet it. She was thrilled at what she felt was the beginning of a new chapter at a low point in her life. She had even got down to the detail of discussing colour swatches with South African designer Dudley Poplak, the man who had been responsible for the interior decor of her apartments in Kensington Palace. In June 1993, the royal protection group, on a second visit to Garden House, were joined by a high-ranking Metropolitan Police officer to assess the property's vulnerability. Their insistence that a team of gun-carrying officers should be free to roam his estate day and night at all times when Diana and her sons were in residence proved unacceptable to her brother.

At the end of the month, he told her of his misgivings and the project was aborted. Diana was shattered, just when she believed there would be a fresh start after so much unhappiness. Her brother's change of heart seemed like yet one more betrayal but, as he explained to the *Chronicle & Echo*, he reached his decision having reviewed the implications of his sister's presence on the estate. 'I did not want the quality of life of my wife and children to be affected by the intrusion of the tabloid press or any outside threat.' Brother and sister barely spoke to each other directly for many months after the Garden House incident.

A funeral Address is hardly the time to highlight it, but 'Diana had a pretty volatile relationship with her brother,' says Anthony Holden. 'She also had a volatile relationship with her mother although I met the two of them over lunch in 1995 and they were getting on terrifically well. It was very charming to see them together during that period of *rapprochement*. But when her mother sold a long interview to *Hello!* in the spring of 1997, that was pretty much the end of the road as far as Diana was concerned.' Despite this, in Diana's will, it was her mother who was named as chief executor and given the responsibility, along with Charles, of looking out for William and Harry on behalf of the Spencers.

Although Charles and Diana were friends again at the end, Holden doesn't believe the siblings were especially close. 'I talked to Diana on many occasions, the last time just the two of us for three hours over lunch at Kensington Palace, and we'd range over the people in her life: her ex-husband, the boys, the Queen, others in the immediate Royal Family, her sisters. But she very rarely talked about her brother in my presence. I would have expected there to have been a stronger relationship, too, between Diana and Victoria. They were sisters-in-law, both with a history of eating disorders. But I was never aware of a great bond there.'

Diana and Charles's nanny, Mary Clarke, also wonders whether the bond between sister and brother might not have been overplayed down the years. Certainly, as young children, it was clear which of the two of them was the dominant personality. 'When Diana was with people she knew, she was very confident, so much so that she would often overshadow her brother when I was looking after them. If the two of them were together, it was Diana you'd notice. She'd sparkle; she was very mischievous. Charles, being quieter and more serious-minded, was only too happy to take a back seat. He was also much less competitive than Diana – or Sarah, for that matter. He did well in team sports like rugby and cricket but he didn't care one way or the other about the diving competitions his sisters would organize. He just wanted to swim for the fun of it.

'He would never have admitted this but I know that Diana was Lord Althorp's favourite. He adored her; she was just so full of life. We'd arrive back from the station when she came home from boarding school, and Diana would be charging all over the place checking on all the animals and asking every imaginable question about everyone she knew. Charles, by contrast, would stay behind to help me with unloading the car. There was an unspoken understanding between the two of us: he and I were together all the time whereas I only had Diana for the holidays. That's why he never minded slightly fading into the background when she was around; I think he felt it was her right, her turn. Nor can I honestly say that there was an exaggerated bond between them. I do think, from what I was told, that she mothered him when their mother had finally left. But, by the time I arrived, the two of them had developed a pretty much normal sort of brother/sister relationship. Being older, Diana would tease Charles.'

The lingering *froideur* between the two siblings was temporarily eclipsed when, on Monday 14 March 1994, Victoria presented Charles with the longed-for son and heir, Louis Frederick John (6lb 10oz and born by Caesarean section at St Mary's, Paddington). The Countess had known for some time, she said, that she was carrying a boy, 'but I didn't tell a soul – not even my husband – as I did not want to take away from his joy on the day. We were hoping for a son,' she added, 'not just for the obvious reason, but because we wanted a more complete family.' The Earl confessed to *Hello!* to being rendered speechless when he realized he had a son. 'The nurses said they couldn't believe the transformation in me. One moment, I was being chatty and the next I was a completely dumbstruck father. I just sat there in the corner with my head in my hands, reeling from shock.' Victoria, he said, had been worryingly good at keeping the secret. 'The most interesting thing is that occasionally we used to feel uncomfortable living at home because, although it's a beautiful place and full of wonderful objects, sometimes it's strange living in a house which feels like it's public property. Now that I've got a son and heir, I've got an added drive to pass it on to him.'

The healing effect of a new baby even extended to a surprise choice for one of the infant Viscount Althorp's six godparents. Alongside Northamptonshire cricket captain, Allan Lamb, and playwright Teddy St Aubyn, Charles invited Peter Shand Kydd, his mother's second husband (now living apart from champagne expert Marie-Pierre Palmer, his third wife), to be little Louis's godfather. The christening, at which former Archbishop of Canterbury, Robert Runcie, officiated, took place at Althorp the day after a party to celebrate Charles's 30th birthday on 20 May. Their family complete, a tenth Earl Spencer-in-waiting safely born, Charles and Victoria were poised for a potentially golden future together.

The first small hint – for those with ears to hear – that all was not as it seemed came in a now-famous remark contained within Charles's speech at his 30th birthday party. In front of his 130 or so guests, the Earl shared a piece of advice passed on to him by his father. 'I once asked him,' he said, 'what I should look for in a potential wife. The ideal bride, in his opinion, was one who would stick with me through thick and thin. Well,' he announced, 'those who know Victoria know she's thick – and she's also thin.' This woefully unfunny bit of *badinage* had guests looking at their inturned toes rather than catching the eye of the waif-like Countess. Charles has subsequently said that this 'joke' was told with Victoria's prior knowledge and approval which, if true, only underscores the depths to which her self-esteem must have sunk.

That apart, the event was a roaring success. The guests, all dressed forties-style, as requested, danced until the small hours to the Piccadilly Dance Band, when they weren't being entertained by cabaret revue duo, Kit and the Widow. Ubiquitous partygoer, actor Christopher Biggins, was thrilled to be invited. He had originally met the Earl and Countess via a Northamptonshire antique dealer, and had then invited the couple to a meal in a London restaurant. 'I thought Victoria was charming,' he said, 'and Charles is obviously very bright. But he was quieter, more introverted than I had expected although a superb conversationalist. He was a terrific host at his party, though.' At one point he noticed Diana was sitting alone. 'In fact, when the band struck up, I saw her sitting rather forlornly at the foot of the main stairs. I don't think anyone quite knew what to do with her so I marched up and asked her to dance. She was so relieved – and, after that, never left the floor all evening.' And Charles and Victoria? 'They seemed to be having a wonderful time,' says Biggins. 'They looked as happy as anything.'

But all was far from well. Or, rather, Victoria was far from well. The eating disorder that had been triggered by a bug she picked up on a modelling assignment in Indonesia, the irregularity of life as an international model and the constant need never to put on weight had all combined to exacerbate her emotional fragility. In April 1995, Earl Spencer, in a short, exclusive interview with Independent Television News, confirmed rumours that had been gathering pace: his wife was an anorexic who was also battling alcoholism. They were to live apart for the foreseeable future. (It is a measure, incidentally, of the continued estrangement between Charles and Diana that the way the Princess first knew of her brother's split from Victoria was, like almost everyone else, via the media.)

Victoria had agreed to become a resident at Farm Place, a

133

clinic in Ockley, Surrey, that was said to charge patients £187 a night. 'My wife would be happy for me to tell you,' the Earl told ITN, 'that she has had a problem with addictions and eating disorders for ten years now, and this has been the first chance I have had to persuade her to have proper, sustained treatment for serious psychological problems. My main concern is to keep her there because obviously she can get the best professional care.'

So was this a blip, however serious, in a marriage that could be retrieved when Victoria had regained her composure and self-confidence? Earl Spencer wasn't ruling that out. 'Nothing is final,' he told the *Daily Mail*'s Richard Kay. 'We will see how things pan out. I wish to stress that I am fully supportive of my wife during this time. She is coping but we know it is going to be a long process.' Friends of Charles, who preferred not to be identified, said he had been close to breaking point when he proposed the separation to his wife. 'He was despairing,' according to one. 'Her anorexia was worsening but she was not prepared to confront it as an illness. He was left with no alternative but to tell her that he wanted a separation. This desperate act worked in that Victoria did finally agree that she needed help. What happens next is anyone's guess.'

In August, a smiling Victoria checked herself out of the clinic and returned to the Althorp estate. Charles told the *Sun* that he had no plans to divorce before adding, 'This is not to say a separation may not become permanent but both parties hope this will not be the case.' Both parties were to be disappointed. By the beginning of January 1996, Earl Spencer, sadly but with some finality, admitted to Richard Kay that the couple would not be getting back together again. 'We are the greatest of friends,' he told him, 'and we will always remain so.' The entire family were based many miles from Althorp by this stage. 'Going away from your home environment does give you a chance to look at things,' he said, 'to get some perspective. But it's not a cure. It's a way of just getting things in proportion. Your problems go with you.'

Indeed they do. Inexplicably, what the ninth Earl Spencer had failed to mention to his estranged wife was his developing friendship with a woman called Chantal Collopy.

10

THE MOVE TO SOUTH AFRICA

Immediately after Christmas 1995, Charles Spencer, his estranged wife and their four children upped sticks and moved 6,000 miles away to Cape Town on South Africa's Atlantic coast. The Countess and the children set up home in a rented house said to cost £150 a day while Charles settled a short drive away on the slopes of Table Mountain in the property of a German tycoon who charged him a reported £10,000 a month. 'We want to start afresh,' Victoria told one reporter. 'We want to find some peace and tranquillity. I am 30 now and I want to be able to look after my children and not be bothered. I don't know why people are interested in me. My husband may be connected to the Royal Family but I am not. We have come to South Africa to escape the ghastly time we had in Britain.'

That tranquillity would be sorely needed. A recovering alcoholic who had yet to conquer her battle with anorexia, Victoria Spencer was still painfully thin, her psychological condition as fragile as her physical state. A break away from the prying lenses of the British paparazzi in a country where the press had a reputation for respecting people's privacy could only assist in her slow recovery; and a spot of winter sun would do none of them any harm, either. It had been suggested, too, that a new start might bring about a reconciliation in the couple's troubled seven-year marriage but Charles was under no such illusions. 'We're not planning on getting back together again,' he told a London television reporter just prior to the family's departure, adding, 'but, at the same time, I am fully supportive of my wife's attempts to get mentally and physically strong again.'

Clearly, there had been many factors to take into account before embarking on the family's move south. The *Daily Mail*'s Peter Younghusband, reporting from the Cape, interviewed two women who had worked as maids, one for Earl Spencer, the other for a friend of one Chantal Collopy. Barbara Mafeleka revealed that Mrs Collopy had been a regular visitor to Charles's rented cottage in Hout Bay the previous summer. 'She and the master would hold hands and kiss,' she said. 'Sometimes, they would go into the bedroom and shut the door and stay there for hours. At other times, they would sit in the garden in the sun, drinking and holding hands and kissing. I could see they were in love. One morning, I came into the house suddenly and they were embracing on the couch. They jumped apart.' When Charles had to return to England, Chantal 'cried a lot and was very miserable', according to Barbara Mafeleka. 'I heard him tell her not to cry because he would come back.'

Then there was the occasion when Earl Spencer and Mrs Collopy were invited to dinner at the house of her friend, Chevonne Morris, near to where Charles was staying. Mrs Morris's maid, Maria Hamza, was told only that a very important person would be accompanying Chantal and that Barbara had been drafted in to help prepare the meal. Both women were warned they should say nothing about this special visitor to anyone. 'From then on,' recalls Maria, 'Barbara and I always referred to him as Mr Top Secret. One day, after Mr Top Secret came back from England, Chantal rushed into madam's house and picked up the telephone. There was a long whispered conversation. I heard her call Mr Top Secret by his first name. They always carried on as though Barbara and I weren't there.'

By April 1996, Charles had obviously decided that the move to South Africa had been a success. He duly invested £800,000 in Tarrystone House, a luxury property in Southern Cross Drive, Constantia – *the* fashionable district of Cape Town, home to Lady Thatcher's son, Mark, and his wife, Diane; zoo owner John

Aspinall also owns a house in the area. Among the rich and famous said at the time to be considering investing in property there, the most frequently mentioned were Cher, Madonna, Sir Tim Rice, Julio Iglesias and Luciano Pavarotti. Lady Spencer, meanwhile, was now just three minutes away in a five-bedroom bungalow on the Silverhurst Estate. Both residences were set in generous, landscaped grounds affording the family much-needed privacy. Indeed, the couple let it be known among their acquaintances that anyone who talked to the press would immediately be ostracized from their charmed circle.

That circle seems to have been almost determinedly non-expatriate. 'I tend not to mix with many English people in Cape Town,' Charles revealed during a local radio station interview. 'I just don't happen to; I have enough friends who are South African. On the other hand, a lot of my English friends come out here to see me. As someone said to me, "You never know how popular you are until you have a house in Cape Town and especially in December and January." Everyone falls in love with it; of course they do. It's one of the most beautiful places in the world and it's a wonderful place to bring up children.' His lack of interest in society life in the snobbish city was confirmed by local public relations executive, Anne Wallis Brown. 'Earl Spencer does not have parties,' she declared loftily to the *Independent on Sunday*, 'and he does not accept invitations to other people's.'

He may not like the *arrivistes* but Charles is keen, it seems, on the indigenous South Africans. 'What I like about them,' he says, 'and I don't want to sound at all patronizing, is their refreshing decency. A lot of it has to do with their relative isolation. Whereas the rest of the world has been totally Americanized, South Africa has managed to hold on to its identity. The average South African respects the proper things in life like privacy, things that I think are morally right. They're fundamentally decent people. And what I *really* like about them is that they set great store by their children. It's very difficult to go into a shop in Cape Town with my children without their being smiled at and talked to and treated like human beings. There are some lovely people in England – of course there are – but, on the whole, people look at children as if they were a time-bomb about to explode at any moment. There's a different attitude in South Africa and it's much healthier, in my opinion.'

Not quite every South African meets with his approval, though. Fanie Jason is that country's most notorious paparazzo – indeed, probably its only serious paparazzo – and the bane of Charles and Victoria's life. A tough-talking Cape Coloured father of two, Jason grew up in Guguletu (a black township just outside Cape Town), one of six children of a blind, unemployed father and a mother who worked as a maid. He scraped by as a freelance photographer acquiring cameras so cheap they had to be stolen. In the eighties, he was to be found at many of the world's trouble-spots – anti-apartheid protests, the genocide in Rwanda, the unrest in Hebron and so on. He was once jailed alongside Archbishop Desmond Tutu. In 1996, while covering a march against the rising tide of crime, he was hit by thirty-eight pieces of birdshot. In 1994, when the former black homeland of Bophutatswana erupted in violence, he travelled twenty hours by minibus to get there because he couldn't afford a plane ticket.

He made it his business to be in the right place at the right time but the pickings, financially speaking, were pretty meagre. When he once photographed Tutu opening his swimming pool to poor children, his local paper bought the shot for just £2. But all that was to change: a number of players on the international stage started settling – or at least taking holidays – in Cape Town and Jason got wise to the possibility of at last earning some decent money. As a result of his efforts over the last couple of years, British tabloids, in particular, have paid him as much as £6,000, he says, in a single month. 'That's abracadabra where I come from,' he told the *New York Times*. 'I have a Toyota now and a computer.'

Quite the biggest fish in Jason's still relatively small pond has proved to be, of course, the ninth Earl Spencer. Nor was South Africa's emergent star paparazzo slow to cotton on to Charles's saleability. When Spencer called in the builders to make certain alterations to his new Constantia home, Jason donned overalls, hid his camera in his toolbox and mingled with the workforce (not something he could have done, as he was later to point out tartly, had he been white). He was stacking some bricks one day when Charles walked by. 'I said, "Hi, baas," [boss] and he nodded and I took a couple of snaps a few seconds later.' But perhaps his biggest scoop to date was the exclusive set of shots he snapped of Charles's mistress, Chantal Collopy. A maid Jason knew tipped him off that her employer ran a bed and breakfast establishment where Charles was due to meet Chantal. He paid his contact to supply the registration numbers of their cars and duly bagged his quarry. Jason's reward was a fat cheque from London's *Daily Mail* (but only once Don Collopy had gone public with the story of his wife's infidelity) and an interdict (the term used for an injunction in South Africa) forbidding him to harass the Earl or any members of his immediate family.

The court file detailed extreme intrusions into the Spencers' life. Victoria stated in an affidavit in September 1996 that, 'Jason's following me became so repetitive that, during some periods, every time that I went out, he would be waiting for me. It has felt as though I have been stalked by someone obsessed, and contrary to what was anticipated by our moving to Cape Town. On one occasion at the shopping mall, he confronted me and said words to the effect that he had seen me the previous Saturday at my home and that I had been sitting by the swimming pool having tea with a friend. This was all said in a threatening manner, the clear implication to me being that he possessed photographs of me and that I ought to co-operate or he would disclose the same. On other occasions, he expressly stated that he had pictures of me swimming alone.'

In October 1996, Jason was given a two-month suspended jail sentence after he flouted the court order when he took a shot of Earl Spencer at a house auction. And yet, he remains, he says, unrepentant. Local South African journalist, Angela Berry, purporting to be a reporter from the *Guardian* (a ruse which Jason soon tumbled), asked him whether he worked alone or whether he had a loose bank of informants providing informa-

140

tion about the movements of the Spencers. 'I have a network of people who work for me,' he replied. 'Also, two of the Spencers' friends tell me what is going on.' Are they paid? wondered Berry. 'I pay the blacks,' said Jason, 'not the whites.'

And no, he says, he sees no reason to back-pedal in his relentless pursuit of the beleaguered family. On the contrary, he accuses Spencer of 'taking the oxygen from my mouth' (via the interdict). 'He wants me to close down,' he told the London *Evening Standard*. 'But I will not give up. I'll just get a longer lens. If he gets a banning order issued against me, I'll become the first person to be jailed for taking pictures in the New South Africa.' In which case, he might do well to contemplate the fate of the *Guardian*, obliged in the summer of 1997 to pay substantial damages to Spencer for a report wrongly implying that he had acted spitefully or oppressively in having the interdict issued against Fanie Jason in the first place. The newspaper accepted that the proceedings had been brought against the photographer solely to protect the welfare of the Earl and his family, and apologized to him unreservedly for the embarrassment and distress which the March 1997 report had caused.

If there's a problem, Charles Spencer meets it head on. There cannot be a husband and father who would not cheer him to the echo for reacting as he did in the teeth of persistent harassment from an unwelcome photographer working to his own self-justified agenda. Perhaps it is this same fearlessness that led to his decision, less than a year after moving his family to the Cape, to accept a commission from *Harpers & Queen* magazine to write a no-holds-barred article on the appalling level of murder, rape and car-jacking currently afflicting South Africa in general, and Johannesburg in particular.

'Pagad started its public protest in Cape Town in August 1996,' Charles wrote. 'It stands for "People Against Gangsterism And Crime". Driving the movement and its offshoot organizations is a strong element of Islamic fundamentalism. When Pagad first appeared, it provoked a swell of support and not only in the Cape Coloured regions where it took root. People in Cape Town had been shocked to see gangsters, openly parading in a street demonstration to protest that their rights as outlaws were being eroded. The consensus was that this was absurd: that, if confirmation were needed that South Africa was in the grip of the criminal classes, here it was.'

And his conclusion was no less hard-hitting. 'Yes, South Africa is beautiful,' he said. 'Yes, the people are hospitable and caring, uncynical and refreshing. But the problem of crime could undo all that and make this yet another African country embroiled in insuperable social problems. Those who have left already, and there are many, clearly see this process as inevitable. The final word should go to Ernie Saks, one-time mayor of Sandton, who wrote the following in the *Sandton Chronicle*: "Take your loved ones, wrap them in your arms and go. The barbarians are not at the gate. They are in our midst." Mr Saks should know. He has been robbed, his son mugged, his sister-in-law carjacked and his son-in-law shot.'

Stirring stuff but it begs a couple of obvious questions: If life is so ghastly in South Africa, why move there, and, what's more, with your whole family in tow? And, who on earth does this parvenu think he is? 'What does he know about the dangers everyone else faces when he lives in such splendid isolation?' spluttered one local gossip columnist. 'He's only just come here and yet he's already spouting off about things he knows very little about. He should keep his mouth shut.' According to one Cape Town resident, 'Earl Spencer was guilty in that article of disinformation and sensationalism – just what he accuses everyone else of.' It was an observation Charles had the good grace to acknowledge.

'That piece didn't go down too well,' he later admitted, 'but it was all true. It was quite well received in England. People were very upset in South Africa, though, and I appreciate that they probably thought, "What's this foreigner doing coming here and saying these things?" To be honest, I was being absolutely straight and we can't really deny that there's a problem. There was resentment because I was the one who had written it and because I was picking on something that wasn't very attractive about South Africa. But I'd been commissioned to do it and the commissioning editor's uncle had just been murdered in Johannesburg. I told the truth. I'd been a news reporter in that city in the eighties while also making wildlife documentaries in Swaziland.

'In fact, that's what I'd like to do again in southern Africa. But, for the moment, I've put everything on hold. Right now, my life is at a crossroads. I'm just considering my options. I run my family's estate in England from Cape Town. There are many varied demands to the job from plain agricultural to what was corporate entertainment although I've put a stop on that because it seems inappropriate to have entertainment in the house and grounds for the time being while it is also a place of mourning. I've been back to England to set up arrangements for the house to be open for two months each summer so that people can come and pay their respects.'

On the other hand, his life is moving ahead, however cautiously, in his adopted country. 'I had been approached by a number of charities since moving to South Africa,' he said, 'but I wanted to establish my family as new Capetonians before I took on anything. I had quite a few offers following my sister's death, one of which was from Stephanie Schutte. She said she liked the content of my tribute at my sister's funeral and that she thought it represented many of the values Lifeline and ChildLine stood for. Would I consider becoming patron?' Clearly, her letter engaged Charles's interest. 'I decided to take a closer look and visited two projects run by the charity. The work I saw fitted in with what I believe in. It's a wide-ranging organization that helps an enormous amount of different interests and communities and I felt this was something I could commit myself to. I've never taken on a charity just to be a name at the top of a piece of writing paper; I've always enjoyed rolling up my sleeves and getting stuck in.'

He doesn't think, however, that he was drawn to this particular charity as a result of Diana's death. 'My sister's death was so recent,' he told Cape Talk listeners in the first week of November

1997, 'that I'm not able to analyse what effect it's had on me yet. To be honest, I'd have treated the offer to become patron of Lifeline/ChildLine in just the same way if it had come three months ago,' in other words, before Diana's death. These were early days but did Charles feel that time would prove to be a great healer? 'Time heals probably to a certain extent,' he acknowledged, 'but, equally, there are certain things that will always scar; and I don't think you can get rid of scars. But I spent nine years as a television journalist and I think that's been a help. It taught me to go into different situations and to analyse what the problem was and to put it across in a succinct way and deal with it. I think that's something I can do as patron: a fresh pair of eyes, a different perspective. I'm not going to intervene in the running of the western Cape branch of the charity; that's not my job. But if I can help suggest things or bring in sponsorship or donations, then that's good.

'Stephanie said originally that she'd be happy if I came to their big annual fundraising ballet and one other event in a year. But that's not really what I'm about. I wouldn't feel that that was a satisfactory role for me or that I'd be doing any good for the charity if I confined myself to the glamorous events. I'd far prefer to get my hands dirty. It's also worth saying, however obvious it may sound, that the reason I wanted to get involved was because of the thought that I can contribute to alleviating a little of these children's suffering. If I'm in a position where I can help, then it's my duty, and my pleasure, to do so.'

In less altruistic vein, Charles is keen, apparently, to reactivate his television career. To this end, he has been in discussion with producer Bonnie Rodini – the more downmarket newspapers additionally speculating at some sort of romantic attachment – with a view to making a series of wildlife documentaries. Meanwhile, he is said to be consolidating his friendship (on a non-physical basis) with former Calvin Klein muse, model Josie Borain, who has a small son, Peter, from her liaison with South African motor racer, Grant Maben. And then there is the pressure imposed by where he and his ex-wife wish their children to be educated. For the moment, the girls are all enrolled at schools in Cape Town with Louis due to join them when he is old enough. But with his name down for Eton (like his father and grandfather before him) and with the entrance exam probably more appropriately catered for by a British schooling, it seems likely that the family will return in time to Althorp while almost certainly maintaining a base in Cape Town. In March 1998, some two years after he first bought it, Charles put his South African home on the market (at an asking price of £1 million) and began looking over smaller properties in the scenic Camps Bay area of the city.

There is also the Earl's role as standard-bearer, on his sister's behalf, of William and Harry's welfare – not one that Charles imagines is his alone but one, nonetheless, that he has told the world he takes very seriously indeed. Royal biographer Anthony Holden recalls a telling moment during the highly successful tour Prince Charles made of South Africa with his younger son a couple of months after Diana's death. An excited Harry was due to attend a concert by the Spice Girls, an informal break from his father's round of official duties. The preceding evening, Holden turned to the rest of the British press pack and asked them to speculate on what the teenager would be wearing at the concert the following day. 'In the event,' says Holden, 'there were few sights more poignant during the tour than that first glimpse of Prince Harry, kitted out in formal suit and tie, to watch the Spice Girls perform. If his mother had been alive, Harry would have been dressed in T-shirt and jeans. I thought to myself at the time, "Charles Spencer, you've lost the battle already." '

On the other hand, Holden freely acknowledges the legacy the Princess has bequeathed to the House of Windsor. 'Look at the walkabout a couple of days before her funeral,' he says. 'We saw not only the Queen and Prince Philip but Prince Charles with both his sons. I believed – and said as much at the time – that what we were witnessing was the House of Spencer taking over from the House of Windsor.' Nor did it end there. 'Since the funeral, the Queen has allowed not only camera but sound crews to accompany her on tours of hostels for the homeless. To some extent, Diana's death, and the extraordinary public reaction to it, continues to exert an influence on the Royal Family months after the event. You could say that the House of Windsor is continuing to be Spencerized to this day.'

11

THE PRESS

If anyone had been in any doubt as to Charles Spencer's views on the press, the statement he read at the gates of his Cape Town home just five hours after the death of his sister would have dispelled them once and for all. 'This is not a time for recriminations,' he told reporters, 'but for sadness. However, I would say that I always believed the press would kill her in the end. But not even I could imagine that they would take such a direct hand in her death as seems to be the case. It would appear that every proprietor and editor of every publication who has paid for intrusive and exploitative photographs of her, encouraging greedy and ruthless individuals to risk everything in pursuit of Diana's image, has blood on their hands today.'

He returned to the same theme in his funeral Address six days later when he spoke of Diana's 'genuine goodness [as] threatening to those at the opposite end of the moral spectrum'. His remarks found favour with Ben Pimlott, the Queen's biographer. 'Earl Spencer's attack on the media,' he said, 'was biting, tight and effective. Whether the newspapers will take any notice is another matter: they seem beyond shame.' Certainly, you'd go a long way before you found someone who argued that all newspaper practices are, and always have been, entirely beyond reproach. And although we now know that the sobriety, or otherwise, of Henri Paul (the French driver at the wheel of the Mercedes) was a significant factor in the fatal crash, the pursuing paparazzi played their part, too.

But Charles Spencer's dislike of the media borders on the pathological. The long-lens photographs taken of his then wife as she walked in the grounds of a rehabilitation clinic are indeed indefensible. News International proprietor, Rupert Murdoch, publicly rebuked Piers Morgan, editor of the *News of the World*, the offending newspaper. 'If ever proof was needed,' Charles was reported as saying at the time, 'that sections of the tabloid newspaper business in this country are riddled with hypocrisy and evil, then it was provided [by this story]. How the sad tale of a mother of four receiving treatment for psychological problems can be treated as news fit for public consumption must be beyond all reasonable people.'

A subsequent statement, issued on behalf of both Earl Spencer and his wife, urged the government to introduce a privacy law. 'It is clearly unacceptable,' it read, 'that powerful businesses, which is what the newspapers are, should have the opportunity to infringe on the most sensitive parts of people's private lives, especially where there can be no justification of "the public interest" in order to increase their profits.' In the wake of Diana's death, this stance attracted overwhelming public backing: in the four days following her funeral, Charles was said to have received 27,000 letters of support. On 12 September 1997, he spent a hastily convened half hour with the Chancellor of the Exchequer, Gordon Brown, to discuss plans for a lasting memorial to his sister and to press his case for tighter privacy laws, emerging from the meeting to tell reporters that 'the final ten minutes of our conversation were devoted to privacy and to possible legislation to protect it. I do appreciate the position any politician is in,' he added, 'because they all need, to some extent, to pander to tabloid proprietors. However, I am confident that such considerations need not preclude sensible measures being imposed.'

It is, moreover, hard to imagine being in a position where you would be forced to go to the High Court, as Charles was obliged to do in Cape Town in March 1997, to obtain an injunction to stop an over-zealous paparazzo from snapping your children on their way to school. And Charles, perhaps more than most, will recall what proved to be his sister's final interview with the French newspaper, *Le Monde*. 'The media is ferocious,' Diana was quoted as saying. 'It doesn't forgive anything. They only point out my mistakes. Each intention is misinterpreted, each gesture is criticized. I think that abroad it is different. I am welcome there. They take me as I am without looking for mistakes. In Great Britain, it is the opposite. I think anybody but me would have gone a long time ago. But I can't. I have my sons.'

And yet, and yet . . . Charles, like his sister, actually has a highly ambivalent relationship with the media. Diana despaired at being chased up hill and down dale by an ever-present throng of freelance photographers and who could blame her? On the other hand, she was happy enough to use reporters like the *Daily Mail*'s Richard Kay as a conduit for stories she wished to leak to the public. We now know she co-operated fully with Andrew Morton when he wrote his first book about her. It was to the BBC and its 'Panorama' programme that she turned when she wanted to hit back at her husband. And she positively glowed in front of the cameras if they were taking pictures of her that would end up on the covers of glossy magazines the world over.

Similarly, Charles, quite apart from having spent the bulk of his career working within the media, has been far from averse to using it to promote his point of view. Witness how he reached for the telephone and dialled Nigel Dempster's number when he wanted to pre-empt the outpourings of his ex-lover, Sally Ann Lasson. And he did not come away empty-handed from his various dealings with *Hello!* magazine. In the late eighties and early nineties, he would have lunch with Nigel Dempster or his deputy, Adam Helliker, perhaps two or three times a year, and very often at the Waldorf Hotel in Aldwych. These meetings were not designed specifically for Charles to place stories in the *Daily Mail*; but they did, quite frequently and with his prior permission, result in diary items appearing in the paper. In 1993, however, Dempster and Spencer were to suffer a terminal falling-out when the doyen of Fleet Street's gossip columnists co-authored a book, *Behind Palace Doors*, in which, among much else, Dempster repeated a remark Charles felt he had made clear was a confidential one – to the effect that Diana, thus far, had not been especially enamoured of the sexual act. To this day, the two men do not speak.

When his sister's marriage finally broke down in March 1994, Charles Spencer chose 'Inside Edition', a less than lofty American television chat and gossip show, to lay the blame for the split squarely at the door of the tabloids. 'I personally believe the British press,' he said, 'is the biggest cancer in society. The tabloid press has a case to answer for the breakdown of my sister's marriage. They are constantly looking at every photo that shows some expression of disapproval.' For some reason, he omitted to mention the existence of Camilla Parker Bowles, Prince Charles's mistress before and during the royal marriage.

Whether or not the press is held responsible by Earl Spencer for the failure of his own marriage is not a matter of public record. His total contempt for them, however, continues unabated. When he realized that tabloid editors had been sent invitations to attend his sister's funeral, he is reported to have hit the roof. A statement issued two days before the service read: 'Lord Spencer has personally asked the tabloid editors not to come because he and his sisters, particularly Diana, would not have wished them to be there. They have kindly agreed to the request although broadsheet and regional papers are welcome.'

Mention of his sisters in that statement prompts the observation that, if Charles Spencer so despises the press, why does he not do as Lady Sarah and Lady Jane and keep his head down? The answer, it seems, is that he would find it impossible. 'If it means people committing suicide or being killed or falling apart or having nervous breakdowns, that's immaterial to [the British tabloids] and I class that as evil. If you grew up in Britain,' he told listeners to Cape Talk Radio in South Africa at the beginning of November, 'you are likely to grow up with a healthy contempt for the media because they are so despicable. The South African media should be more selective about using stories that were in the British press; it's absurd to believe they are true.'

Since this is a theme to which he repeatedly returns with such unabashed ferocity, you would think he might have spotted the correlation between his public utterances, his private behaviour and the enthusiasm with which both are picked over and pursued in the popular prints. He may shrug his shoulders and say he couldn't care less what the hated hounds of the press say about him (in which case, why does he bellyache about them so incessantly?) but there's no escaping the double standards some commentators divine in what Charles says and does. Henry Porter, for instance, writing in the *Daily Mail*, took an altogether sceptical line about the Earl's call for tighter privacy legislation. 'What is becoming increasingly plain,' wrote Porter, 'is that the most vocal advocates of a privacy law are also those who have most to hide ... Indeed, it ill-behoves such people to call for legislation in such strident terms when they have so much to gain personally from a media that is gagged by politicians and judges.'

Sir Nicholas Lloyd edited the *Daily Express* from the mid-eighties to the mid-nineties, a decade when the presence of Princess Diana on the world stage did no harm whatever to newspaper sales. In considering Earl Spencer's attitude towards the press he goes right back to the first time he met Diana at the British Embassy in Washington in 1984. She and Prince Charles were on an overwhelmingly successful tour of North America and Lloyd was then working for Rupert Murdoch in New York. 'To be honest, I wasn't bewitched by her from the word go,' he recalls. 'I found her a bit gauche, a bit awkward and not very bright.'

But, at that very first meeting, there was a brief illustration of the woman she was to become and, to some extent, the person she must always have been. 'Almost the first thing she said to me was: "What's on the front pages of the London papers this morning?" I replied that I wasn't totally sure but that I suspected it would be Joan Collins who had married her fourth husband, Peter Holm, the previous day. To which Diana replied: "Not jocked off by Joan Collins!" I admit I was a bit thrown by this reaction from an allegedly coy and shy princess.' Clearly, says Lloyd, Diana was already conscious of her cover-girl star quality, an early awareness that matured down the years. 'In time, she gradually became much more accomplished, much more tuned in to how to make the media machine work for her. She became cuter altogether.

'She read everything about herself. She could quote quite long tracts of newspaper stories back to you. I found that surprising and a little unhealthy. You would think, by the nineties, she'd have transcended the need to devour every small mention of herself.' The explanation for what looked to the objective onlooker like something of an obsession may have been prompted, says Lloyd, by her attitude to the Palace old guard. 'I think she felt – and she may well have been right – that They were out to get her, whoever They might be. She felt she was being denigrated behind her back. She had a kind of conspiracy theory about it all.'

Occasionally, Sir Nicholas would be invited, along with other Fleet Street editors, to have an off-the-record briefing session with Diana about ways in which their newspapers could co-operate better with her and respect her privacy more. 'There wasn't too much I could do for her other than tempering bits of the coverage. But then I think she knew I was a Prince Charles man in that I felt – as I still do – that, if you're going to have a monarchy, you have to support the institution itself; and that, in one way or another, she was trying to undermine it. I think she'd fallen out of love so completely by then, not only with her prince, but with the system, that she was trying to bring them all down.

'She was very aware of her power in a way that I wasn't. I was the classic cynical newspaperman, forever questioning the depth of her relationship with the great British public. But Diana had no doubts. She felt she had the people on her side – and that William would have, too. She was convinced she could take on the rest of them and win. Her death showed that she was right and that I was wrong. She was far, far more important to the public, far, far more in tune with them than perhaps we gave her credit for.

'By 1993, Diana felt that her marriage to Prince Charles had irretrievably broken down and that she had to look after "my boys", as she always referred to them. She felt the Royal Family

Charles Spencer heading for marriage - with his best man, Darius Guppy, 16 September 1989.

A truly traditional wedding, September 1989.

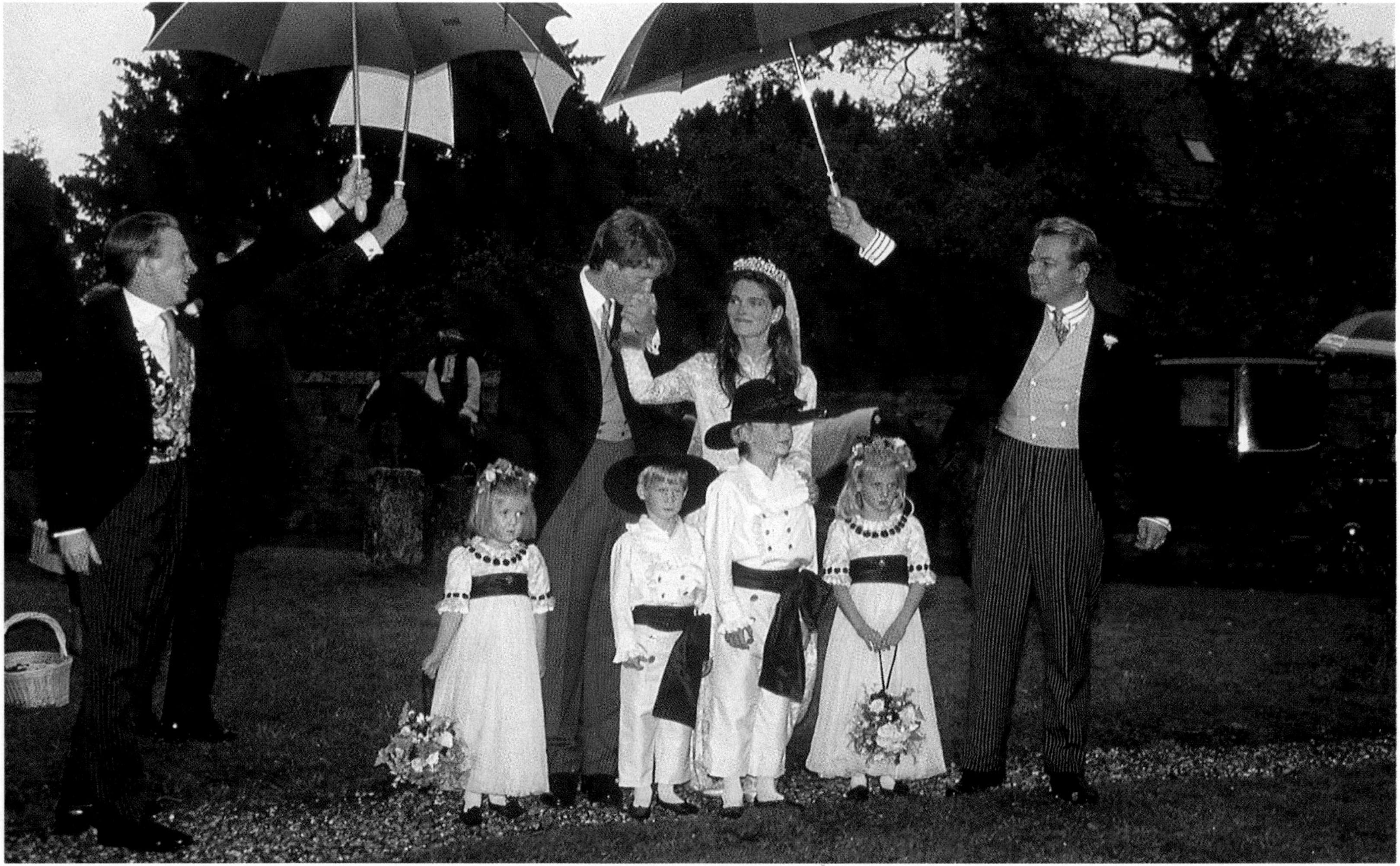

The growing family; Charles and Victoria pose with Kitty, Lizzy and Katya at Althrop, 1993.

© ALPHA

A proud day – with their newborn son and heir, March 1994. © DAVE CHANCELLOR/ALPHA

A relaxed family day in the
country, 1994.

A day out in town with Mum
and Dad, Grandma and Aunt
Diana, 1994.

Outside Charles' Cape Town home, where the world's press were waiting for his reaction to the tragedy that shook the world, 31 August 1997. © PA NEWS

Once more, Earl Spencer speaks to the grieving millions – at the funeral of his sister, Diana. © PA NEWS

6 September 1997, the day the nation stood still.
© REX FEATURES

Earl Spencer and Prince William walk amongst the floral tributes to Diana, the Queen of Hearts.
© ALPHA

The faces of the future; the parent and the protector meet in Cape Town, alongside Nelson Mandela, November 1997.

© TOPHAM PICTURE POINT

had been brought up in a certain way that made it difficult for them to convey normal human emotions and she was determined to redress that balance. Hence, the trips to McDonald's, to theme parks and so on. She wanted to ensure they didn't lose sight entirely of the real world. This was a real mission of hers. She wanted to make William better able to do the job of being King than she felt Charles ever could. And it was this selfsame mission that her brother felt compelled to tell the world at Diana's funeral that he would undertake in her name.'

Lloyd is no fan of Charles Spencer's. The two first crossed swords when Charles took exception to the reporting of his friend Darius Guppy's involvement in an insurance swindle that resulted in the latter's being sent to prison. 'I'd pick up the telephone in the office and Charles would be on the other end of the line ranting away. As on all similar occasions (such is the lot of a tabloid editor, it seems), I'd start by being almost excessively polite, assuring him, absolutely genuinely, that I'd look into his grievance. But that was never enough. He'd never let up on his attack. "Don't you know who I am?" he'd bellow. Naturally, that would get anybody's back up. I found him quite difficult to deal with, a very, very self-assured young man with an enormous belief in his own position and worth . . . He was still in his early twenties at that stage and I found it slightly puzzling, I must say, as to why he should be taken quite as seriously as clearly he felt he should. I said to him at one point, "Hang on, aren't you now in the media yourself? You've become a journalist. You understand the rules and regulations. Of course we try to get everything right but we probably only ever see 180 degrees not 360 degrees. We do our best, though." At which point, he got very aggressive indeed and told me not to be so preposterous.'

If Charles Spencer was, at best, brusque in his dealings with Lloyd, Guppy took matters a stage or two further. 'He'd write to me from prison threatening me with physical violence on his release; long diatribes about how he was the innocent party and we were the most trashy of all the tabloids and that if he could do me personal injury, he personally would.'

You would expect him to say this, says Lloyd, 'but I truly

believe the press weren't, and aren't, the mischief-makers. The mischief in almost every instance connected with the modern royals had already happened and Charles, along with the rest of them, knew much more about that than I did. Take the whole royal romance and its unravelling. The newspapers were vilified for running what turned out to be a belated version of the story. I'm really not willing to give Charles Spencer – or anyone else – the benefit of the doubt on this. He and his family, in its widest sense, knew what was going on and there was a general tendency on their part to mislead, to try totally to fool the media. We were miles behind the action. I used to have my leg pulled at the paper as yet one more incredible royal revelation emerged. On each occasion, I'd say, "I just don't believe it." And, on each occasion, it turned out to be true.

'I would go so far as to say that if you wanted a defence of the tabloid press in Britain in its dealings with the Establishment, there's not much better an example of what we reported about the relationship between the Prince and Princess of Wales. We were attacked from almost every quarter but, in the end, it was shown we'd got it totally correct. If anyone wants an example of when the British press earned a measure of respect for what it tries to do, I believe it was this unfolding story: the fairy-tale that ended up a nightmare.'

Mary Clarke, Diana and Charles's last nanny at Park House, would not underestimate, she says, the powerful effect of the press on people in the spotlight. 'I've always believed that the last occasion Diana and Charles spent time together had a profound effect on him. He made mention of the time his sister came to visit him and his children in South Africa in March 1997. They went to great lengths to avoid the press and they succeeded. I think it was that visit which impressed upon Charles the constant pressure Diana had suffered from being pursued down the years since she became a public figure. I think the pressure she'd been under really dawned on him then.

'When he heard at the end of August that his sister had been killed while being pursued by the paparazzi, it must have confirmed his worst opinions of the press. They had hounded Diana to her death. We now know that the fault may have lain with the driver of the car but Charles's fury when he issued that statement hours after his sister was killed was perfectly under-standable. He spoke from his heart, as he did later in his funeral Address. He blamed the press for making Diana miserable and he wasn't about to hide those feelings.

'It was perhaps inevitable that the papers should have had such a field day over Charles's divorce from Victoria but I'm certain he wouldn't have taken that into account when he spoke out about the press being at the other end of the moral spectrum. I don't approve of philandering and it looks foolish, with hind-sight, for Charles to have proposed to Victoria after knowing her only a few weeks. She had all sorts of problems which have been well documented but I think it's too easy to imagine that Charles, mindful of his own parents' failed marriage, would have stopped and thought before he rushed headlong into his own marriage. He was young, impulsive and presumably believed he'd found the right woman for him.

'Having said that, it was Diana I remember as the impetuous one. I know for a fact how bitterly she regretted doing that book with Andrew Morton. She told me so. I said to her, "That's typical of you. You always were so impulsive." I'm not suggesting that Morton came by the facts in some underhand way; Diana co-operated with him throughout. But she was at her most vulnerable at that time, at her lowest. How many times have all of us read again something we've written – perhaps a letter – and thought better about sending it? But, with Diana, it was too late. I shudder to think how much more bitterly she would have regretted it if she'd known the speed with which Morton was going to update the book after she'd died. I was absolutely horrified at what he did. I understand people wanting to make a penny or two but he'd already made millions out of her, albeit in a straightforward and ethical way. He must have known, though, how much she wouldn't have wanted him to reveal the extent of her co-operation in the project. Did he really have to release her annotated corrections to his manuscript?

'He asked her to help him with a second book he was writing while she was still alive – and she refused. Following that, he didn't waste an opportunity to ridicule her; he was ridiculing her up to two weeks before her death. I find that totally despicable. And then for him to justify the revised version of his first book as being the correct history of Diana is contemptible. It wasn't her correct history: it was one sad chapter of a poor, vulnerable woman trapped in a loveless marriage who was desperate to tell the world what she was going through. So to try and fossilize her in that period is quite, quite wrong. She had already come so much further by the time she died; she wouldn't want to be remembered like that. Each of us should look at the lowest point in our lives and ask ourselves if we'd want to be remembered like that – and of course we wouldn't. She was really sorry about doing that "Panorama" television documentary, too. But that was Diana for you: act first, think later.'

Morton himself, when researching his iconoclastic book, had cause to interview Charles Spencer in the winter of 1991 at the Earl's London home in Notting Hill. The Countess was also in attendance though very much in the background, says Morton, but he found the interaction between husband and wife amused and affectionate. 'I had a long list of questions, almost all of which centred on Diana's childhood and, therefore, of course, on Charles's, too. I found him very honest, very candid, almost recklessly so, a characteristic of which I was vividly reminded in his funeral Address. Indeed, the more I researched the Spencers, the more I realized that this thread of recklessness is a family trait. The eldest child, Lady Sarah McCorquodale, to take just one random example, once led a horse into her grandmother's house for a bet. Charles himself accepted a £100 bet to throw his stepmother, Raine, into a swimming pool,' (though she got wise to the caper and made herself scarce).

Sally Ann Lasson, Charles's lover before and during his marriage, describes the Spencers as 'a flouncy family', and it's a description Morton recognizes. 'These are people who wear their hearts on their sleeves. When Diana and her brother famously fell out after Charles reneged on his promise to allow her the use of a house on the Althorp estate, the two barely spoke to one another for many months. Diana told me, for instance, that the first she knew that Charles and Victoria were to divorce was when she read about it in the papers; hardly an illustration of sibling love and closeness.' When Morton first came to interview Charles, brother and sister had not yet fallen out. 'When we met, he was refreshingly open. There was no holding back; he just gave it to me straight from the shoulder. There's little doubting that he's clever but it's combined with the same sort of naivety his sister possessed; additionally, there seems to be a streak of other-worldliness about the Spencer family. In Charles's case, though, the reckless naivety is allied to what I would describe as his own code of honour.

'Take Guppy.' Darius Guppy was Spencer's best man in 1989, a favour Charles returned when Guppy married Patricia Holder in 1994. This was the occasion when the Earl announced, accurately, as it turned out, that the brilliant and glamorous Guppy, would either be a millionaire by the time he was 30 – or in prison. In the event, he went down for five years for an elaborate insurance fraud involving a bogus burglary in a New York hotel room, in which Darius and former fellow undergraduate Benedict Marsh claimed they had been tied up and relieved of a stash of expensive jewellery.

And what did Charles Spencer do when his friend was comprehensively and publicly disgraced? 'He stood by him,' says Morton. 'There is a sort of nobility about that which is not inconsistent with his agreeing to talk to me in the first place: it demonstrated a solidarity with his sister. Not that he was sentimental. He was tart, acerbic, honest. In other words, he didn't sacrifice his own standards. He told his own truth. He was consistent in what he said, as we saw at Diana's funeral. But then that, too, was true of her. People try to maintain that she had somehow changed her opinions between 1992 and 1997. It's not true. Her view that Prince Charles will never become King never wavered. She was also consistent in her view of the monarchy. I see now, looking back, that Charles Spencer was equally consistent and trusting. I was a relative stranger engaged in what might have seemed a high-risk enterprise; a lot of people would have thought once or twice before talking so openly to me. So, my conclusion is that brother and sister had rather similar qualities.'

Anthony Holden takes a less forgiving line. 'Charles knew his upcoming divorce case was going to attract some pretty lurid headlines about the other women in his life,' he says. 'On the one hand, it was quite cunning of him to take up an anti-tabloid position and to withdraw the invitations to the tabloid editors. On the other, he must have been aware that he was throwing down the gauntlet and that those same newspapers would stop at little to tear him to shreds if they were provided with the appropriate material.' His espousal of the need for tighter laws on privacy, therefore, looks slightly suspect, says Holden. 'Rich people can use these laws to silence the press and that's all wrong.

'The one thing he could do, though, and with some credibility, was to make a pledge in front of what was almost half the world's population in which he declared that the Spencers would play as much of a role in raising William and Harry as the Windsors. But terrific hit that the speech was – vivid in the memory are those images of people applauding in Hyde Park, the applause rolling through the Abbey, and quite devastatingly for the royals – the follow-through from Charles has been sporadic, to say the very least. Smart political advisers should have told him that he must be seen to deliver his promise although you might imagine that he could have worked that out for himself.'

Two months after his ex-wife died, Prince Charles took their younger son, Harry, with him on a state visit to countries in southern Africa. Charles Spencer, self-appointed standard-bearer of his nephews' future well-being and a resident of Cape Town, never saw his sister's son while he was on African soil. Holden can only shake his head in wonder. 'It seems extraordinary to me,' he says, 'that the Palace machine had not liaised with Spencer and somehow organized his being more involved in that trip.' As soon as Prince Charles and Harry arrived in Swaziland, Tiggy Legge-Bourke, Harry's nanny, took him and a schoolfriend off on safari for three days.

'Now, that would have been a perfect chance for Spencer, living in South Africa, and without the embarrassment of being with Prince Charles, who was anyway performing official duties, to spend some quality time with his nephew out in the bush and to follow up on his Abbey pledge. All the royal press were there. He would have got a lot of positive publicity. It struck me as a bizarrely missed opportunity to the point where one has to assume that relations must still have been pretty strained between the two Charleses.' (Earl Spencer acknowledged this very point when he spoke to the *Cape Star* newspaper in November. 'The pledge I gave [to look out for William and Harry] was on the family's behalf and we have honoured it and will continue to do so,' he said. 'The boys spend most of their time in boarding school and are not accessible on a daily basis. But they have my number, and my sisters and my mother are there.')

During the royal trip, Charles Spencer was over in England on business connected with his Althorp estate and the fund set up in his sister's name although he also found the time for what looked to fellow diners like a lengthy and enjoyable lunch one day with a group of friends at the fashionable Kensington Place restaurant in west London. By the time he returned to Cape Town, Harry was back at school in England. Even then, Spencer managed to irritate the royal party – although this went unreported – by arriving more than fifteen minutes late for a reception at the city's town hall for President Mandela and Prince Charles. 'Everyone – Spencer included – knows what a crime it is,' says Holden, 'to arrive after royalty at a royal event. And it wasn't as though he could have been unaware of the car parking facilities.'

Constitutional historian David Starkey is characteristically jaundiced on the subject of Earl Spencer's relationship with the press. 'The fact that Charles was able to deliver so devastating a soundbite from outside his Cape Town home, just five hours after his sister had been killed, merely reinforces my contention of his solipsistic world view.

'Then again, at the funeral, anyone else in his position of knowing that he was only weeks away from what could turn out to be a messy divorce might not have taken on the press. It was as though he somehow thought he could cloak himself in the same armour his sister so effectively donned. Whatever Diana did, we still went on loving her. She was Teflon woman; nothing bad ever stuck to her for long.

'But if Charles truly imagined he could emulate his sister's example, he was wrong. The fact that he had increased his profile so enormously beforehand simply made the story of his divorce an even bigger one than it might otherwise have been. I was reminded of that wonderful phrase of Feste's in *Twelfth Night* when he says: "Thus the whirligig of time brings in his revenges". The whirligig, in the case of Charles Spencer, took very little time indeed to catch up on him. He loves attention despite what he might protest to the contrary. I think he would have liked to have been a politician. As it was, he chose the media and that tells its own story.'

As the interface between client and press, Shelley-Anne Claircourt sees Charles's position rather differently. 'His relationship with the media had been strained ever since Diana got married to Prince Charles,' she says. 'The spotlight was on Charles Spencer for no other reason than that he was Diana's brother. For those who seek publicity – pop stars, actresses and so on – fine; but for those who have it thrust upon them, it must be very, very difficult. Becoming famous by default is a different kettle of fish. That's why Charles went to Strasbourg to have the laws on privacy in Britain tightened. [He failed, the European court refusing to refer his claim to a higher authority on the grounds that he hadn't yet exhausted all the available channels in Britain. His ill-advised initiative was said to have cost him £50,000 in legal fees.] When Victoria was secretly photographed walking in the grounds of Farm Place rehabilitation clinic, that really started the ball rolling for him; it got worse as the press continued to hound his sister so relentlessly. He's the sort of person who is going to say what he's feeling and say it then and there. When it seemed to him that the paparazzi had been so directly responsible for Diana's death, who could honestly blame Charles for speaking out as he did?

It's a point Earl Spencer acknowledged to Lisa Chait in her Cape Talk interview. 'I have no interest in or desire for personal publicity in any way, shape or form,' he said. 'I'm a very private person. On the other hand, if you ask me a straight question, I'll give you a straight answer. And the fact is, I've developed a hearty contempt for the British media. I really can't emphasize that enough. When I used to read the South African papers – though I gave up reading all papers in September '97 – I'd read ridiculous stories picked up from the UK, whether through wilful ignorance or whatever, and printed as though they were the truth. The main body of tabloid journalism in Britain is evil in its entirety. It wants to destroy. It's not something I'd say if it wasn't true and it's totally true. They operate on a level of sensationalism and destruction with no concept of the human soul. They're only interested in increasing circulation and in making their proprietors richer. These are despicable people.'

He is not, however, above having dealings with certain sections of the press – both as a television journalist and as the beneficiary of allowing magazines to photograph him and his family in his home. Sally Cartwright is publishing director of *Hello!*, the weekly magazine dedicated to the lives and loves of the rich and famous. 'In 1992,' she says, 'we were approached by Working Title Television – an independent production company and a subsidiary of Polygram – with a view to putting together a television version of the magazine in the UK. Eduardo Sanchez Junco, son of Antonio Gomez, who first launched *¡Hola!* in Spain in 1944, was and remains cautious about this general idea.

'He wondered how well the magazine would translate to the screen. An attempt had been made to do just that in Spain some years earlier – and it had not gone well. It's one thing having a journalist and a photographer interviewing and taking pictures of a celebrity; quite another if there's a television crew present and a bank of cameras. The level of intrusion escalates. However, what made this latest approach more interesting than most was that it came with a main presenter already in place: Charles Spencer. Now that, of course, put a whole different spin on proceedings. We took it very seriously. He was well-connected, he was working as a professional television presenter for NBC at the time and he was married, as far as we knew, perfectly happily.'

A couple of meetings took place with Working Title, Charles Spencer and Sally Cartwright. 'We discussed how the show could be handled and the restrictions Charles felt he'd have to impose in view of his immediate family. He couldn't exploit any family members, a position we understood absolutely. That said, by taking on this job, if it should ever materialize, he inevitably would have been exploiting the position in which, by accident of birth, he happened to find himself.'

What did she think of Charles Spencer? 'He was professional at all times. I wondered, though, if he had quite the right light touch. But he seemed a perfectly normal sort of guy if terribly conscious of his own position. I can't say I would have trusted him: he seemed arrogant, not your average kind of television presenter. But then he *wasn't* your average kind of television presenter. He was courteous and possessed the ability to charm; it's just that he didn't seem to feel it necessary to bother to turn it on. I found that a little irritating.'

In the end, what scuppered any plans to bring *Hello!* to the small screen was the unexpected death of Johnnie Spencer. Overnight, Charles became the ninth Earl Spencer and his elevation made the prospect of hosting a television series that took viewers behind a series of celebrity front doors irreconcilable with his new status. So it was that Shakira Caine, Catherine Oxenberg, the late Lady 'Kanga' Tryon (one-time confidante of the *other* Charles), Sky TV's Kay Burley, and the Annabels Giles and Croft, among others, were no longer to be considered as possible co-presenters with Earl Spencer – the project was aborted.

In his non-professional capacity, of course, Charles Spencer has been no stranger to the pages of *Hello!* That same year saw him and Victoria, along with their three daughters, splashed across the cover and nineteen pages of the magazine as the Spencers threw open the front door of Althorp House. 'I feel enormous love for the house,' Charles told *Hello!*. 'I am prepared to devote my entire life to making it a wonderful place for future generations of my family to grow up in and enjoy.' The decision to move to South Africa, presumably, had not yet entered his head. But then he also doubtless meant it when he told the magazine, 'I certainly pray that Victoria and I never get divorced because I couldn't bear to put my children through that sort of pain.'

And yes, says Sally Cartwright, a fee was indeed paid by *Hello!* for the interview and photographs that made up this extensive feature although, in keeping with company policy, she declines to confirm that it was the widely rumoured sum of £250,000. A fee was paid again (£100,000, it was said, although again *Hello!* refuses to comment on the amount) when, two years later at St Mary's Hospital in Paddington, Countess Spencer gave birth to the longed-for heir, and the happy couple posed for photographs. Both these issues sold reasonably well, says Cartwright, even though, by the time the second one appeared, rumblings of marital discord between the Spencers had begun to surface in the tabloid press. The word on the street was that Victoria had been treated latterly as little more than a brood mare and that the strain on her was beginning to tell.

If *Hello!* was prepared to pay inflated sums to Charles Spencer in return for his co-operating in carefully controlled picture spreads, that was their business. What subsequently complicated the cosy arrangement, however, and attracted unwelcome criticism of the Earl in the tabloids, was the dilemma of a man on the one hand fighting via the European courts for a tighter privacy law in Britain, and on the other continuing to talk to *Hello!* about future lucrative collaborations involving his family. The Earl denied any direct communication with *Hello!* after the

British satirical fortnightly magazine, *Private Eye* made certain allegations. Copies of letters and faxes written by both Earl and Countess Spencer came into the hands of *Private Eye* editor, Ian Hislop – supplied, it is rumoured, by a disgruntled former employee of *Hello!*. They purport to show that the Spencers continued to be in correspondence with the Marquesa de Varela, the legendary 'fixer' associated with *Hello!*.

In an undated letter thought to have been written a little before the Spencers decamped to Cape Town on 28 December 1995, the Countess floats the notion of 'an in-depth interview' with her in the magazine. 'There are things I would like to say,' she wrote, 'on the subject of my disease [anorexia] and my recovery (since this would benefit others), the British press, and my marriage (in support of Charles).' In a subsequent note to the Marquesa, Victoria claimed, 'I've discussed everything with Charles. He is in the middle of fighting the British government in Strasbourg for a privacy law in Britain – he is fighting it in my name. Therefore we simply cannot even contemplate or consider doing an interview for less than £250,000 to me. To do this would completely destroy my case in fighting for a privacy law in Britain which is why the fee must be so substantial. Otherwise it is just not worth my while, as I'm sure you'll appreciate.'

Sixteen days before they emigrated, Charles Spencer sent a fax to the Marquesa. 'Dear Neneta,' he wrote [they were on first name terms]. 'I am afraid I really feel most uncomfortable with your proposal concerning Victoria ... Please don't follow through with your plan.' He had acted honourably, clearly uneasy about what he considered would have been a clash between his public pronouncements and his wife's private plans.

More was to come. The couple had not long been in South Africa when Victoria Spencer wrote again to the Marquesa. She was thinking of 'coming out of retirement', as she put it, to pose for some fashion shots for the magazine. But she was adamant that there could be no accompanying interview or references to her private life. 'I could be severely criticized,' she wrote, 'for even modelling for you, since everyone knows of my desire to lead a private, anonymous life out here, so it would certainly have to be worth it for me.' Scrawled across the top of a letter from *Hello!* on this very subject is Charles's response to Victoria's request for advice on whether or not she should proceed. 'If you do this,' he wrote, 'get a letter in advance confirming that you will not be quoted on anything other than modelling – and get a huge fee!'

Charles's own approach to the Marquesa arrived on 21 March 1996. In a fax from Cape Town headed 'Subject To Contract', the Earl offered the magazine the exclusive story and pictures of a proposed party to celebrate the restoration of Althorp House. For a yet-to-be-negotiated fee, *Hello!* would get photographs of Charles with 'a few of my family (my mother, for instance), some of my friends, plus the restoration team'. The fee was earmarked for the Althorp House and Park account.

Charles Spencer subsequently rebutted the idea that his privacy campaign had been undermined in any way by his dealings with *Hello!*. 'I have not been involved in any such negotiations,' he wrote to *Private Eye*, 'neither has anyone on my behalf. On the contrary, I have spent a lot of the nearly two years we have lived in South Africa protecting my family's privacy: in particular, my wife and I have had to obtain restraining orders against one member of the paparazzi who harassed my children repeatedly.

'At no stage have I ever contemplated allowing any intrusion into my family's privacy in Cape Town. I think it a pity that my sincere wish to help this country's fight against the culture of intrusion should be sneered at so dishonestly in *Private Eye*, and I would be grateful if you could therefore acknowledge your fault. I am sure *Hello!* will confirm that it has had absolutely no contact with me during the entire time that I have lived in South Africa.' He may have been splitting hairs but Charles Spencer was right in what he said: the Marquesa works autonomously and independently of the magazine, her direct line of communication being to Eduardo Sanchez Junco in Madrid.

If he were to make contact with the magazine again, via the Marquesa or not, Cartwright would be delighted, she says.

'Charles Spencer is a figure of genuine interest to our readers and we would take the view, therefore, that it would make an interesting feature. I don't think there's anything hypocritical about our stance. We would never use intrusive pictures without people's knowledge or consent. On the other hand, if someone in the public eye wishes to open his doors to us and to our 2.4 million readers, we'll go through those doors – and happily.'

Cartwright acknowledges that *Hello!*, along with every branch of the media to a greater or lesser extent, must share a degree of responsibility for contributing to a climate which allowed paparazzi on motorbikes to pursue the Princess of Wales's car on its final, fateful journey in Paris on 31 August 1997. 'But, speaking for *Hello!*, we have never run the kind of photograph of which the Princess – or her brother – would have disapproved.' Indeed, Eduardo Sanchez Junco is said to have bought a set of photographs of Diana which showed her naked breasts, her bikini top having fallen down when she stood up too quickly while sunbathing on a balcony. He then sent her the photographs to prevent their being published anywhere, a gesture that was said to have irritated the Princess who felt herself being patronized: she didn't need *Hello!* to act as her moral guardian. Diana's relationship with the press – and it's true, too, of her brother's, says Cartwright – was highly inconsistent. 'You cannot invite them in on a Tuesday and then lock the door on a Wednesday. It really was a case of if you sup with the devil, you should do so with a long spoon. That said, nothing justifies her being chased through the streets by motorbikes or hounded as she was in London.'

The magazine also had dealings with Frances Shand Kydd. 'Diana knew her mother had given a long interview to *Hello!* to be published in two parts,' says Cartwright. 'There was a huge reaction to the first piece, most of the newspaper coverage suggesting that the Princess was extremely unhappy with what her mother had said.' Diana was then offered the opportunity to read the second instalment and to edit out anything she didn't like. 'We were always at pains never to upset her.' The text of the concluding part of the interview was duly despatched to

Kensington Palace the day before Diana was due to fly out of London on an official trip to Pakistan. 'In the event,' says Cartwright, 'she claimed she didn't have time to look at it which was curious since it takes ten hours to fly to Pakistan, ample opportunity to read what her mother had said. Her excuse suggested one of two things: either, that she genuinely wasn't troubled by what her mother might have said or, that she didn't want the responsibility of having looked at it and then possibly having to tackle her mother on certain points contained within it.'

When journalist Ingrid Millar was commissioned by the Marquesa de Varela to interview Patricia Guppy, wife of Charles's disgraced best man, for *Hello!* magazine, she had not expected that she would be dealing through a middle man: the Earl himself. 'Darius had been sent to prison for five years for his part in an insurance swindle,' says Millar, 'and Patricia had just given birth to the couple's first child. Charles and Darius were very close and, in her husband's absence, I think Charles wanted to ensure that Patricia was well looked after by the magazine. On the day of my interview with Patricia Guppy, I had to meet up with Charles and the Marquesa at the Marquesa's house just round the corner from Harrods in Knightsbridge. This was a big story for which the magazine, it was rumoured, had paid £80,000 – and that in itself produced adverse comment. Should a man who has been convicted of a crime then be entitled to benefit from selling his story?

'I was really struck by Charles when we were introduced. He's so large, a great big teddy bear of a man with sandy-coloured hair; I found him very attractive, much more so than photographs of him suggest. He wasn't effusive but he was pleasant and charming, somebody who wanted to get the job in hand done. He explained that he would be taking me to Patricia's rented house in south London, after which I assumed he'd leave. But he didn't; he hung around. I got the strong impression that he was looking after her for Darius. I have no way of proving this but I'm certain Charles was involved only as a favour for a close friend; I'd be amazed if he received a fee for acting as broker. I do know that he'd offered Patricia a rent-free cottage on the Althorp estate where she could live with her baby daughter but she wasn't going to take up the offer at that moment. What struck me was that Patricia stoutly maintained that Darius had been the victim of a miscarriage of justice. But then she was very much a woman who stuck by her man; as Charles was evidently a man who stood – resolutely, defiantly – by his friends.

'Whatever else you may say about Charles – and I have no quarrel with him whatever – you'd have to acknowledge that he is intensely loyal to his friends. A lot of people in his position might have made an excuse or two when their close friend got himself into so serious a scrape. Not Charles. He was as honourable and protective as he knew how. You might question his judgement in choosing Darius as a friend in the first place but, having done so, he certainly stuck by him.

'That extended to Charles insisting on seeing what I had written before I submitted it to the magazine. That's very unusual. Quite often, the interviewee asks for what is called copy approval but I've rarely known a middle man demanding it as well. He could have confined himself to ensuring that everything went according to plan in regard to the financial arrangements. But it was more than that. He wanted Darius and Patricia to be absolutely happy with what was said in the article; and they were. When Charles finally got back to me, he didn't have any corrections to the text which he'd obviously read in some detail. He'd done his job as he'd promised he would.'

Another female journalist worked with Earl Spencer when she was sent by her newspaper to cover him filming a report for a television station. 'I found him to be an odd mixture,' she says. 'He managed somehow to be both shy and arrogant. I remember him recording a piece to camera and turning to me afterwards to ask my opinion. I said that it had seemed fine with the exception of one sentence which had sounded ungrammatical. His mood changed instantly. His eyes flashed and he snapped at me, "I wasn't asking you to comment on the content. I was interested in your opinion of its presentation." I just arched an eyebrow, turned my back and started talking to the crew. Then there was the occasion when he seemed to be sulking in his room so I was despatched, rather against my will, I might say, to take him a glass of champagne. His initial reaction was to say that he hardly drank the stuff but, in the end, he took it and, of course, he did drink it. I kept thinking that what I'd like to do was give him a good slapping and tell him to grow up. He seemed far more conscious of his title and his position than any of the rest of us were. He was terribly hard to love.

'At one stage, he wrote my telephone number in his book; we were getting on quite well by this stage and I think he realized that I wasn't there to stitch him up in any way. He jotted down the number and then my initials. "I won't put your full name," he said, "because my wife goes through everything." The implication was that a woman's name with a number next to it would strike Victoria as highly suspicious. That seemed a bit sad. Then he kept asking everyone on the plane home when they'd lost their virginity. I'd made it very clear to him from the start that I was engaged; I didn't want him thinking I was out to get him into bed. But when I'd told him that, he asked me if I'd been married before which I thought was rather odd since I was only in my twenties at the time.

'Not, I might say, that I found him remotely attractive. Being a journalist, I've met a lot of famous men so my head isn't easily turned by power or position. Even so, I found it difficult to believe his ex-wife's courtroom allegation that he had had twelve lovers while she was recuperating at a clinic. The man lacks charisma.'

It is Charles Spencer's contention that less than one-tenth of any articles written about him are totally accurate. So it was not hard to predict his reaction to a story run by the *Daily Express* in 1994. This one concerned the whereabouts of the money that the convicted Guppy had been paid by an insurance company following the apparent theft of jewellery from his New York hotel suite. New evidence, fed to the *Daily Express*, seemed to suggest that there was more mileage to be had out of the story. But there was no question, as the newspaper was at pains to point out, that Earl Spencer either knew something he wasn't disclosing or that he had in some way benefited from Guppy's crime.

That, however, was not Charles's view: the Earl issued a libel writ and made a statement in the wake of the newspaper story of 9 April 1994. 'I have no knowledge,' it read, 'of Darius Guppy's criminal activities nor the whereabouts of any alleged gains from these activities. Nor have the police at any stage intimated to me that I might be able to assist in their inquiries into these matters. Of course, I would be happy to meet the officers involved in the case to assure them personally that I know nothing that they do not already know.' Although the *Express* legal team were confident that the paper's coverage in no way defamed the Earl, they eventually settled out of court.

Charles has since said that, no matter where in the world he might be living, he will seek out any publication that questions his honesty and integrity and pursue them through the courts. This is, of course, his entitlement but it is hardly a recipe for a carefree life. As every parent knows, the best advice to give a child being teased by a sibling is for the victim to ignore the baiter who will quickly get bored and move on to something – or someone – else. The mystery continues as to why the ninth Earl Spencer persistently fails to accentuate the positive, not least because it would make him so much happier, free him from so much unresolved anger. The alternative is to continue to react as he did in January 1993 when he extracted an apology from the *Daily Telegraph* – hardly a publication to be found at the 'wrong end of the moral spectrum' – for a caption it ran alongside a picture of his daughter in something called the Tiny Hats Calendar. Lady Kitty, who featured as a model in the calendar, was described as 'wearing only a blue hat', a line that, inexplicably, enraged her father who insisted it be made clear that it was a 'head-and-shoulders study and that she was otherwise clothed'.

At the time of the photographic session, Lady Kitty was just two years old.

12

THE DIVORCE

They had given us first The Wedding, then The Divorce and, ultimately, The Funeral of the late twentieth century. Now, the Spencers were ready to re-stock the pages of the smaller newspapers with the larger circulations (and not a few of the broadsheets, either) with a second round of high-profile family tragedies. When the ninth Earl stood up in that Westminster Abbey pulpit and shivered the very timbers with the power of his oratory, he cannot have been unaware that, in a matter of months, he was likely to be splashed across precisely those same publications he was so busily denouncing.

To many, Matthew Engel's remarks in the *Guardian* that Spencer's funeral Address was a model of 'disingenuousness bordering on mendacity' seemed too harsh. If only in that Charles Spencer has always been sufficiently sure of himself – it strikes some people, undeniably, as arrogance – to say what he thinks, when he thinks it, and then deal with the consequences. However, it is hard to believe that the man who delivered it can have been so naive as to imagine that the imminent severing of his marriage would pass by largely unremarked simply because the drama would be unfolding in South Africa.

For all that, though, even he might have experienced an initial sharp intake of breath when it became clear that his estranged wife had chummed up sufficiently with his ex-mistress that they were prepared to present a united front to courtroom and camera alike. Certainly, his public relations spokeswoman, Shelley-Anne Claircourt, recalls, with chilling clarity, the moment at which she realized this dissolution of a quasi-royal marriage was going to be something of a messy business.

172

'A couple of weeks before the date was announced for the court hearing which would decide where the divorce would eventually be heard,' says Claircourt, 'I received a couple of rather aggressive press enquiries. Then one newspaper printed a report that Victoria had asked to see Diana's will because, it was suggested, if Charles was to be a substantial beneficiary, it would be within Victoria's interests to know to what extent. [As it turned out, Charles was named in his sister's will as a guardian of the young princes, alongside his Mother, in the event of Prince Charles' death.] I began to get a mounting sense that the court case in Cape Town was going to turn pretty unpleasant. David Horton-Fawkes, general manager of Althorp, and I both offered to go to South Africa if Charles felt it would be helpful. I remember him saying, "Yes, I think we're going to have rather an *interesting* time." He wasn't wrong. Shortly afterwards, someone told me that Chantal had been paid £50,000 by the *News of the World* newspaper for an interview with her.

'Divorce is never a pleasant business so I had every expectation that this was going to be pretty ghastly. But what shocked me was the venom with which the press pounced on every last word said in court. I'd speak to journalists who'd be perfectly charming to my face and who would then go away and write the most vilifying reports for their newspapers. It was unbelievable. I'd ring London to find out what the coverage had been – this was at a point when the South African press was banned from reporting the case – and, to be perfectly honest, I didn't repeat most of it to Charles. It was totally unconstructive and not in any way helpful to what we were doing. One journalist admitted to me that, once Charles had branded the British press despicable and evil, the British press, in its turn, was hellbent on proving the same thing about Charles. It was a vendetta, no question about it. One tabloid journalist said to me after the case that, in the match between Charles Spencer and the British press, the score was now deuce.

'Now, I don't for a moment deny that Charles Spencer was unfaithful to his wife. That was widely reported at the time and he is, after all, human, like the rest of us. But the idea that he had up to a dozen lovers while Victoria was in Farm Place is ludicrous. If there *had* been all these women, don't tell me that the press, dedicated, as they were, to rooting out any small nugget of scandal to throw in Lord Spencer's face, wouldn't have uncovered at least some of them. And yet not one has ever been unearthed. What's more, that piece of information was presented to the world as something Charles had said to Victoria. But that simply wasn't the case. Victoria's counsel claimed that a friend had told Victoria that she had heard from a third party of Charles's multiple infidelity. This was hearsay of the most tenuous kind but still the British press, in particular, presented it as an incontrovertible fact.

'Through the two weeks in court, when the spotlight remained so relentlessly on Charles, I saw him experience some terrible lows and some corresponding highs. But he's a very strong character; I never felt he would go under. I think his feeling was that he would meet strength with strength; in other words, if the other side were going to say the things they said, he wasn't going to let those things go by unchecked. And yet, never once did Charles's side leak any information that was detrimental to Victoria. He felt he had nothing to hide. His past behaviour was no secret and this was an open court. But little did he imagine the viciousness with which half-truths and lies would be reported in the British press. At one point, I counted twenty-six British journalists sitting in the courtroom and twenty-eight film crews and photographers circling around outside it. It was like constantly being followed by an all-seeing mob. Personally speaking, I felt I had discovered where hell was.'

The case opened on Monday 24 November 1997. Charles's last-minute offer to his estranged wife the previous evening – the fourth such attempt, apparently, designed to head off an ugly and revealing courtroom battle – had once again been rejected by the Countess. Jeremy Gauntlett for Lady Spencer began proceedings by branding Earl Spencer a serial adulterer who, according to his estranged wife, had confessed to sleeping with up to a dozen women while she was undergoing a five-month programme at the £187-a-night Farm Place rehabilitation clinic in Surrey.

Gauntlett went on to describe a little of the background of his client to the judge, the Honourable Justice Mr Ian Farlam. A successful model, Victoria's work had taken her, at an impressionable age, to New York where she had begun experimenting with drugs. But it was a subsequent trip to Indonesia in the late eighties that was to prove decisive. 'She picked up a disease,' explained Gauntlett, 'that sparked off an eating disorder and she became dependent on hard drugs.' Victoria Lockwood married the ninth Earl Spencer in September 1989 but, before she did so, she had told him everything about her former drug habit and eating disorder. 'She gave up drugs before she married,' said her counsel, 'and she has never resorted to them since. The eating disorder is a continuing problem.'

Although the family had lived in Cape Town for almost two years, the Countess felt that the dissolution of an English couple's marriage should be heard in an English court. (It was widely suggested, whether accurately or not, that Victoria might have secured a more beneficial settlement back in Britain.) Arguing against Earl Spencer's contention that, as South Africa was where the family had settled, the full divorce hearing should be heard there, Jeremy Gauntlett quoted from a Northamptonshire parish magazine in which Charles had spoken proudly of twenty generations of his family tending the Althorp estate. 'Twenty generations?' he said. 'This is the family that has moved permanently to Cape Town?'

He also pointed to the Earl's funeral Address in which he had pledged to help Diana's two sons. 'He has made a public commitment to what he specifically termed his blood family to do whatever he can to care for these nephews. Althorp is where his late sister is buried, and there is to be some special place of remembrance for people to visit and where they can express that enormous outpouring of grief we all witnessed. That is going to impose additional commitments and responsibilities. The plaintiff has tenuous ties in this country. They have no family here; they have no job here.'

British matrimonial law expert Mr Jeremy Posnansky, a witness for the Countess, told the judge that Earl Spencer's personal fortune had been calculated at £6 million and that he had family assets valued at around £100 million. He maintained that the Earl's annual income before tax was approximately £1 million – some £600,000 after tax. Victoria had originally requested a lump-sum settlement of £3.75 million or £5,000 per child per month; her estranged husband had offered £300,000. Shelley-Anne Claircourt was at pains to enumerate subsequently what Charles claimed he had offered on top of that sum. There was to be £30,000 maintenance a year for his ex-wife, 'an offer relating solely to her,' said Claircourt. 'This was to be totally separate from all expenses relating to the children, including food, clothing, nanny and educational needs which are provided for by Earl Spencer.' Victoria was to be given the five-bedroom bungalow, worth £250,000, in which she currently lived, as well as her four-wheel-drive Isuzu car plus private medical insurance.

It was revealed in the Earl's own sworn affidavit that he was unwilling to offer any more – and for a reason. 'I am most fearful,' he said, 'that should Victoria receive significantly more money from me than she does at present, she will be unable to resist the lure of the substances to which she is/was addicted and/or unprincipled individuals who may seek to take advantage of her, with the result that she will relapse to the detriment of the children.' At a later point in the same affidavit, Charles Spencer claimed, 'Our marriage became unhappy and although I appreciate that the purpose of this affidavit is not to ascribe blame or make allegations, it is a matter of public record that Victoria's mental and physical health (and reliance on drugs) were material factors in the breakdown of our marriage. I have done everything in my power to support her and to assist in her recovery which, while fragile, is a cause for considerable relief.'

The second day of proceedings was overshadowed in terms of newspaper coverage, by the release of the intimate letter Charles had sent to his mistress, Chantal Collopy. Earl Spencer, meanwhile, was fighting a rearguard action to prevent the local

South African press from reporting the case by taking out an injunction against the *Cape Times* and the *Cape Argus*. In his legal notice, Charles said the reporting was affecting his children and, particularly, his six-year-old daughter, Kitty, at school in Cape Town. 'Kitty is able to read,' said her father, 'and the *Cape Times* posters referring to "Spencer's Other Women" were displayed on many lampposts. When I asked her how she knew about this, she told me that all her friends at school were talking about the matter.' (Days later, Earl Spencer capitulated in his fight with the South African press. Not, he said, because his views had changed but because the wrangle had turned into a matter that could only be resolved at Supreme Court level and he had no wish for his already troublesome divorce case additionally to 'turn into a constitutional football'.)

If Charles had wanted a discreet end to his marriage, he had failed spectacularly. The gloves were off now and Lady Spencer had a smile on her face and a detectable jauntiness in her step as she turned up to court in a succession of chic little outfits. UK press coverage focused on reports that she had claimed she had become 'very scared' of her husband as their marriage began to come seriously unstuck. 'He is an extremely domineering man and I was never allowed an opinion or a voice.' She went on to claim that he became 'intolerant and angry and he increasingly criticized, undermined, bullied and belittled me until eventually I lost all confidence and became very scared of him.' Her twenty-eight-page document, made available to the court, details a marriage of violent mood swings, marked by periods of 'great happiness intermingled with stormy fights', usually after both partners had embarked on heavy drinking sessions.

When, in August 1994, Charles apparently told his wife that their marriage was over, Victoria believed that the reason for its disintegration could be laid at her door; her eating and drinking disorders, she believed, were the root cause of the couple's problems. But when she consulted her psychiatrist, it was suggested that Charles had another woman. 'I replied that that was impossible because I firmly believed that the respondent would not dare to attract that type of adverse publicity again . . .' (a reference to his minutely reported affair with cartoonist Sally Ann Lasson, just six months into his marriage). The following April, Charles suggested a reconciliation but Victoria refused. 'I was no longer keen on the idea,' she revealed in her sworn statement, 'and, in any event, I have recently learned that at the time the respondent made this suggestion, he had already proposed to Chantal Collopy.'

You did not have to open the newspapers to read the wretchedly intimate details of the death of the Spencer marriage: they were splashed all over the front pages. But the traffic, it seemed, was flowing only in one direction. Charles Spencer – by the fourth day of proceedings, at least – was remaining resolutely tight-lipped on the subject of Victoria's problems. It was left to David Horton-Fawkes, his fellow Old Etonian and, latterly, general manager at Althorp, to speak up on behalf of his friend and employer and to do so, he made a point of emphasizing, off his own bat. There was no question whatever, he insisted, that he was being used by Spencer as a mouthpiece.

Reading from a prepared statement on the steps of the courtroom, Horton-Fawkes denounced both Victoria and Chantal in an angry and emotional outburst. He had known Charles for twenty years, he said, and had worked for him for the past three; he was godfather to one of the Spencer children. Although it was not his habit to put his head above the parapet – he had, for example, declined the Earl's offer to be best man at his wedding – he had been so incensed by what he believed to be the 'lies we have been forced to read that I am prepared to endure any exposure to set the record straight and speak out independently. I was living at Althorp after Charles and Victoria were officially separated and their marriage had broken down. Charles was looking after his four children single-handedly when allegedly a dozen women were supposed to have been cavorting with him. I am utterly amazed by these allegations.'

He went on to address the letters written by the Countess while she was receiving treatment in Farm Place. 'Far from claiming Lord Spencer was brutal, she lovingly and touchingly thanked him for his tolerance and support – generosity and support, which those of us who know him well recognize and admire. In my opinion, her welfare and that of his children has always been his utmost concern and will continue to be so. Charles is confident of clearing his name in court.' As a postscript, Horton-Fawkes reiterated that 'Earl Spencer has not seen this statement. I asked him if he would be offended if I made a statement and he said no. This is me speaking, not Lord Spencer.'

The following day – Friday 28 November – five of those letters, handwritten on Althorp-headed writing paper, were produced as last-minute evidence by Earl Spencer and lodged with the Cape Town court. Victoria's legal team were incredulous. A member of her team was reported as having said, 'These letters were written at the lowest point of her life. He waved them at her across the courtroom. The Countess is very unhappy about it.' So unhappy indeed that she issued the following statement: 'I do not wish to comment on the public offers of a divorce settlement in South Africa which Earl Spencer has chosen to disseminate through press conferences held through his media agent in the back of the court. I simply wish to state in response to what is said by – or, perhaps, through – Mr Horton-Fawkes that it is in material respects quite untrue.

'I am a private person and I wish to keep my privacy. I have accordingly kept my silence in relation to our marriage, as I am advised I should do so, until the court has heard my evidence. I still wish to do so. My husband chose to sue me in South Africa for divorce and for the custody of our small children without warning when we had been involved in negotiations through our English solicitors for many months with a clear view to divorce in England. My struggle before the Cape Town court is to have my future, and that of my children, determined by the law of the land where we were born and to which we shall return. My husband declared in a letter of April 23, 1996, which is before the court, that our stay in South Africa was temporary.'

It was hard to see how things could deteriorate further, short of Victoria and Chantal Collopy each taking the witness stand in the second week of a divorce case the whole world seemed to be watching. Clearly, this was a prospect that alarmed Earl Spencer who agreed to a dramatic end to proceedings as the clock struck midnight in Cape Town on Monday 1 December. After eleven hours of behind-the-scenes talks between the warring couple and their representatives, an out-of-court settlement was reached in which Victoria received a lump-sum settlement of £1,815,000, (slightly under half her original demand), her Cape Town house and its contents, and joint custody of the couple's four children. (Less than two months later, Victoria issued a writ against the Family Law Consortium – a London firm of solicitors, from whom she'd sought advice, reportedly on the recommendation of her ex-husband – demanding a seven-figure sum in compensation for the more generous divorce settlement she says she would have won via the English judicial system.)

In a joint statement, the couple said, 'The fundamental term of the agreement is that we undertake to the courts of South Africa and England not to breach our marital confidences or to give further details of this settlement. Accordingly, no further statements will be made on those matters and we hope that our privacy will be respected. For the greater part of the three years for which we have been separated, we have had an amicable relationship. This has been primarily for the sake of our children. For that same reason, we now aim to rebuild a civilized and friendly arrangement whereby our four children will continue to prosper. For this reason, too, we unreservedly withdraw all allegations made in relation to each other. We recognize that we have both contributed to the sad breakdown of our marriage. We now intend to look to the future and our main motive is the welfare of our four young children.'

As he left the court, Charles told reporters, 'It's over and I'm very happy. I am delighted that the case has been settled in South Africa and Victoria does not have to be cross-examined.' Victoria, who had left ten minutes ahead of her ex-husband, looked composed but declined to make any additional comment. The most high-profile divorce case in recent history was all but over; the headline writers began casting around for fresh sources of inspiration.

Mary Clarke, by then living in France, followed British newspaper coverage of the Spencer divorce battle a day late and with what she calls a healthy dose of cynicism. 'When I read all those lurid headlines about Charles's divorce, I knew that that was all they were: just headlines designed to sell newspapers. I acknowledged there must be a little bit of truth in them but, basically, I didn't believe a lot of it. The Charles I knew through to his early teenage years could not have changed so completely to have become the sort of person we were being asked to accept he was. I personally felt that he was quite deliberately keeping back some of the facts to protect Victoria; and, in doing so, leaving himself open to these adverse press comments. And as for Chantal ganging up with Victoria; well, you know what they say about a woman scorned? I imagine Chantal was very bitter. She'd lost Charles *and* she'd lost her husband.'

Mary Clarke does not deny, however, that the hostile coverage of his divorce must have had a damaging effect on Earl Spencer's reputation; and nor could that coverage have been more comprehensive, precisely as detailed and dirty as he must have feared only in his most vivid nightmares. Charles Spencer is an intelligent man, wise, presumably, to the ways of the international media. So the mystery remains as to why he ever imagined he'd be able to keep his divorce case low-key by having it heard in Cape Town. It is not as if he is without advisers although any amount of wise counsel counts for little if it goes unheeded. 'He miscalculated,' a friend told *The Times*. 'Victoria is so paranoid about her private life, he was sure she would panic. His biggest miscalculation was in failing to notice how strong she had become – and how badly she wanted revenge.' He also failed to understand the depth of the fury felt by Chantal Collopy, the unexpected 'star' of what the *Daily Mail* billed The Divorce of the Decade.

Chantal Collopy has since recalled the moment she swept into Cape Town's oak-panelled Court 17 and both Charles and his counsel, Leslie Weinkove, spotted her at the same moment. 'I don't think Charles was sure whether I would be there or not,' she says, 'but, when I walked into the courtroom, he and his lawyer looked at me and exclaimed, "Oh!" to each other. "Oh, there's Chantal."' She had been subpoenaed to appear as a witness by the Countess's lawyer, Jeremy Gauntlett, so she had no choice but clearly Earl Spencer must have been sending up a silent prayer that she wouldn't appear – nor provide so public a show of support to the woman whom she'd supplanted in his affections.

'Seeing Victoria and me together must have made him feel very vulnerable,' Chantal later confessed to *Hello!*, 'but she and I will always have a bond now. Before I met Victoria, I already felt sympathy for her, having read Sally Ann Lasson's story of her affair with Charles six months after their wedding. Victoria was painted as insecure, immature and incapable and, if you're told those things enough, you begin to believe them. But I've seen her going through some of the most stressful times of her life and she says I've helped her find strength. I think Charles thought Victoria would back down long before going into court but, although she will always have that vulnerable, rather appealing side to her, she has a stronger personality now and I don't believe Charles realized that. But I always told him not to underestimate her.'

He would have done well to listen. Here was the woman who approached Victoria in a local bookstore in Constantia, some months after Charles had terminated their affair, and who had made it her business to befriend his estranged wife. In time, that friendship progressed sufficiently well to encourage Chantal to show Lady Spencer the love letter Charles had sent to her as their romance had burgeoned. 'I showed it to Victoria,' Mrs Collopy subsequently revealed to Sky News, 'because I wanted her to know that it wasn't me who had pursued her husband and broken up her family.' She is adamant, however, that she was not the person who made the letter available to the press. 'It may have been my letter but Charles still retained its copyright in the eyes of the law.'

However it became 'public property', it is hard to believe that Earl Spencer could imagine the letter's content would reveal him in a sympathetic light. Here is what it contained:

My darling,

Do I want to spend the rest of my life with you? Yes. When I was with you, everything was so clear. You've been wonderfully patient with me and, as for sensible – well, you couldn't have been more wise and considerate.

For someone who's screwed up a major part of his life by charging into something he feared and didn't understand – marriage – your control of the situation has prevented me repeating my error. I feel truly sorry for Victoria, for Don, and for all six children involved. I never intended to put my children through the hell of a divorce but I hope these divorces will be more civilised than those of my parents.

If I can't learn from their mistakes by avoiding divorce, I can at least prevent the unpleasantness that accompanied it. It sounds selfish but you are everything I need. You make me feel loved and valued, an equal yet ultimately your man, and you make me laugh, make me happy.

I have to balance my quest for happiness – which I know, despite your reservations, would lead to my making you happy – against my duty to my children, and my wife. Deep down, I've always known my marriage was a mismatch, a terrible error, an impulsive whim that I compounded by adding more and more children to my family.

There have been good times but the bad ones have been chillingly awful. I'm not sure whether Victoria can remember them all but I can and I never want to go through such desperate lows again. Part of the problem has been having an immature wife, one who is incapable of dealing with a husband with a strong character, except by going on hunger strike, an alcohol binge or resorting to drugs.

The other side of the problem is that I cannot deal with a woman who does these things to herself and I can't respect such negative reactions, and therefore found love drifting away. There wasn't an abundance of it in the first place.

This is why your uncomplicated character is so refreshing. Yes, you're a pretty face but there's a lot more besides. You're clever, you're sensitive and you're strong. Like me, you are in an unsuitable marriage in many ways because I know much of you is unappreciated, and most of the rest is taken for granted.

I would appreciate you and value you. Thanks to Dr Peck [Chantal had encouraged Charles to buy *The Road Less Travelled*, a book on relationships by Dr Scott Peck], we both know the limitations of the 'hearts and flowers' stage but we both know what lies beyond that.

To be loved by you is the greatest gift I could ask for. I know you are basing your love (or, rather, your suppressed love) on instinct but the intensity of an emotion that has lasted seven-and-a-half months held together by a telephone line is not to be denied.

I am ashamed to have hurt you in the past. Only when I was with you did I fully understand what I have put you through. I had no right to ignore you. I abused the power I have, through being able to dial you, and I feel bad that you were hurt by my thoughtlessness.

I have spoken to my lawyer who has told me the press will have a field day. I meet him tomorrow at 8am to discuss tactics. In the evening, I'm seeing the sisters.

My excitement at moving two steps nearer to you is balanced by the thought of how bloody the time will be for me when I end this marriage – and how Victoria will collapse. I know it sounds cowardly but I have to be honest. At least the children will be too young to understand or to be bothered by the papers.

I have been a dreadful bully to Victoria. I've been callous and vicious, trying to force her out of my life. She deserves better than that – a good man, who will love her, give her security and help her deal with her shortcomings.

I've just spoken to you for nearly an hour and you were very down. I'm glad because it means that you are taking the whole matter very seriously. It's not just me who has to think, and then act on those thoughts, any more. You realise that everything is no longer a distant dream and that you have to work out how you truly feel. The pressure is on!

Anyway, relax – it'll work itself out, one way or the other. I've got your philosophical approach. It is a time of turmoil but the potential for happiness is there, and neither of us is happy at the moment.

You must still protect yourself because nothing is certain from either end but I want you to know how truly sincere I am; and, if we don't pull this off, I'll regret it for the rest of my life.

All my love, Charles

In a long career answering tens of thousands of letters sent to her by readers of a host of publications, both newspapers and magazines, Virginia Ironside has become well-versed in reading between the lines of her correspondents' anguish. The letter that Charles Spencer sent to Chantal Collopy reveals much, says Ironside, but not always what the Earl intended. Had the letter turned up in her postbag, this is what Britain's leading agony aunt, well known for her strongly worded style, would have written in response:

Dear Charles,

On behalf of all the women you have loved and left, I feel compelled to reply to your love letter to Chantal Collopy. At least, I think it was a love letter to her. At times, it sounded more like a love letter to yourself, a navel-gazing piece of diary, spewed out in a fit of self-indulgence. Interestingly, there are twice as many references to yourself and your own feelings as there are to hers (I know; I counted). Never a good sign, if I may say so. It is always the loved one who should be the centre of attention, not the lover.

But enough of that. Let's go through your letter carefully. You say you feel sorry for Victoria and the children; you say she was immature, incapable of dealing with a husband who has a 'strong character', that you can't respond to her negative reactions – anorexia, alcohol, drugs. In other words, to put it more neatly, your wife doesn't understand you.

Oh, poor you. Did it never occur to you that it was *you* who didn't understand *her*, that it's natural for a wife to have negative reactions to a man who, by his own admission, was callous and vicious and tried to force her out of his life? Even when you view the end of your marriage, you can only think of how 'bloody' it will be for you when Victoria collapses.

But thinking of others is just not your style which is why your love letter rings so hollow. Like all damaged children – for, like your sister, you're a damaged child yourself – you look to others to make you happy rather than looking to yourself. You say that Chantal will make you happy and that, by being happy, you will make her happy. No one, Charles, can 'make you happy'. If you have been, as you admit, cowardly, thoughtless and bullying, then no other person can change those things in you. This is a battle you have to fight on your own.

Fantasy weaves itself through your letter like a black thread. It's clear that this affair has been sustained, incredibly enough, by seven-and-a-half months of talking on the telephone only. How could any man in his right mind believe that this was a love affair built on the loyalty and strength of love you get by living together day by day?

And what true lover gets any pleasure out of the other person being down? True lovers are happy only when their lovers are happy; when their lovers are depressed, they feel their agony for them.

Love letters, like poems, or letters to the newspapers,

should be short and preferably rewritten several times to make certain they hit the mark. They should be well-honed cupids' darts, not whacking great sledgehammers aimed against a rock that throws out splinters and stones in every direction.

The speech you gave in the Abbey was a brilliant piece of emotional oratory. It deserved the round of applause it got. Any prime minister would have been proud of it. Perhaps you should stop writing love letters, however, because, when you write them, you seem only to spread your own hurt into the lives of everyone around you.

Virginia

The grand passion, which Chantal truly believed, she says, would lead to marriage, began inconspicuously enough in the summer of 1994. She and her husband, Don Collopy, a man who had made a small fortune in the fashion industry, had flown to England to attend the 40th birthday party of their friend, ex-pat England cricketer, Allan Lamb. Earl Spencer, cricket enthusiast, was a friend of Lamby's too. 'I was standing leafing through some photographs at the party,' recalls Chantal, 'and almost the first thing Charles said to me was, "Are you happily married?" To which I replied, "Aren't we all supposed to be?" Looking back now, I realize it was a rather flirtatious exchange.' There was a mutual attraction – that much was clear – but, as Chantal told him at the time, there was little point pursuing it since they were separated by thousands of miles and she was, anyway, a married woman with two children. 'Then I asked him how old he was and when he told me, I said, "Oh well, I'm five years older than you." So that was the end of that.'

Except, of course, that it wasn't. Charles, wherever he happened to find himself, began calling Chantal – she'd given him her number – long calls that lasted a minimum, she says, of an hour and were often much longer. 'He was immensely charming and a little shy. I felt rather sympathetic towards him; he seemed burdened by the huge responsibility [of Althorp].' In

February 1995, Charles flew to South Africa for a documentary series he was making on the world's ten most beautiful houses – in this instance, his wine-maker friend Hannes Myburgh's Meerlust Estate at Somerset West. 'I remember calling round for him the first time we went out together,' Chantal told *Hello!*, 'and we had lunch in a little town outside Cape Town called Stellenbosch. I had the photographs with me taken at Allan Lamb's birthday party and we laughed a lot as we looked through a pile of them.'

It was not until a subsequent visit in April that Chantal and Charles finally became lovers. 'His wife was in a clinic and my husband was away for the weekend. I had arranged for Charles to stay in a cottage which belonged to a friend of mine. It was there that we consummated our relationship. I felt that it was right. It was very passionate. He told me he really loved me very much.' Their emotions were running away with them. 'With me being the way I am and with Victoria getting more and more insecure, I'm sure Charles just couldn't cope with the emotional support that she needed. He saw me as such a strong person and Victoria was totally different.'

On his return to Britain, Earl Spencer asked his wife for a divorce and suggested that it would be a good idea for the family to move to South Africa. By December 1995, the entire Spencer brood had decamped to the fashionable Constantia district of Cape Town. 'Even though the feeling between us was very strong,' says Chantal, 'we did try not to see each other. We effectively ended our relationship because I wanted to try and make my marriage work.' Nor did Spencer attempt to contact her. Then, one day, they passed each other driving in opposite directions and he blew Chantal a kiss. When she reached a friend's house, Charles had already called to ask after her – and the state of her marriage. 'That's all it took and that's how we got back on track again,' she says. 'That same evening, my husband was out and I just picked up the phone and called Charles.'

Don Collopy, aware of his wife's infatuation with Earl Spencer, began taping her telephone conversations. Barely six months after Charles's arrival in Cape Town – 'I knew he was here to stay,' says Chantal, 'the moment he flew out his two dogs, ridgebacks called Delia and Sybil, from Britain' – her husband heard Spencer say how much he loved her in a phonecall. 'Then Charles asked me if I loved him. My husband heard my clear response. "Of course I love you," I told him.' It was pretty much the end of the Collopy marriage. 'Don's immediate reaction when he confronted me,' Chantal revealed in *Hello!*, 'was that he didn't want to stay married to a woman who loved another man.' This, she later told Sky News, without any hint of self-irony, she found very hurtful. She was shocked, apparently, because she hadn't yet had time to consider divorce.

Don Collopy was assailed by no such doubts. 'My husband was angry and hurt and wanted to expose my new relationship. In South Africa, you cannot name a third person in a divorce so the only way he could make my affair with Charles public was to take advantage of an ancient civil law and sue Charles for "alienation of affection", [or enticement, by any other name]. The claim was settled out of court at the end of February 1998. Perhaps the reason he did it was to humiliate Charles. He was very vengeful, a man seriously scorned.' Don Collopy told local reporters, 'From the moment Charles Spencer set eyes on my wife, he hasn't left her alone. He acts as if he thinks he has the authority to go round and do whatever he wants; and he's destroyed my family. He has just steamrollered over all our lives. He is an arrogant sod and should remember he isn't royalty himself.'

Rather than signalling a fresh start for Chantal and Charles, this proved to be the beginning of the end. 'At the height of our affair, he'd said to me, "I don't understand why you don't leave your husband." Six times on one day, he'd said, "Promise me you'll marry me, Chanti." He was putting me under tremendous pressure to marry,' she told the *Sun* newspaper in London. 'I had to tell him to take things more slowly. But we even went house-hunting together. I had no doubt that he would marry me. I was very angry when I later found out he had told our friends that he'd ended the relationship because I was pressuring him into marriage. Nothing could be further from the truth.

'Then, when my divorce was imminent [it came through in November 1996], Charles suffered a sort of panic attack, telling me he couldn't guarantee me a future. I suppose I got into quite a tearful state which is when I began to see a different side of him. I suddenly started feeling very insecure,' she told Sky News, 'and worrying about the way I looked and my weight. Charles had once asked me to promise that I would never get fat, the last thing a man should say to a woman. He'd always regarded me as strong and yet I'd become emotionally needy for the first time. He saw that I could also be vulnerable. He just couldn't cope with that.'

The crunch came at Christmas 1996. Charles had invited Chantal to come to Althorp where he was staying for the annual festivities. By then divorced and with her two sons spending the holiday with their father, she arrived in Northamptonshire on 20 December. 'It wasn't long before I realized the atmosphere wasn't right,' she says. 'Back on his home ground, Charles was different towards me, not nearly so needy, and I just hadn't anticipated it.' But it's a baseless rumour, she says, that she stumbled across another affair in Spencer's life. 'It was more that, once back in his own home and surrounded by his four children, Charles realized, I think, what a lot of responsibility he had taken on.' It didn't take long for matters to come to a head. At the end of a day when Chantal had barely seen him, he confronted her with the fact that he would never be able to accept her two sons. 'He just said, "Look Chantal, I'm going to be honest. I could never accept your children." I replied, "Well then, we don't have a future." We ended things just like that.'

She spent a couple of days with a friend in London and then flew back to South Africa on Christmas Day. 'All I could think was that I was divorced, my boys weren't with me and I was all alone on an aeroplane on Christmas Day. I was totally devastated, a complete wreck. I was in a desperate despair. When I arrived home, I couldn't believe Charles could cut off from me just like that. He didn't even pick up the telephone to see if I'd arrived safely or to wish me Merry Christmas or Happy New Year.'

Nor did it end there. 'What angered me even more after he dumped me,' she later disclosed to the *Sun*, 'was that stories started appearing in newspapers – which I believe that Spencer was behind – claiming that Princess Diana didn't approve of me and that's why I was ditched. That was the biggest load of nonsense I've ever heard. I never met Diana.' Soon after they split, Chantal claims Charles asked her to sign a confidentiality agreement under which she would never speak publicly about the relationship. 'He didn't want anyone ever to hear about the affair. I refused then and I refuse now. I would never sign such an agreement.' She was in touch with him one more time, however, the morning she awoke to the news of Diana's death. 'I called as soon as I heard. Obviously, he was in shock. I told him to go to a particular cupboard in his kitchen and take a herbal remedy I remembered having put there. I also told him that he must try and mourn, that he must shed a tear. If he didn't, it would affect him a lot in the future.' Chantal called back a few hours later. 'Charles told me that he had cried but that he was trying to cope with it.'

Now, with the benefit of hindsight, Chantal has all the time in the world to look back on an affair which destroyed her marriage (although rumours began surfacing in the spring of 1998 that she and Don were at least back on speaking terms, not least for the sake of their two sons, and even contemplating a trial reconciliation). And yet she has no regrets, she says, the single exception being the effect the whole episode has had on her children. 'I've probably had the best of Charles,' she told Sky News, 'in that it was a very mature relationship, extremely romantic, extremely civilized and very respectful. He said he had never experienced that kind of relationship before. I will always have fond memories of him. He was extremely good to me. The good times outweighed the bad and I really don't like to think of the bad times. Yes, I'll get over it and I'll learn from him.'

Psychologist Dorothy Rowe regards the lovers' diverging expectations towards the end of their relationship as being all too depressingly familiar. 'Men and women have a very different attitude to sex,' she says. 'Men can compartmentalize it. Commonly, a lot of men divide women into two groups: madonnas and whores. Charles has grown up in a generation of great sexual freedom, a time when women have been much more generally available than in previous years. You don't have to be heir to an historic estate to believe that, as a man, you can go on and on having lots of women, lots of sex, while at the same time being married; *and* sleeping easy. You're a handsome young man; girls fling themselves at you; what's a guy to do?

'The trouble is if, as a result of your upbringing, you've learned not to value yourself, you focus on yourself all the time so that you don't learn about other people; you don't even develop an interest in other people. You don't notice what other people do. Consequently, you never develop the habits of sussing somebody out and being able to predict what that person might do or feel or think. And yet that's an essential skill in life and in business and, certainly, in marriage. He said in his letter to Chantal Collopy that he knew, almost at the point that he married Victoria, that it was the wrong thing to do. That seems to suggest he has a capacity to be aware of other people but a capacity that he uses only in an instinctual way rather than developing skills in assessing people and summing them up; and because he hasn't developed those skills, he makes terrible mistakes and then doesn't feel the need to correct himself. Some people prefer not to think things through; they believe they can rely on their instincts. But that's just lazy.

'At one level, Charles knew his marriage wasn't going to work. He could have done one of two things: not get married in the first place or get married and then try to make a go of it in sensible ways. It didn't surprise me that he revealed in his letter to Chantal that Victoria's eating disorders and general attention-seeking were an irritant to him whereas the same type of behaviour in his sister appeared to be something, in his view, that we should all have felt sympathetic about. The point is, Diana wasn't doing what she did for her brother; she was doing it for her husband. The same is true of Victoria; she was trying to have her needs met by *her* husband.'

Throughout it all, though, Charles has been at pains to do what he feels is right by his children, the innocent casualties of their parents' unhappiness. In his Cape Talk radio interview, he spoke fondly of his three daughters – and of his son, Louis. 'I'll be very sad,' he said, 'when my children stop hanging on to my legs but I suppose that when my boy gets to about six, that's when he'll start to want his independence. He'll stop wanting to be hugged but then, like all boys, he'll probably start to gravitate more towards his father in terms of looking for a role model. He'll go from that nursing stage to learning to be a little man and that'll be an interesting process in itself. As to the keys to successful parenting, I wouldn't be arrogant enough to suggest I know. But, from my point of view, I'd say it was to do with love and security and setting boundaries within which they feel safe and secure and able to operate but boundaries, too, where they know when they've overstepped the mark; not in a ghastly puritanical way but an understanding that certain things are acceptable and certain things aren't.'

It is his children, he says, who have helped him as much as anyone to get over the grief of Diana's sudden death. 'It's not like Victorian times when there was a set year of mourning and you changed the colour of your clothing accordingly. If there's one thing I've learned, it is that children are the best antidote to adult depression and grief. Their lives and needs are immediate; they keep you going. Normally, people are almost embarrassed to bring up the subject of grief. I discovered that when my father died in 1992. But Diana's death was such a public thing and people were so united in their grief, I haven't found it a problem.'

Dorothy Rowe, meanwhile, remains unconvinced by Charles's track record to date as a father. 'He hasn't done too well so far. Marriages break up because two people discover they don't want to live with one another any more. But there's enough information around nowadays for any adults on the point of splitting up to tell them how they should behave in front of the children. Charles's actions tell me that he hasn't demonstrated enough concern for Victoria; he hasn't looked after her when she's needed looking after; and that will have impacted on their children. We are judged by our children not on what we say but by what we do. Not words but actions.'

For all that living through a divorce – especially a bitter one – can be an extremely stressful experience, Dr Rowe does not believe that Earl Spencer will have been plunged into the depths of despair. 'I don't think Charles would be depressed now because depression only sets in with people who blame themselves for any disasters that may have occurred. The fact that he blames the press so vociferously suggests that he's good at turning the blame outwards on to other people. When a disaster befalls you, you always ask yourself why this has happened; and there are only three possible answers. One is that it was your fault. One is that it was somebody else's fault. And the third is that it happened by chance.

'If you believe that we live in a just world where goodness is invariably rewarded and badness is punished – something that every religion teaches – then, in a just world, nothing happens by chance. So my guess would be that Charles is only ever faced with two possibilities following some personal disaster: that it was his fault or someone else's. In other words, depression or paranoia. His funeral Address was very strong on apportioning blame – to the Royal Family, to the press and so on – but never to Charles himself.'

On Wednesday 3 December 1996, in a six-minute hearing, the marriage of Charles Spencer and the former Victoria Lockwood was finally and formally brought to an end. When it was all over, when the dust had settled on the private tragedy of this public uncoupling, those wicked lads at *Private Eye*, Britain's long-standing, satirical fortnightly magazine, felt compelled to publish the following:

APOLOGY

In common with all other newspapers we may have given the impression at the time of the funeral of Diana, Princess of Wales, that her brother, the Earl Spencer, was in some way a noble and upstanding figure who was giving the nation a moral lead. Headlines after his speech at his sister's funeral such as, 'Well Said, Your Lordship', 'Top Marks For Spencer – The People's Earl' and 'String Up The Windsors – Let's Have The Spencers Instead', may have reinforced the view that we in some way regarded the Earl as a towering moral leader who was giving the British people a new sense of values in their hour of grief.

We now recognise that these tributes were entirely without foundation and constitute a baseless calumny on the reputation of the Earl Spencer . . .

We say: Come off it . . . pay up the money to Vic and don't try coming back to Blighty – 'cos you're not welcome!

We apologise to our readers for any confusion that our earlier tributes to Earl Spencer may have caused.

13

THE FUTURE

The tragic and unexpected death of his sister moved Earl Spencer, whether he liked it or not, firmly centre-stage. As the head of the family, there was much to consider, the complicated funeral arrangements apart. It was on the journey from central London to Althorp, for instance, on the very afternoon following the service at Westminster Abbey, that Charles's brother-in-law, Sir Robert Fellowes, first floated the notion that Diana's HRH status could be restored posthumously. The suggestion was rejected. 'Diana would not have wanted it,' Charles was reported as saying, 'and it is not what we want, either.'

Buckingham Palace confirmed this reaction in a formally worded statement. 'There has been speculation in the media,' said a spokesman, 'about the restoration of the style, Her Royal Highness, to the Princess of Wales. Buckingham Palace has confirmed that it consulted the Spencer family on the afternoon of her funeral regarding this matter. Their very firm view was that the Princess herself would not have wished for any change to the style and title by which she was known at the time of her death. The Spencer family itself also did not wish for it to be changed.'

Then there was the thorny question of how best to remember Diana. Initially, her brother ruled out the possibility of a permanent museum at Althorp, dedicated to her life and work. But the public clamour demanding a lasting memorial proved irresistible and Charles changed his mind. So it is that, from 1 July to 30 August each year – that is, from the anniversary of her birth to the eve of the anniversary of her death – Althorp will be open to those members of the public wishing to remember a woman who reached out to the lives and hearts of so many. (Touchingly, Prince William, it was reported, wanted his own memento of his mother and asked particularly to be given her sapphire and diamond engagement ring which, he believes, symbolizes a period of true love between his parents and which Diana continued to wear long after her divorce from his father.)

The 12,000-square-foot, honey-stoned stable block at Althorp is being converted – under the eye of designer Rasshied Din – to house an extensive exhibition celebrating Diana's life and achievements. 'I think a lot of people associate museums with being old and fuddy-duddy, dark and dingy,' Spencer told the *Guardian*. 'We want it to highlight her life and not be mausoleum-like.' It is Din's intention to make the Grade II listed building feel contemporary. 'It is a large space which is divided into lots of small spaces. We are working closely with English Heritage and the solution is going to be quite ingenious. We want to sustain people's interest. It is a difficult space to move through.' Within the 1730s Palladian building will be cafés, a shop and myriad visitor facilities. In addition, the Spencer ancestral home, Althorp House, replete with priceless works of art, furniture and china, will also be open to visitors.

The exhibition area will focus on the childhood of the former Lady Diana Spencer and the public life of Diana, Princess of Wales. There will be considerable cine-footage taken by her father and items from the Spencer childhood. It is intended, says Rasshied Din, to accomplish a clean, modern approach situated within an historic building. Nor is architect Giles Quarme blind to the problems involved. 'Roger Morris's original design is particularly appealing,' he says, 'combining elegant Palladian detail and proportions with a no-nonsense functional simplicity. The stable block, which is externally almost unaltered, is, therefore, being treated with the greatest respect.' Charles Spencer is overseeing the conversion, both its interior redesign and the content of the permanent exhibition itself. Working alongside a curator, he has personally selected items for display, his experience as a television journalist proving useful in the preparation of the audio-visual content.

These plans were generally welcomed although certain elements attracted criticism. A pop concert in June, in anticipation of the opening of the museum celebrating Diana's life, was felt by some to be an inappropriate way to raise further money for her memorial fund, particularly since it was to be staged in the grounds of Althorp, her final resting place. There were dissenting voices, too, following newspaper reports that Charles was to make available for sale memorabilia incorporating her image. And then there was the battle of the car park. Plans for a 500-space car park outside the walls of the estate to cater for tourists visiting Althorp were shelved following lobbying from local residents. Members of Great Brington parish council favoured a park-and-ride scheme or even the re-opening of Althorp's defunct railway station. Said council member Nora Jones, 'Were this car park to have gone ahead, it would have had a ruinous effect on our village.'

Althorp's garden, meanwhile, has been re-landscaped to form a natural route to the arboretum where a collection of rare trees has been planted by members of the Royal Family, successive Earls Spencer and their families since the accession of Queen Victoria, and by Charles, his two surviving sisters, Diana herself and her sons. The arboretum surrounds the lake – the Round Oval, as it is known – and an island that will be the focal point for visitors to Althorp. A memorial on that island will be clearly visible across the narrow stretch of water, home to four black swans. The 'temple' at the lake's edge, brought by the fifth Earl Spencer from the gardens of Admiralty House in London, is being restored and dedicated to Diana's memory. Here, individual members of the public can pay their respects and leave their floral tributes in sight of the island where the Princess was laid to rest.

Assuming, of course, that she is. Persistent rumours, both in the drinking taverns in and around Little Brington and Great Brington, the two villages closest to Althorp Park, as well as in media circles, suggest otherwise. Diana's long-held wish, it is said, was that she should be buried next to her father in the family crypt at the twelfth-century village church of St Mary the Virgin in Great Brington. This had originally been the intention of her family, headed by the ninth Earl, and the crypt was duly opened in anticipation of the introduction of Diana's remains. But then Charles had a public change of heart: a small parish church, he suggested, was not equipped to withstand the ceaseless pilgrimage of members of the public wishing to pay their respects to the People's Princess. How much better to accord her the unique privilege of a final resting place on the island in the middle of the lake in Althorp Park?

Which is what the world assumed had duly happened. But then a number of stories began obstinately recurring. According to local historian, Alan Burman, an estate gamekeeper told him that Diana was cremated and that the urn containing her ashes had been placed inside the Spencer family crypt in the church. And what of the account of the taxi driver who saw a plume of smoke in the dead of night, emanating from the chimney of the nearby crematorium at Milton Malsor? Then there is the problem of interring a coffin in what is probably wet or swampy ground on the island site: burying the body beneath the water table almost certainly would have meant the construction of a waterproof vault. Given the suddenness of Diana's death, could such a vault have been constructed, it is being asked, in the short time-frame that existed between Earl Spencer's apparent change of mind and the interment itself?

The vicar of St Mary's, the Rev. David MacPherson, is adamant that Diana is buried on the island in the middle of the lake. 'I know it is a widely held belief in Northampton,' he told the *Observer*, 'that Diana is in the church but the wet concrete [seen by several local parishioners] around the vault can be explained. After Diana's death, it was opened in preparation and then closed when the Earl changed his mind. If the Princess is not buried on the island, my bishop and a lot of other people have been made a fool of.' Charles's public relations spokeswoman, Shelley-Anne Claircourt, was also insistent that the Princess was buried in the middle of the Round

Oval. 'The decision to bury the Princess on the island was taken early on,' she said, 'partly to protect Great Brington. A bridge was built out to the island to take the coffin there. The Princess is definitely buried on the island. I was there on the day.' (Claircourt was indeed a frequent visitor to Althorp, personally participating, for instance, in the transfer of floral tributes from the mainland to the island but she did not attend the burial service itself.)

The rumours came to a head in the middle of January 1998 when the Rt Rev. Ian Cundy, Bishop of Peterborough, in whose diocese Althorp stands, took the highly unusual step of releasing a copy of Diana's burial certificate. It states simply that, 'on the 6th of September 1997, Diana, Princess of Wales, aged 36, was buried in an extra-parochial place, namely at Althorp Park in the County of Northamptonshire in the grave previously consecrated by the Bishop of Peterborough on the island in the Oval Lake.' It was signed by a Sussex priest, the Rev. Victor Christian de Roubaix Malan, the man in charge of the burial.

The Spencer family also had to contend with the persistent pronouncements of Mohamed Al Fayed, owner of Harrods and father of Dodi, that Diana and his son were not the victims of a terrible car crash but perhaps of something more sinister. His conspiracy theory, fuelled possibly by a tortured grief – the driver was, after all, on his pay-roll – suggested that the British establishment could not countenance the prospect of the United Kingdom's future monarch having an 'outsider' for a half-brother or sister, assuming Dodi and Diana had married and produced children. Whatever else this theory achieved, it may not have assisted Mr Al Fayed's long-cherished ambition to be granted British citizenship.

In the middle of February 1998, Lord Spencer issued a short, dignified statement asking for his sister to be allowed to rest in peace. 'I have one question,' it read. 'Is there any good in all this speculation? I ask because there is clearly a lot of harm in it. All we, her family, ask is that Diana's memory be respected, and that sensational speculation be left out of the public arena where it undermines all our aims to come to terms with our loss; a process that is, naturally, still ongoing – as I imagine it is for Mr Al Fayed and his family.'

Despite all this, there can be little doubt that Althorp will for ever remain a magnet for the millions of people the world over who felt Diana spoke to them, the people who felt a personal sense of loss at her going. The future of the ninth Earl, however, is less easy to predict. But before we turn for the final time to our panel of expert witnesses, let's consult two other experts – one a graphologist, the other an astrologer – to discover whether his handwriting or his chart can provide any significant pointers, both to his character and to what lies ahead for him.

Julie Hinton is a member of the Graphology Society and has been a trained graphologist since the beginning of the eighties. She uses her skills for recruitment purposes (helping assess shortlisted candidates for particular jobs), compatibility, general character analysis, counselling and advising career suitability. She also teaches and has published a book on the subject.

For the purposes of this exercise, Julie Hinton was provided with a sample of Earl Spencer's writing but was not made aware of his identity. However, in response to her request, she was told the age and sex of the subject. From the material available, this is what she deduced.

'Independent in outlook, he is a mature, strong-minded individual who likes to see matters through from beginning to end, preferably without interruption. Shrewd, the writer has a highly developed critical sense. He is personally organized, sharp-witted and tenacious in his pursuits. There was, however, some degree of ambivalence and internal conflict at the time of writing, resulting in a feeling of being pulled in different directions.

'Cultured and intellectual, he can be rather guarded and evasive at times, someone who likes to keep his options firmly open. Emotionally, he can be rather intense. There is a degree of inhibition present: he does not always find it easy to really let go; some caution exists but he likes to have the final say on matters. A stubborn streak is evident; he is not a person easily deflected

201

by others' ideas. His thoughts proceed in a systematic, methodical and logical sequence. He is analytical in outlook and one to calculate likely results from a particular action, coupled with great powers of concentration.

'Tending to strip matters down to the essentials, he likes digging for facts and knowledge. The writer is a tough negotiator, quick to assess and go straight to the hub of an issue, generally in a direct manner. He is a stickler for accuracy and does not want for determination but he can be inflexible and seek to impose his will at times.

'Essentially, he accepts his own nature and expects other people to accept it, too. Elaborations are seen as unnecessary; his clear-sighted vision could sometimes prove ruthlessly critical. The writer needs to be continually stimulated, otherwise he is likely to become restless within. He is a person who is fast and intuitive, yet orderly and circumspect. Idealistic in his approach, he thinks quickly and objectively, coupled with a focused, alert mind, creative potential, intelligence and perception.'

Shelley von Strunckel, the first astrologer to be featured in a British broadsheet when her column started appearing in the *Sunday Times*, and the chosen successor to the late Patric Walker, considered Charles Spencer's chart but not before setting the interpretation of individual horoscopes in their proper context. 'Often, people are afraid of learning about their birth chart,' she says, 'frightened that they'll hear about a future that they don't welcome and can't change. But while an individual chart or horoscope can be eerily accurate in its depiction of the future, there is still plenty of room for free will, whether that means saying no to opportunities or turning around difficult circumstances.

'This is particularly the case with Charles Spencer, whose destiny has been as much dictated by fate as it has been determined by his actions. His chart is like any other person's in that it portrays his assets – the talents and potential strengths on which he can draw – as well as revealing his weaknesses. These characteristics are indicated by the positions of the planets on his birthdate; thus, while he might be similar to another Taurus, it is only those born on 20 May 1964, who share a similar birth chart. In every chart, each planet signifies a type of energy – for example, Mercury is communication, the Moon, mother and all women in an individual's life. The signs these are in, and their position in relationship to other planets, indicate how those energies are likely to be employed.

'While the planetary positions in birth charts never change, the ones in the sky shift on a daily basis. These movements are the basis for newspaper and magazine horoscopes. Whether they read star sign columns or not, everyone experiences their influence. For an individual such as Earl Spencer, these planetary movements, usually called transits, appear as events. But it is how he reacts to those events that has made news – and will in the future.

'Charles Spencer was born on the last day of Taurus in 1964. And with four of the ten heavenly bodies in Taurus, he is heir to its benefits, charm and simplicity, as well as its major liability: self-indulgence. Of greatest significance is not so much the number of planets there but the combination. Mercury, planet of communication, is next to the inquisitive, well-travelled Jupiter, which is near the volatile warrior planet Mars. This line-up indicates an inclination for journalism and suggests a quick mind and forthright way of speaking – and a ferociously independent streak. The same goes for the three planets in the usually quite restrained sign of Virgo: the Moon, key to the women in his life, is near Pluto, which indicates the potential for intense dramas that include sexual obsession and power struggles – but also a powerful need to tell the truth – and to Uranus, planet of the unexpected. These alone would indicate a strong personality. However, three planets in the sensitive water signs, including Venus in Cancer, soften this; he is both intuitive and uses those instincts to connect with others.

'He's a practical earth sign. But he still tends to think quickly and to make emotionally-based decisions before that earth sign side takes over. After the fact, however, he analyses both situations and the individuals involved clearly and comes up with creative resolutions for problems.

'The real key to understanding Earl Spencer's chart is Neptune, the planet of hope and idealism – and of disappointment and disillusion. Neptune also figured prominently in the chart of his sister, Diana. In Spencer's birth chart, Neptune sits exactly opposite all his planets in Taurus. This means that, while he can have moments of dazzling inspiration, he can simply refuse to acknowledge what he doesn't want to be true. Neptune also accents those in need and charities. This is where free will comes in. Diana learned that by helping those in need, she could not only relieve her personal pain, she could achieve a great deal for others. Neptune is a tricky planet, however, and if the individual doesn't give voluntarily, life itself tends to arrange it for them. Someone around them – partners, colleagues, or loved ones – seems constantly to be in trouble, if not in crisis. Fate has taken a hand in dealing with this in Charles Spencer's life. Diana's death has involved him in what is suddenly a world-class charity. But will this continue to be the centre of his life? Is there more?

'The past can be instructive about the future. From November 1983 until November 1993, the uncompromising Pluto was positioned in Scorpio, opposite all Spencer's planets in Taurus. During times like this, an individual seems to be almost hypnotized into taking life's most extreme options. That cycle left a broken marriage, scandals and conflicts with the press behind him. After Pluto's departure in late 1995, the focus shifted to Uranus, planet of innovation and the unexpected. Then, early in 1998, Neptune (already an important player in Spencer's birth chart), moved into position, taking the starring role in the drama. But it could be said that Diana's death was the culmination of his old pattern of destiny. Nearly every one of the transiting planets on that day triggered sensitive planets in Spencer's own chart. And the events that followed not only changed his life but are likely to have brought about fundamental alterations in his understanding of himself and outlook as well.

'If so, then he could exchange the old planetary pattern that involved Uranus and Neptune, the planets that in the past have signified so many difficulties in his life, with a far more positive approach. Uranus and Neptune could, instead, bring a new spark, innovation and promise. And instead of battles with both loved ones and the press, Charles Spencer will become a light for others and for the future. Personally, he's likely to discover that an entirely new kind of woman suits him, one who has suffered herself and, having learned through it, can stand her ground with integrity.

'And his role in the world? He has proved that his words can both sway hearts and make people think. Once the complexities of his sister's heritage and estate are settled – and they will be, although it may take until 2003 – he is likely to return to the world of business. A reborn and newly qualified Earl Spencer could easily turn his unique experience to the world of communications – advertising, journalism or even writing. In time, that experience will make him an elder statesman, a position no more comfortable for him then than it would be now. For, once all is said and done,' concludes von Strunckel, 'Charles Spencer is a modest man.'

Sir Nicholas Lloyd, perhaps unsurprisingly, sees the ninth Earl's future in more pragmatic terms. 'To put it bluntly,' says Lloyd, 'it is one of the ironies of this extraordinary story that, through the death of his sister, Althorp's financial problems are a thing of the past. Having said immediately after her death that he would not agree to a museum being built at Althorp in Diana's memory, he then announced that the grounds and house will be open to the public – initially for two months every summer, maybe for longer later – and that a permanent exhibition area will be devoted to the memory of his sister's life and work.

'Althorp Park and the estate – although, I accept, not Charles in any personal sense – are bound to benefit from the money that will pour in via the huge numbers of visitors who will stream to Althorp.'

For PR spokeswoman Shelley-Anne, her client has other, more pressing considerations. 'At the moment, most of his efforts are directed to ensuring that Althorp House and its grounds will be ready to open on 1 July for two months each year so that people can come and pay their respects to Diana. It's a huge undertaking. Charles is very much hands-on in every aspect of all this work; he's going through all the potential material for the museum, for instance. Two months may seem like a short time but, by limiting the number of people and days open, we can ensure that the whole area retains dignity and tranquillity, somewhere you can remember Diana without feeling you're being hurried through on some sort of conveyor belt. There is to be a limit of 2,500 people a day allowed into the house and grounds, each visitor paying a little under £10. It's also worth pointing out that, at the end of the day, Althorp does remain a private home so it is perhaps understandable if Charles doesn't want it overrun every day of the year. He has real commitment to that house. He's looking always to the future for the estate and particularly in respect of his son, Louis. I think he feels as if the house and all it contains are on loan to each Earl Spencer.

'For all that, I know he has plans in other areas of his life. It's difficult, though. A lot of people want him to carry on almost from where Diana left off but he's very much his own man so I can't see him pursuing that path unthinkingly. He can't do things in the same way Diana did for the very good reason that he isn't Diana.

'If anything, and as a result of the divorce case, I hold Charles now in higher regard than I did before. You might think that, as someone who is paid by him to be his public relations mouthpiece, I might well say that. But that doesn't stop it being true. I just didn't feel he deserved what he was put through. He's an incredibly fair person; he could have done an awful lot of damage during the trial if he'd wanted to. But, on the contrary, he was completely honourable and very dignified throughout it all. I think history will judge him differently from the way perhaps he might have been perceived in the last months of 1997.'

Agony aunt Virginia Ironside takes a different view. 'Charles is still very bitter,' she says. 'He seems remarkably lacking in self-awareness. I think he'll continue to be a damaged man. From the moment his mother left the family home, his life has been marinaded in loss and rage at some level. It would be very difficult for him ever to trust anyone again. If your mother dies, it's pretty tough but you can eventually come to realize that she didn't mean to go. But when a mother leaves, it must be hugely difficult to come to terms with.

'Most mothers don't leave without their children. They fight like tigresses never to be parted from them. They kill for their children. For most women, that instinct is primeval. How could he not be damaged? We all saw the effect it had on Diana. She was quite open about her eating disorders. Charles has never had any eating disorders, as far as we know, but he's always somehow surrounded himself with people who do. That's very handy. It means they can have the eating disorders for him. People who haven't ever resolved their emotional problems inevitably have someone close to them who's suffering all the misery and depression and nervous breakdowns on their behalf.

'To this day, and it's not hard to see why, Charles Spencer is full of righteous anger. I don't like him but it's hard not to feel sorry for him. I think his life will be dogged by him rejecting people and people rejecting him. I can't see how it can be otherwise unless, in some way, he starts to comprehend the pattern of his life and his relationships and works with all his might to break the mould.'

Former nanny Mary Clarke arrives at much the same point, albeit from rather a different angle. 'I think Charles will spend more time at Althorp,' she says, 'particularly as the children get older. He is extremely proud of his heritage and his home and he will want to ensure that the estate is suitable for his son to inherit when his time comes. I feel certain he will want all four children to be educated in Britain when they reach secondary-school age and maybe beforehand. I'd like to see him forming a new permanent relationship with someone more suited to him than Victoria. He's intelligent enough to learn from his mistakes. I think he's earned the right to be free now, to have a good time. Why shouldn't he – as long as he's tactful and discreet about his private affairs as his father was before him? Everyone deserves happiness and Charles is no exception. If he's sensible, he should leave a long gap before settling down again; he needs to make sure before choosing another wife.'

Earl Spencer's mother, Frances Shand Kydd, is also keen that her only son should meet another woman he'd like to marry but there are other considerations, too, as she told *Hello!*: 'I'd dearly like to see Charles happy,' she said, 'and also Victoria. I'm devoted to her and always have been. They are immensely considerate, good friends who have a beautiful quartet of healthy, happy children who are an enormous credit to both of them. It was right that they should part, though; they are both much happier living separately from each other. Charles has a tremendous loyalty; it's a wonderful part of his character. He's a rescuer of people and he doesn't worry what the personal cost will be. If he thinks it's the right thing to do, he does it. In the case of Darius Guppy, his best man who served a jail sentence for fraud, he really saw the need to protect and support Patricia, his wife. She needed a home and he offered her one. He does believe, as I do, that friendship is for all seasons, particularly when the clouds descend. If we're guilty of standing by someone who's wrong, so be it. I'd rather have that than be guilty of abandoning a friend.'

Psychologist Dorothy Rowe has other concerns: the future pattern of Charles Spencer's life – and whether it has been informed in any significant way by his past. 'The Spanish philosopher, Santayana, wrote something important,' she says, 'in *The Life of Reason*. He said, "Those who cannot remember the past are condemned to repeat it." And it's the same with our lives; what we do is to repeat patterns established early in childhood. People who marry more than once almost always choose the same type of person with the same disastrous result. Charles's letter to Chantal, which was, in many ways, rather gentle, revealed that he sees a woman as someone who will look after him. But that then complicates matters because you're not supposed to have a sexual relationship with someone like that. How can you have a passionate affair with somebody who's busy mothering you? Victoria clearly had her frailties but she mothered Charles to the extent that most women mother their men; they're taught it as a kind of politeness. It's all part and parcel of learning to be an attractive, acceptable, feminine woman.

'A lot of men are very simple-minded, to say the least. They find it impossible to build up a complex set of ideas about a woman; they fail to understand that a woman can be mothering one moment, ferocious the next and then perhaps not interested in them at all. They find it difficult to think of this as all one person.

'Another of the problems facing chaps as they start to get older is that, if they've married a woman the same age as them, they've married someone who in time will cease to think that all men are wonderful. Charles is now in his thirties and someone who must be scared of women, given the hammering they've meted out to him. It's quite something when your wife and your ex-mistress gang up together against you, isn't it? So he's unlikely to choose a new partner of his own age because she will be experienced enough to suss him out. He's likely to go for a younger woman who, initially at least, will adore him unconditionally.

'On the other hand, he might try to learn from this experience. But I doubt it. Charles doesn't seem to be interested in trying to understand the unresolved problems of his childhood. Children who had less than happy upbringings fall into two categories: they either do to other people what was done to them, sometimes without necessarily meaning to or being able to help themselves; or they learn from their experiences and work hard to prevent history from repeating itself.

'Diana was trying – particularly towards the end – to understand what had happened to her; and she was very protective of her sons, completely devoted to them. In her work, she saw herself as someone who sought out people with whom she felt some sense of identity; they were suffering as she had suffered.

209

But she didn't seem to have changed in the essential way she felt about herself. Look at her choice in men. If you don't think much of yourself, you tend to choose partners who aren't as wonderful as you'd like them to be but are, simply, as wonderful as you think you deserve. Clearly, she didn't think much of herself as she ended up with a pretty useless collection of men. She may have channelled some of her anger into good causes, into being the self-declared Queen of Hearts, and that was good. But she hadn't got to the point of believing she deserved better than what she had so far been given.

'She was grateful to Mohamed Al Fayed's son for his attentions. But her long-term relationship with Dodi was doomed to disaster because he was not a man who was going to be faithful to her. Where people were concerned, she wasn't stupid but she was grateful when someone paid attention to her. A woman tells herself she's in love with a man if she's having an affair with him; it's very rare for women to go into a sexual relationship just for the sex. That's a male preserve. And the fact Diana was giving Dodi presents tells me that she was telling herself that she was in love with him. She told herself that she had this wonderful capacity to be with people, to be healing, but she wasn't thinking in terms of how she could channel any of this in any controlled sense, say, by training to be a therapist, presumably because she didn't feel she was bright enough; and that's sad.'

Similarly, says Dr Rowe, if Charles had learned anything from his life, he would have taken care when he got married in his choice of wife. 'But he married someone he'd known a matter of weeks which tells me that he demonstrated no signs that he had learned from his own experience. I see him as a very proud man but then, for me, pride is the deadliest of the seven deadly sins. It prevents people from standing sufficiently far back to see themselves and trying to make changes that might be necessary. They're so proud of what they've achieved or, simply, the fact they've survived, that it confers on them a sort of arrogance. They think, "Well, I've been through all of that and I'm still here. I don't need to change." Will Charles Spencer learn from his experiences and change? Nothing he's done so far suggests as much.'

'The future for Charles Spencer?' asks constitutional historian David Starkey. 'God alone knows. Clearly, it was preposterous of him to stand in that pulpit and speak of himself as a sort of standard-bearer on behalf of Diana for her beloved boys and then, two days later, fly halfway across the world back to Cape Town. The more you think about what he said, the more implausible it becomes. Did *he* believe it and, if so, is he a self-delusionist?

'I think Spencer will be seen in time as a footnote to the whole royal saga, albeit an interesting one. I think he was responsible for much of the atmosphere on the extraordinary day of Diana's funeral. With the possible exception of Verdi's *Requiem* and Elton John's song, the only element that anyone will remember in a service that was dull to the point of being banal – the Church of England at its worst – was Charles's oration. He found a language that acted as a conduit to people's emotions. In that sense, he did something profoundly memorable.

'But it will turn out, I think, to have been the only thing he's ever done that has mattered, for whatever reason.' Furthermore Starkey predicts that the press will consider him as 'a steady source of increasingly sordid stories for increasingly sordid newspapers. His speech was tacky if effective but then there were an awful lot of tacky emotions flying around. Why otherwise were people leaving bottles of champagne and teddy bears outside the gates of Kensington Palace? It's given to very few of us to seize history in that kind of way, and seize it he did. Charles Spencer had his six and a half minutes of fame. But that's it.'

Royal biographer and journalist Anthony Holden takes a more pragmatic line. 'I would guess Charles would return to Britain and take up his role as custodian of Althorp – and become quite rich on the proceeds, though in the general not personal sense. His private life is harder to predict. Whether he's capable of settling down in a stable marriage, I have my doubts. I suppose becoming the self-appointed keeper of Diana's flame will be his life's work.

But the King Uncle, as it might be, should be seen to have a home life that is above reproach. His past doesn't bode well, though. Prince Charles, for all his own hanky-panky, almost certainly takes a dim view of the way that Charles Spencer has conducted his private life. Charles Windsor is quite morally rigorous – even if he doesn't inevitably apply those same strictures to himself.'

When Diana, Princess of Wales talked to author Andrew Morton, at what turned out to be the depth of her unhappiness, she was typically open and direct in her estimation of her younger brother and his likely prospects. 'I so understand him,' said Diana. 'He's very like me as opposed to my two sisters. Like me, he will always suffer. There's something in us that attracts that department whereas my two sisters are blissfully happy being detached from various situations.'

Andrew Morton characterizes Charles as being defined by a sort of noble recklessness. 'I think, in many respects, he's made a rod for his own back. If he'd wanted to be a private person, the drama of that funeral oration moved him from being a sprig of the aristocracy to being a main branch, one of the men of the moment, someone firmly positioned centre-stage. The trouble with Charles – and it seems to be true about other members of his family – is that "cautious" is not a word that occurs in his lexicon. He can demonstrate courage and nobility but shrewd judgement is alien to him.

'If we consider the statement he gave to the press outside his Cape Town home just five hours after the death of his sister, we see that, like the funeral Address the following Saturday, the language he chose to use was rich and vivid although not neces- sarily accurate or fair. That is typical of the man. But then here was the person who told almost half the world's population that he would strive to ensure William and Harry's souls "could sing openly". He's going to have his work cut out achieving that aim if he remains in South Africa for long. He's a great one for making statements on the hoof and then having to retract them. Caution, as I say, should be his watchword.'

*

212

Whether Charles Spencer becomes resident custodian of Althorp or continues to divide his time between South Africa and Britain; whether he pursues his interest in documentary film-making or takes up writing seriously (he is said currently to be tackling a full-length work of fiction); whether he plunges headlong into a new relationship or whether, newly single, he chooses to play the field – only time will tell.

What remains unambiguous is that he will continue to run at life with that curious blend of courage and confidence, arrogance and anger, decrying the press hounds from hell while being unable to stop himself from supplying them with the tastiest of morsels. And, throughout it all, looking out for those 'two exceptional young men', the Princes William and Harry. 'You can't go far wrong if you deal in honesty and communication,' he told his Cape Talk interviewer two months after Diana's death. 'We see things and we feel things and we think things from a certain perspective and if other people were more straightforward with us and we understood what they were feeling, I think there'd be less tension than there is in families or businesses or in any part of our lives.'

Honesty and communication. Charles Edward Maurice Spencer has everything to play for.